THE POLITICS AND ECONOMICS OF DEFENCE INDUSTRIES

The Begin–Sadat (BESA) Center for Strategic Studies at Bar-Ilan University is dedicated to the study of Middle East peace and security, in particular the national security and foreign policy of Israel. A non-partisan and independent institute, the BESA Center is named in memory of Menachem Begin and Anwar Sadat, whose efforts in pursuing peace laid the cornerstone for future conflict resolution in the Middle East.

Since its founding in 1991 by Dr Thomas O. Hecht of Montreal, the BESA Center has become one of the most dynamic Israeli research institutions. It has developed cooperative relationship with strategic study centres throughout the world, from Ankara to Washington and from London to Seoul. Among its research staff are some of Israel's best and brightest academic and military minds. BESA Center publications and policy recommendations are read by senior Israeli decision-makers, in military and civilian life, by academicians, the press and the broader public.

The BESA Center makes its research available to the international community through three publication series: BESA *Security and Policy Studies*, BESA *Colloquia on Strategy and Diplomacy* and BESA *Studies in International Security*. The Center also sponsors conferences, symposia, workshops, lectures and briefings for international and local audiences.

The Center for Defense and Peace Economics at Bar-Ilan University is the only centre in Israel dedicated to the study of defence economics. Since its founding in 1994, it has become very active in sponsoring research on issues regarding defence and peace economics in Israel and abroad. Research results are disseminated via publications, symposia and national and international conferences. Israeli and international advisory boards of prominent economists (including Nobel Laureates Professor K. Arrow and Professor L.R. Klein) guide the Center's research.

THE POLITICS
AND ECONOMICS
OF DEFENCE
INDUSTRIES

Edited by
EFRAIM INBAR
Bar-Ilan University

and

BENZION ZILBERFARB
Bar-Ilan University

Routledge
Taylor & Francis Group

LONDON AND NEW YORK

Published in 1998 in Great Britain by
Routledge
2 Park Square, Milton Park, Abingdon, Oxon, OX14 4RN
711 Third Avenue, New York, NY 10017

Transferred to Digital Printing 2011

Website http://www.routledge.com

Copyright © 1998 Contributors

British Library Cataloguing in Publication Data

The politics and economics of defence industries. (BESA
    studies in international security, no. 5)
    1. Defence industries – Political aspects   2. Defence
    industries – Economic aspects
    I. Inbar, Efraim, 1947–   II. Zilberfarb, Benzion
    338.7'6'23

ISBN 0-7146-4852-3 (cloth)
ISBN 0-7146-4410-2 (paper)

ISSN 1368 9541

Library of Congress Cataloging-in-Publication Data

The politics and economics of defence industries / edited by
    Efraim Inbar and Benzion Zilberfarb.
        p.   cm.
    Includes index.
    ISBN 0-7146-4852-3 (cloth). – ISBN 0-7146-4410-2 (pbk.)
    1. Defense industries. 2. Economic conversion. I. Inbar,
    Efraim, 1947– . II. Zilberfarb, Benzion.
    HD9743.A2P58 1998
    338.4'6233–dc21   97-37993
                                                                      CIP

Publisher's Note
The publisher has gone to great lengths to ensure the quality of this reprint
but points out that some imperfections in the original may be apparent.

To our parents:
Devora, Shalom, Shlomo
and in the loving memory of Clara

Contents

Notes on Contributors

Ian Anthony of the Stockholm International Peace Research Institute in Sweden is a leading expert on the global arms trade. He holds a doctorate from the University of London, where his thesis dealt with the *International Arms Trade: Case Studies of India and Pakistan, 1947–86*. Among his recent publications is a book entitled *The Future of the Defence Industries of Central and Eastern Europe* (1994).

Michael Brzoska is Research Director at the Bonn International Centre for Conversion. He has lectured at the University of Hamburg and has served as a project leader at the Unit for the Study of Armaments, Development, and Wars. Dr Brzoska has also been a consultant for the United Nations, the World Bank and the European Parliament.

Gil Feiler, senior lecturer in political science at Bar-Ilan University and lecturer in economics at Tel Aviv University, specializes in political and economic development, Middle East economic cooperation and Arab markets and economies. He is a consultant to the Israel–America Chamber of Commerce and his work *From Boycott to Economic Cooperation: The Political Economy of the Arab Boycott of Israel*, has recently been published by Frank Cass Publishers.

Keith Hartley is Professor of Economics and Director of the Centre for Defence Economics at the University of York. He is editor of *Defence and Peace Economics*, and has been published widely in the fields of defence economics and applied economics.

Efraim Inbar is Director of the Begin–Sadat Center for Strategic Studies and Associate Professor of Political Science at Bar-Ilan University. He is a leading expert on Israeli national security and defence strategy, and the evolution of Israeli public opinion and leadership perspectives on the Arab–Israeli conflict. He is currently preparing a book on the late Israeli Prime Minister Yitzhak Rabin.

Michael Intriligator is Professor of Economics at the University of California, Los Angeles, where he is also a Professor of Political Science and Policy Studies. He has prepared numerous papers on economic theory, econometrics and international relations addressing such issues as the arms race, arms control and global security.

Aharon Klieman is Nahum Goldmann Professor in Diplomacy at Tel Aviv University, specializing in Israel's foreign policy and US Middle East policy. He is a senior research associate at the university's Jaffee Center for Strategic Studies, and has also received grants from the Ford Foundation in Israel and the National Science Foundation (USA).

Ann Markusen is Director of the Project on Regional Industrial Economics at Rutgers University, where she is State of New Jersey Professor of Urban Planning and Policy Development. She has authored several books on high technology and American economic development. Her current research explores the impact of military spending on American technology, industry, economic and foreign policy.

Yitzhak Shichor is Associate Professor of Political Science at Hebrew University and an expert on the economy and security of China, and Chinese relations with the Middle East. He is currently pursuing research at the Sejong Institute in South Korea.

Etel Solingen is an Associate Professor of Political Science at the University of California, Irvine and a former Faculty fellow at the

University of California Institute on Global Conflict and Cooperation. The author of many works on nuclear proliferation and arms control, Professor Solingen received the 1995–96 MacArthur Foundation Award on Peace and International Cooperation.

Benzion Zilberfarb is Director of the Center for Defense and Peace Economics at Bar-Ilan University and an expert on the Israeli economy and issues of privatization. In the past he has served as a consultant to the Bank of Israel and the private banking sector, Israel's Securities Authority. His current research investigates the anticipated economic benefits to Israel resulting from the Middle East peace process.

Introduction

Efraim Inbar and Benzion Zilberfarb

Security problems are a constant challenge in the unpredictable international community. The Iraqi assault on Kuwait, the civil war in the former-Yugoslavia and the conflict in Chechniya are only a few recent examples of the kinds of conflagrations that can break out at any moment. As a result of such uncertainty, states throughout the world must prepare for the real possibility of involvement in military conflicts, and they must therefore develop the armed forces necessary for such circumstances. As a result, the production of military weaponry is a perpetual necessity.

In coping with so tumultuous an international system, the states of the world have pursued a variety of policies. Some have chosen the course of domestic weapons production, while others have preferred to purchase their means of defence from others. Of importance in determining the outcome of this calculus is the knowledge that in times of crisis it can be far too dangerous to rely on the good graces of others, as well as the awareness that the ability to field a people's army equipped with home-made weaponry is a source of pride and an expression of national development. In addition, the international arms market can be good business: a lucrative export venture with the bonus of extensive domestic technological advancement and political profit.

However, the post-Cold War international environment has not been friendly to the weapons emporium or to the local weapons producer. The new non-belligerent relationship between the countries of the West and the former Soviet alliance has made irrelevant the vast fortifications and extensive armies which once faced-off across the European front, while the end of the bi-lateral contest over influence and world dominance has dried the once endless wells of foreign economic and military assistance. A different international security arena has been formed, and as a result, across Europe and Asia, in South America and within the United States, national champions and sub-systems manufacturers have been forced to cope with the challenges posed by shrinking domestic demand as well as downward trends in the international arms market.

Unable to find enough buyers at home, those companies – state or privately owned – which have chosen to continue their production and sales efforts have turned outward, entering the hotly contested international export market. Buyers can be found, especially among the oil producing countries of the Gulf and the 'Tigers' of the Far East, although here too sales are not easy to achieve. As the costs of sophisticated weapons systems continue to escalate, buyers find it increasingly difficult to pay for their armament programmes.

Confronted by these challenges, the industries and the countries in which they reside have sought remedies as diverse and numerous as the industries themselves and the weapons they produce. Often, they have resorted to corporate consolidation and massive personnel layoffs, if not the complete cessation of operations. In many cases the side-effects have been as damaging as the illnesses themselves. Tens of thousands of workers – once heroes of the national defence effort – have found themselves without work or pay, and as a result the communities in which they live have had to face widespread unemployment and societal dislocation. Other industries have attempted to convert to the production of non-military goods. However, even the much heralded conversion process has not proven to be the panacea for the industries' woes.

The military industries represent a web of political, strategic and economic considerations. Their past development and future existence are of primary international importance. Recognizing this, the Begin–Sadat Center for Strategic Studies and the Center for Defense and Peace Economics, both situated on the campus of Bar-Ilan University, convened an international conference entitled, 'The Politics and Economics of Defence

Industries in a Changing World.' What follows is a collection of the papers presented at the conference. The contributors, heralding from various countries and experts in their fields, address a wide range of topics of primary importance in the academic discourse on the military industries.

Combined, the chapters of the volume provide a comprehensive look at the state of the worldwide arms sector. The volume begins with a look at global issues, and then reduces its focus to individual countries, beginning in the West and then moving beyond. The United States, the world's leading arms producing state, is analysed, as are second-tier countries in Europe, South America and Asia. International economic trends, political developments and strategic considerations are linked to provide a comprehensive and policy-relevant analysis of the subject matter at hand.

In the first chapter, Ian Anthony presents an overview of the general state of the international arms sector. His discussion focuses on the need to align production levels with the demands of the current market while maintaining defence capabilities and technological sophistication. In line with this focus, Anthony presents the broad trends shaping the environment: force posture planning, public and military expenditure, military technology development and export prospects. He then explains how the industries should respond to the challenging circumstances of the post-Cold War world.

In the next chapter, Michael Intriligator looks at a number of issues related to defence conversion in an environment of reduced military expenditures. Among the subjects he reviews are reduced defence budgets, defence conversion, the peace dividend, conversion costs, disarmament as an investment process, arms exports, the economics of conversion in the Western industrialized nations, the former socialist countries and the rest of the world, and, lastly, the implications of the discussion for policy. Intriligator notes that with informed policy making supplemented by new arms control initiatives, disarmament could bring substantial long-term economic return with a minimum of military and societal conversion costs.

Ann Markusen, in chapter 3, reviews the evidence regarding

the restructuring efforts of US defence industries during the 1980s and the first half of the 1990s. She argues that the debt-financed build-up of the 1980s increased industry dependence on the defence sector. In addition, she highlights the different strategies chosen to confront the challenges posed by recent reductions in defence outlays, and she reviews claims against the recent trend of mergers and acquisitions. Markusen notes that in contrast to the 'dual use' posture of the US government, its efforts are ineffective and inadequately funded, and that as a result, the wall of separation between the civilian and military markets has grown higher and more difficult to overcome.

In the following chapter, Michael Brzoska looks at the conversion efforts of the European military industries. He notes that, combined, the European military industries appear to be a strong international power: diverse, competent and technologically advanced. However, these same qualities, upon a closer look, are detrimental. In the face of reduced defence budgets and the consolidation of the European Union, these industries are overly redundant, with excessive capacities, and in need of extensive restructuring. Brzoska reviews the dilemmas facing the European industries and sheds light on the challenges and efforts facing the individual countries and companies. He notes that as a result of the complicating factors of the European context, relief for the industry's woes remains elusive.

Keith Hartley, in chapter 5, takes a look at the state of the defence industries of Britain, presenting an overview of the United Kingdom's defence industrial base. Hartley examines the performance of Britain's industries and considers the prospects of the defence sector joining the Single European Market. Following a review of possible scenarios for UK defence market restructuring, he notes that the concept of a centralized European Armaments Agency has the greatest potential among possible solutions to the problems of Britain's and Europe's military industries. However, he stresses that many factors ultimately could undermine this all important restructuring process.

In chapter 6, Aharon Kleiman addresses the military industries of a small yet important producer of military equipment, Israel. He states that in spite of Israel's disadvantaged status in the arms market – its almost total lack of strategic and industrial raw materials, its small domestic base, local defence cuts and international political constraints – the Israeli military industries remain viable contenders. Kleiman reviews the reasons for why Israel's arms companies have survived as well as the forces involved in their future success or failure. In all, he notes that drastic steps by Israel will become of increasing necessity, and that in the face of international and domestic constraints, considerable political courage will prove of no less importance than other factors.

The military industries of China are the subject of chapter 7, written by Yitzhak Shichor. He explains that success of the Chinese conversion process may not be as incredible as some claim; political considerations, cultural and behavioural norms, collective historical memories, and a dialectical philosophical bent are as important as economic indicators in explaining Chinese military industry policy. In detailing this point, Shichor reviews the development of China's industries and the factors which influenced this process. He then addresses the Chinese industrial conversion effort and the concomitant People's Republic military build-up, both of which followed the death of Mao.

In chapter 8, Gil Feiler looks at the military industries of the Arab states in the 1990s. He addresses the characteristics of their military industries as well as their efforts at industry conversion. In addition, Feiler looks at experiments of the Arab countries in the joint development of military materials. He notes that, in general, the arms sectors of the Arab states are not very advanced. The oil boom of the 1970s and early 1980s provided extensive capital and fuelled the development of import based economies at the expense of a local industrial base. However, the more recent fall in the price of oil has led the Arab states to develop local industries, although these efforts have met with very little success. Indeed, as a result of these and other factors, Dr Feiler suggests that the Arab states have given up on indigenous conventional arms industries and have turned instead toward the development of unconventional weaponry.

The final chapter, by Etel Solingen, covers the military

industries of Argentina and Brazil. She examines the causes behind the development of these South American weapons industries, focusing on international market and political conditions, domestic economic and political determinants, and regional contextual factors. Solingen then presents the domestic, regional, and international dimensions which caused the near-collapse of the arms sector in Argentina and Brazil. She explores this dramatic contraction and its potential implications, including the impact of the rise and fall of the Argentinian and Brazilian industries on the countries of the Middle East.

The collection of authors included herein make up the brightest minds in the academic discourse on the military industries, as well as some of the nicest people with which we, the editors, have had the chance to work. Their attention to deadlines and willingness to accept our comments and criticism was most refreshing and made this academic effort a pleasure to complete. Indeed, rarely has a collaborative project been completed with such a spirit of camaraderie. This volume and the conference which preceded it bear testimony to the potential of inter- and intra-university cooperation and to the adage that two minds are better than one.

We would like to thank all those who facilitated the compilation of this volume: Chaya Beckerman for her editing skills, and Hava Waxman Koen and Alona Brinner-Rozenman for the administrative assistance. In addition, we would like to express our gratitude to Avi Rembaum for his tireless dedication, without which this project would never have seen the light of day.

Politics and Economics of Defence Industries in a Changing World

IAN ANTHONY

INTRODUCTION

Prior to the end of the Cold War in 1989–90, the defence budgets of major powers were already under pressure. In the United States, military expenditure peaked in real terms in 1985, while within the NATO alliance as a whole, expenditure peaked in 1987. The economic capabilities of the Soviet Union were completely stretched in the 1980s – a factor which many consider to have contributed to President Mikhail Gorbachev's decision to initiate a reform programme after 1985. With the end of the Cold War there has been an enormous reduction in the levels of military effort by the major powers. This reduction in effort has in turn been reflected in the diminished demand for military equipment. While there is no single indicator that captures the scale of this change, sales and employment figures for the largest defence companies are perhaps indicative. Arms sales by the hundred largest arms producing companies in the OECD (Organization for Economic Cooperation and Development) and developing countries fell by 15 per cent between 1991 and 1994.[1] According to the Bonn International Centre for Conversion, worldwide employment in the arms industry has fallen from 17.5 million workers in 1987 to 11.1 million in 1995. More than 90 per cent of the reductions have occurred in member countries of NATO and the former Warsaw Treaty Organization.[2]

If the current environment in which the defence industries of the major powers must operate has changed dramatically, there is still uncertainty about the precise nature of the future demand for military equipment – reflecting the deeper uncertainties of political, technological and economic conditions in the major centres of arms production. In these major centres – North America, Europe, and the former Soviet Union – there is still a broad consensus that armed forces are required to deter an attack on national territory, or should deterrence fail, defeat the enemy. In the present environment of threat, however, existing forces are sufficient for the purpose of territorial defence.

Whether the armed forces will be required to do more than defend national territory and, if so, where and under what conditions military operations will be performed is still an open question. The period 1991–95 has seen the deployment of large multinational military formations for very different purposes. The coalition which expelled Iraqi forces from Kuwait represented an enormous concentration of offensive power. The coalition of forces participating in the IFOR under the framework of the Dayton Peace Agreement has an entirely different composition and mandate.

The armed forces of at least some states are expected to be flexible and capable enough to achieve a variety of objectives. Similarly, a defence industrial policy will have to provide the equipment necessary to carry out these tasks at minimum cost.

In several parts of the world, states remain unable to regulate their relations by peaceful means. In China, on the Korean peninsula, and, not least, in the Middle East, the risk of conflict remains a constant factor in inter-state relations. In certain countries in the Middle East and Southeast Asia, military expenditure is increasing, in contrast to the global trend. However, demand from these relatively small states cannot compensate industry for lost markets among the major powers. On a global basis, therefore, the central issue for the 'traditional' defence industries – manufacturers of conventional arms, delivery systems and platforms – is how to reduce production capacities in line with the reduction in demand.

At the same time, there is interest among many states in raising the technological sophistication of their armed forces and adding new technical capabilities. Therefore, it may be that demand is not depressed for all equipment types, despite shrinking global military expenditures.

The 'defence industry' is by no means homogeneous.[3] While sectoral industrial classifications are usually based on the characteristics of the product, adopting this approach in the defence area confines the sector to items specifically designed, developed, and produced for military purposes and which have no alternative use. This creates a discrete sector of arms and munitions along with a small number of dedicated delivery platforms and target acquisition systems, but it excludes many products that are of growing importance to military capability. The alternative is to classify the sector by the nature of the customer and the end-use to which a product is put. However, many producers sell the same or similar products in both civil and defence markets. These definitional problems contribute to the fact that defence-related trade and production have never been disaggregated in national and international economic data according to standard procedures.

A cash-rich producer of digital telecommunications equipment that is part of a global private sector corporation has a different environment from a heavily indebted producer of mortar bombs. Clearly, a broad brush approach cannot do justice to all of the issues involved in the micro-economic environment of any company. This paper will attempt to identify broad trends shaping the environment in which the defence industry has to work. Specific questions related to individual products and companies are not addressed.

The defence market is determined by government, and therefore this is essentially a demand-side approach. Defence equipment producers have to consider at least the following issues (most of which are closely inter-related):

• Trends in defence planning and force posture
• Trends in public expenditure and, within that, trends in military expenditure
• Trends in military technology development
• Prospects for successful exports

The remainder of this chapter will look at each of these sets of issues in turn and offer a brief summary of different responses by industry.

TRENDS IN DEFENCE PLANNING AND FORCE POSTURE

Following the end of the Cold War, arms procurement and the impact of political and military changes on the defence industry have not been a high priority in the discussion of international security. Governments have centred their attention on broad issues of security and defence policy and assumed that appropriate procurement choices will flow logically from the outcome of those debates. At the international level, discussions have focused on the future shape of the international system. At the national level, the debate has focused more on how to shape a new 'grand strategy' for the new international conditions than on defence industrial issues.

Even within the national debate on narrower defence issues, equipment has not been a dominant issue. Defence down-sizing has required manpower reductions and the relocation of large numbers of military units and personnel. Many military bases have been closed.[4] Several countries have discussed whether they will retain conscription as the basis for their armed forces or try to establish smaller armed forces with fully professional personnel.

Russia in particular has seen massive upheavals in its military environment. During the Cold War, large numbers of Soviet forces were deployed far forward, in support of the prevailing doctrine. By the end of 1995, Russia had withdrawn more than 700,000 men and women and 45,000 pieces of equipment from the Baltic States and Central Europe. Nevertheless, a large number of Russian troops, and infrastructure to support them, remain stationed outside the territory of Russia. Each of the major branches of the Russian armed forces (Ground Force, Air Force, Air Defence Force, Navy, and Strategic Rocket Force) has drawn up a development plan that sets objectives for fundamental reform and reorganization to be achieved by the early years of the next century. None of these plans is yet final and several key variables are not yet known.[5] However, one objective is the implementation of the military doctrine approved in 1993, which includes among its objectives the capacity to conduct defensive and offensive operations under the conditions of massive use of present and future weapons.[6]

Within NATO, the main preoccupation of member governments was the elaboration and implementation of the new Alliance Strategic Concept approved in late 1991. Subsequently, the dominant issues within the alliance have concerned the establishment of new relationships with both former adversaries and European neutral and non-aligned countries.

The United States, Canada, and most Western European countries take many of their most important decisions about strategy and force structure in the framework of NATO. The new Alliance Strategic Concept provided a framework for subsequent decisions about a new NATO force structure that is not based on the defence of a fixed front in Central Europe. These decisions began to be implemented in 1994 and were being completed in early 1996.[7]

The new structure is built around the idea that participating members contribute discrete units – divisions or brigades – to larger multinational formations. The goal of these changes is to allow members maximum flexibility in their decision-making. Not only the United States, but also the larger European countries are still trying to retain the widest possible range of independent military capabilities. For this reason they prefer to avoid creating interdependence in key operational tasks. Such interdependence could make it difficult or impossible for one government to use force without the consent of another, or alternatively, may create pressures to assent to the use of force at the request of a partner.

Outside the framework of NATO, the same approach underpins the Franco-German Eurocorps established after May 1992. This force is intended to form the core of a future European Security and Defence Identity and was joined by Belgium and Spain in 1993. Belgium will also contribute a discrete unit – a mechanized brigade – to the force, as will Spain

– a mechanized brigade that will be upgraded to a mechanized division in 1998.

In January 1994 NATO approved the concept of combined joint task forces. These forces deployed self-contained elements of existing national forces, in 'packages' tailored to specific scenarios. However, the task forces might include non-NATO forces. The further discussion of details regarding these task forces has become an important element of the NATO Partnership for Peace initiative.

In January 1994 NATO heads of government also approved the idea of enlarging the alliance by admitting new members. Managing this enlargement has now become one of the central issues facing NATO governments. In particular, since this process of enlargement has been strongly opposed by Russia, it has been necessary to think through and discuss the future implications of enlargement for relations with Moscow and the impact on the security of countries that do not join the alliance.

From the perspective of defence industries in Europe, an additional factor to be considered is the process of political union taking place in the framework of the European Union. While the evolution of a common foreign and security policy in the framework of the EU has potentially important long-term implications, thus far moves by government to establish new practices for arms procurement have been very tentative. Decisions of this kind are currently still taken at the national level in all countries.

The idea of a European Armaments Agency able to take collective decisions on arms procurement was approved as a long-term objective of the European Union in a declaration on the Western European Union (WEU) annexed to the Maastricht Treaty.[8] Clearly, such a step would have very important implications for the defence industry. However, no such agency has been established so far and government discussions have been limited to harmonizing national requirements for any given system and combining certain administrative aspects of project management where a system is to be jointly procured. Efforts of this kind have a long history within NATO.[9]

For European defence industries – including those in countries considered to be export-oriented – the most important single line of communication remains that with the domestic ministry of defence or armed forces procurement agency. The close ties that have developed over many years, between national producers on the one hand and their ministries of defence and armed forces on the other, still offer a channel for information exchange about future requirements that allows industry to tailor products to the needs of the customer.[10] In order to improve their access to information and to decision-makers, many companies have established teaming arrangements with foreign partners through whom they tend to market their products. In some cases companies may also share technology with a foreign partner or share the financial risks involved in developing new products together. However, for the most part these remain arrangements for cooperation between independent companies. The major cross-border rationalization of the European defence industry anticipated in the early 1990s does not appear to be taking place, and there remain significant political and legal obstacles to international take-overs in the defence sectors.[11]

Elsewhere in Europe, the dissolution of the Warsaw Treaty Organization and the end of the Cold War also transformed the strategic landscape for former member states. The need to counter a putative threat from NATO disappeared – the focus of defence planning for nearly four decades – taking with it the central rationale for maintaining enormous defence establishments. The defence planning problems are now of an entirely different character: eliminating surplus military equipment, personnel, and industrial production capacity; and adapting national armed forces to an unsettled security environment lacking an immediate or well-defined threat. As Curt Gasteyger has observed, in meeting this new security environment Central and East Europeans have little, if any, guidance as to how they should define a security policy that is politically feasible, militarily credible, and financially sustainable.[12]

Prospective NATO members – Poland, the Czech Republic, and Hungary – initially believed that defence industrial issues would be an important element of NATO membership. It was assumed in these countries that NATO membership would require the armed forces to invest heavily in new equipment.

However, it is increasingly recognized that replacing major platforms currently in service with the armed forces is neither practical nor necessary in order to operate alongside NATO forces.

Central European arms industries were developed to supplement the Soviet industry. While political control independence has been achieved, these countries retain the legacy of technical dependence. They would undoubtedly like to add some new industrial capacities to secure access to technologies previously supplied by the Soviet Union, but financing their development from local resources is likely to be impossible. The likelihood of major economic assistance from Western powers for the purpose of arms procurement is also very low, given their other needs and priorities.

Recent studies in the United States have suggested that most of the costs associated with enlarging the alliance are related to the relocation of forces and the necessary investment in new infrastructure. The equipment-related expenditures considered necessary do not involve major new platforms, but rather adapting existing forces to make them inter-operable with those of other NATO forces.[13] For the most part, this would mean adapting platforms to use NATO communications systems, weapons, and ordnance. Major new purchases of, for example, fighter aircraft or main battle tanks would be deferred until well after the year 2000.

Outside the major industrial powers, several other countries are also planning significant force structure changes. In both Southeast Asia and Latin America, states have been faced with the task of military reform in response to changing security environments. In Latin America, armed forces which played a central role in domestic politics defined their tasks to include internal security. However, after the transition to democratic governments in Argentina, Brazil and Chile, the armed forces may be limited to more traditional external defence tasks. In Southeast Asia – where counter-insurgency was a major mission for the armed forces – Malaysia, Thailand, Indonesia and the Philippines are also beginning to see external defence as the primary or exclusive task for the armed forces.

In some cases, new capabilities have been acquired to meet new mission requirements. States have sought to upgrade air defence, maritime patrol, and sea denial capabilities, which had been given a low priority while the primary need was counter-insurgency.

TRENDS IN PUBLIC EXPENDITURE AND DEFENCE EXPENDITURE

In wartime or in an acute crisis, economic policy is likely to be subordinate to defence policy. However, as a finance ministry official in the United Kingdom has noted, in most countries at most times, 'before deciding its priorities for particular programmes any government has to take a view of what is the total of public expenditure which can be afforded. That is a judgment which is taken in the context of the government's overall economic strategy.'[14]

TABLE 1.1
SELECTED DATA FOR NATO MILITARY EXPENDITURE, 1986–95

1. Military expenditure in millions of (1990) US dollars

	1986	1987	1988	1989	1990	1991	1992	1993	1994	1995
NATO	527,305	529,356	520,159	518,185	504,092	464,008	470,851	451,057	430,271	407,738
USA	335,048	331,215	323,860	320,427	306,170	268,994	284,116	269,111	254,038	238,194

2. Expenditure for the NATO category 'Equipment', in millions of (1990) US dollars

	1986	1987	1988	1989	1990	1991	1992	1993	1994	1995
NATO[a]	118,127	120,886	112,886	111,352	102,088	99,209	88,118	84,581	98,083	90,435
USA	86,442	87,772	80,317	81,068	75,930	73,435	65,063	59,204	74,179	65,980

[a] Data exclude France and Canada.
Source: Derived from Table 8.1 and Appendix 8A, SIPRI Yearbook 1996, World Armaments, Disarmament and International Security (Oxford: Oxford University Press, 1996).

For countries that belonged to the former Warsaw Treaty Organization, this subordination of defence readiness to other goals has been a recent phenomenon. However, the data in Table 1.1 underline that across NATO downward pressure on military expenditure pre-dated the end of the Cold War. Overall spending was reduced by 23 per cent between 1987 and 1995. Meanwhile, spending on equipment declined by 30 per cent between 1987 and 1993. Whereas during the Cold War it may have been possible for ministries of defence to argue that they had special reasons to override broader public expenditure targets, this is no longer the case.

In the past two years, however, there has been some evidence that the reductions in military expenditure in the United States – which still accounts for approximately 60 per cent of all military spending in the alliance – have ended. By the year 2000 it is intended that the modernization account of the United States Department of Defense will reach $67 billion.[15] Added to roughly 30 billion dollars worth of research, development, testing, and evaluation, this would mean procurement spending of roughly $100 billion – close in real terms to the levels recorded in the mid-1980s.

Among some of the most important European members of NATO – including France, Germany and the United Kingdom – an upturn in military expenditure is unlikely in the next several years. In the UK and Germany, changes in the approach to public expenditure were already visible in the early 1980s.

In the United Kingdom (in 1979) and the Federal Republic of Germany (in 1982) the governments that came to power put a high emphasis on controlling the growth in public expenditure in order to reduce the deficit between government spending and income. These policies have continued.[16]

During the period 1979–85, the British government increased military expenditure only because the prime minister personally intervened to overrule an effort by the Treasury to ignore the NATO target of annual increases of 3 per cent after inflation.[17] However, military expenditure has been falling since 1985.

In the Federal Republic of Germany military expenditure was broadly constant in real terms between 1980 and 1990. After 1990, when the special circumstances created by unification began to take effect, military expenditure declined by 25 per cent in five years.[18]

Although defence spending has been under pressure in France since the early 1990s, major cuts were postponed until 1995. In that year the new French government of Alain Juppé made a sudden mid-year decision to reduce defence expenditure.. These cuts were not restored in the 1996 budget and may signal the beginning rather than the end of the downturn in French defence spending.

In 1991, when the Italian government made the control of public expenditure a central aim of its structural reorganization programme, defence spending was to some extent shielded from the process. A rise in the defence budget, from 1993, was planned. In fact, the budget for 1993 was reduced from the amount agreed upon mid-year in 1992 and fell by 8 per cent in the following two years.[19]

European Union governments have emphasized the control of public expenditure, deficit reduction and reducing public debt as elements necessary in bringing about a convergence in approaches to economic policy. In February 1992, in article 104c of the Treaty on European Union (the Maastricht Treaty), EU governments bound themselves to avoid excessive government deficits.[20]

The changes in aggregate NATO expenditure on equipment do not reflect uniform behaviour by the European allies. Table 1.2 indicates the shifting national trends and shares of equipment spending by the European members of NATO.

It illustrates that the distribution of equipment expenditure among these countries has changed in some significant ways in recent years. Whereas in 1986 Germany accounted for 28 per cent of the spending on equipment, by 1995 this per centage had fallen to 15 per cent. By contrast, whereas in 1986 Turkey accounted for only 3 per cent of spending on equipment by European NATO members, by 1995 this share had risen to 9 per cent.

There are many methodological difficulties in measuring the absolute value, or even the trends in Russian military expenditure, but significant public information is now available. In 1995 Russia reported its military expenditures for the years 1992–94 through the United Nations Reduction of Military Budgets mechanism. This report provides a matrix in which states can desegregate their military budgets as well as providing total expenditures. According to the report, Russian military expenditure was 900 billion rubles in 1992, 7.6 trillion rubles in 1993, and 43 trillion rubles in 1994.[21] The impact of the enormous inflation experienced by Russia in recent years is clear in these numbers. Few meaningful conclusions can be drawn from this official data about the level of Russian spending, as a share of national economic activity (gross domestic product) or even as a share of government expenditure. Moreover, the additional problem of finding a satisfactory exchange rate makes it difficult to say anything very useful about Russian expenditure in international comparative terms.

In Central Europe recent economic developments have been more dramatic, more complex, and have contributed to a much steeper decline in military expenditure than what is seen in

TABLE 1.2

THE DISTRIBUTION OF MILITARY EXPENDITURE FOR EQUIPMENT AMONG
EUROPEAN MEMBERS OF NATO, 1986–95

Equipment expenditure in millions of (1990) US dollars

	1986	1987	1988	1989	1990	1991	1992	1993	1994	1995
Belgium	643	657	577	468	367	375	308	250	277	232
	2%	2%	2%	2%	1%	2%	1%	1%	1%	1%
Denmark	353	397	391	347	395	426	471	387	411	371
	1%	1%	1%	1%	2%	2%	2%	2%	2%	2%
Germany	8,137	8,155	7,767	7,628	7,491	6,118	5,014	3,772	3,445	3,459
	28%	27%	26%	27%	30%	26%	24%	16%	15%	15%
Greece	610	663	950	836	827	744	891	918	922	759
	2%	2%	3%	3%	3%	3%	4%	4%	4%	3%
Italy	3,714	4,676	4,943	4,982	4,091	3,864	3,451	3,978	3,496	3,357
	13%	15%	16%	18%	16%	16%	16%	17%	17%	15%
Netherlands	1,515	1,352	1,542	1,344	1,328	1,126	1,019	923	1,068	948
	5%	4%	5%	5%	5%	5%	5%	4%	4%	4%
Norway	653	702	617	836	767	724	871	918	990	854
	2%	2%	2%	3%	3%	3%	4%	4%	4%	4%
Portugal	95	158	183	217	193	164	44	137	78	282
	0	1%	1%	1%	1%	1%	0	1%	1%	1%
Spain	2,083	2,469	1,934	1,769	1,150	1,132	884	1,191	969	1,133
	7%	8%	6%	6%	5%	5%	4%	5%	5%	5%
Turkey	811	911	856	756	1,063	1,240	1,425	1,455	1,820	2,012
	3%	3%	3%	3%	4%	5%	7%	6%	9%	9%
UK	10,803	10,513	10,324	8,974	7,120	7,971	6,722	9,441	8,651	9,215
	37%	34%	34%	32%	29%	33%	32%	40%	39%	41%

Note: Data exclude France and Luxembourg.
Source: Derived from Table 8.1, SIPRI Yearbook 1996, World Armaments, Disarmament and International Security (Oxford: Oxford University Press, 1996).

Western Europe.[22] The effort to reduce the importance of public expenditure within overall activity is by definition a central characteristic of economic policy in all Central European countries as they move toward a market economy. In some cases policies aimed at tight control over the budget were prompted by international financial institutions – notably the International Monetary Fund – while others – in the Czech Republic, for example – these were the preferred policies of the national government.

Against this background of approaches to public expenditure, levels of military expenditure have fallen significantly across the region. Moreover, within these declining defence budgets, the distribution of resources has also been changed. The priority assigned to restructuring and relocating the armed forces has meant that the share of the budget allocated to the procurement of equipment has been reduced dramatically.

To summarize, while the overall equipment expenditure within NATO fell sharply after 1988, the recent pattern has stabilized largely because of developments in the United States. Turkey is one NATO country where there has been a consistent increase in levels of spending on equipment. In Central Europe and the former Soviet Union, expenditure reductions have been especially sharp.

TRENDS IN MILITARY TECHNOLOGY DEVELOPMENT

There is widespread agreement that 'a number of new technologies are now in public view which, if fully developed and deployed, could have implications for existing military capabilities'.[23] Some technologies appear to have matured – for example, it is unlikely that any major new breakthrough will be achieved in military applications of nuclear technology – while others are still in a period of rapid development. Among these rapidly developing technologies three – communications, data processing and biotechnology – appear to have the greatest potential military significance. These areas of technology share the characteristics of not being inherently military in character.

13

In contrast with the past, in these areas of technology development is being undertaken primarily in the hope of developing major civilian applications. Nevertheless, each has potential applications in the military area.

In 1991 operations by US forces against Iraq underlined the impact that technological change could have on military operations. However, while the United States is now committed to implementing a 'revolution in military affairs' (one element of which is a 'military technological revolution'), European countries still face the decision of whether or not they have either the need or the desire to follow the United States across this threshold.

The United States is now building a new force structure on a platform of expenditure at around 6 per cent of GDP sustained for almost ten years. European governments would find it difficult to justify these levels of expenditure. More likely than a revolution in European military affairs is an incremental pursuit of some trends already set in motion in the framework adopted in the 1980s by the Follow-On Force Attack, a NATO concept.[24] These trends highlighted operational mobility (the ability to move armed forces quickly within and beyond Europe), increasing the firepower available to relatively small units; and increasing the flexibility of field commanders (i.e., their ability to fight successfully in a variety of different geographical conditions against a range of different enemies).

Some European countries have been discussing a greater emphasis on mobility (especially air mobility) for several years. In France, the Force d'Action Rapide (FAR) was created in 1983, as the culmination of plans initiated in 1977. The United Kingdom began to investigate the creation of air-mobile forces in 1978, and by 1986 it had established the experimental Air Mobile Brigade. In Italy a relatively small rapid reaction force – the Forza d'Intervento Rapido – was created in the late 1970s. In Spain the Fuerza de Acción Rápida underwent its first exercise in 1988. Mobility is an equation that depends on three factors: first, the availability of transport by air, land or sea; second, the volume and mass of items to be transported; and third, the infrastructure (ports, airports, terminals, railheads, etc.) needed to receive and distribute the flow of goods and people into the area of operations.

Achieving greater flexibility in the armed forces has also become a major technology development challenge. Sensible decisions about appropriate armament require information about the forces to be faced. Whereas the European theatre created a clear framework for operations during the Cold War, governments are now thinking about conditions in which armed forces must be prepared for deployment at short notice, against unknown adversaries, in places where knowledge of local conditions may be limited. Under such conditions it is considered essential that commanders have access to the surveillance, command, and control assets required to make an accurate and rapid evaluation of the situation in which they find themselves.[25]

Another trend that became visible from the late 1970s on was toward improved 'military productivity'. The argument was advanced that 'trends in accuracy, reduced size, and increased destructiveness mean the devolving of true combined arms capability (including air defence) to smaller and smaller units. It is not inconceivable that units comparable to today's battalions will have the capability of today's brigades or divisions in terms of the type and number of targets they will be able to attack.'[26]

It should be noted that these developments are likely to be pursued within the European theatre (meaning Western and Central Europe) either in the framework of NATO or as part of national defence. Unlike in the United States, where there is a determination to retain power projection capabilities, it has not been decided whether European governments should plan for operations further afield (other than traditional UN peacekeeping operations).

The technologies most often listed as central to the objectives of mobility, flexibility, and enhanced productivity are information technology, space technology, and materials technology. It has been pointed out that these technologies are not specifically military in nature and that the pace of their development is likely to be at least as fast in the civil as in the military sector.[27] Moreover, in several cases they are process technologies (that is, the organization of existing products organized in a system that enhances their efficient use) rather than product technologies (the invented new products).

Certain specialist areas remain military-specific – for example, few civilians are thinking about how to penetrate a hardened bunker and detonate an explosion powerful enough to destroy its contents or how to track, intercept and destroy multiple objects, each travelling at Mach speeds. However, some processes have evolved at least as fast in the civil as in the military sector. In terms of mobility, the capacity to move large volumes of goods and people quickly and efficiently is a key element in modern life. Continuous expansion in trade and tourism is likely to ensure the continuation of this trend.[28] In terms of flexibility, the ability to collect, process and transfer large quantities of data in a rapid and secure manner is also a key element of civilian economic development.

The integration of civilian and military industrial production is also heavily influenced by these trends. Before 1945 the ability to increase the volume of production of military goods in times of crisis or war was regarded as a strategic necessity. However, the growing complexity of military equipment developed during the Cold War, together with the introduction of nuclear weapons into the European theatre, seemed to make notions of a 'surge' in production impractical or redundant. Through the 1950s and 1960s, the production of major platforms required the integration of more and more sub-systems – jet engines, electronics, guided weapons – each of which in itself grew progressively more complex. Even if these systems could be produced in significantly larger numbers, training the manpower to operate them and integrating them into the armed forces would be a lengthy process. Moreover, the presence of nuclear weapons made the notion of an unlimited war impractical. As one observer expressed it: 'Multiply the concept of unrestricted warfare by the power of the hydrogen bomb to obtain the apocalypse'.[29] Under these circumstances the retention of surplus capacity increasingly became a waste of resources.

There is some evidence, however, that new defence industrial policies may emerge among the major powers to compensate for the fact that neither industry nor government is willing to sustain redundant production capacities against the contingency of an unspecified future crisis. All governments take into account the impact on domestic industry of taxation, tariffs on trade, support for research and development, and other economic policies. Nonetheless, economic policies that have an impact on industry do not amount to industrial policy, which has been defined as a complex of policies concerning protection of domestic industries, development of strategic industries, and adjustment of the economic structure formulated and implemented by government agencies in the cause of the national interest, as defined by the responsible officials.[30]

A team of researchers at the RAND Corporation has suggested that if the production lines used to manufacture certain major platforms are closed, it may not be impossible to restart production at a later date.[31] Jacques Gansler of the Analytical Sciences Corporation has suggested that facilities could be designed that permit production of some items to switch from civil to military and back again, according to demand.[32] In Europe, the chief executive of Dowty Aerospace has said that some form of integrated planning for the defence industry would be welcome if it did not undermine existing economic and market philosophies.[33]

The kinds of ideas proposed are somewhat reminiscent of the Ministry of Supply and similar agencies that grew up in the United Kingdom under the 'ten year rule,' which stated that aggressive action against the British Empire within the next ten years was 'not a contingency seriously to be apprehended'.[34] A Principal Supply Officers Committee, established in 1924, was tasked with liaison to industry through a series of sectoral sub-committees which drew personnel from other government departments. The responsibilities of these sub-committees included, for example, discussions with industry about which kinds of machine tools and production equipment were likely to be most useful in future defence production.

These sub-committees faced some problems that may still apply. While it was relatively easy to identify generic technologies of interest, it was difficult to predict which specific products would be critical ten years into the future. Similarly, today everyone would acknowledge the growing importance of information technology. However, these products have a life-span measured in months. Secondly, when the effort was made to restart production of warships in the 1930s, it was discovered that skilled labour was not available in the parts of the country where it was required.[35] Some recent discussions have also led to the question of whether developing prototypes or technology demonstrators is sensible if these cannot be produced when needed.[36] Nevertheless, despite its shortcomings, the policy pursued in the 1920s is believed to have worked. Brian Bond and Williamson Murray concluded that 'by the late 1930s, the Committee of Imperial Defence (CID) and its sub-committees had compiled comprehensive blueprints for the conversion of industry and manpower to military needs and the acquisition and stockpiling of vital raw materials'.[37] This contributed to the subsequent rapid increase in defence production.

PROSPECTS FOR EXPORTS

Prospects for overseas sales are the fourth factor of growing relevance to the planning processes of defence producers. Given the scale of the reductions in procurement spending noted above, few defence producers would be able to compensate through foreign sales for the loss of this domestic market. Yet there is a view among producers that overseas markets are becoming relatively more important in the short term, though reliance upon them can be questioned as a long-term strategy.

As suggested earlier, the approach of offsetting reduced domestic demand by increasing exports is difficult to pursue in a shrinking global market. Moreover, this strategy is constrained by political as well as economic factors. At the level of major systems, the international arms market is still dominated by a small number of rather stable bilateral relationships which are as much politically as economically motivated. For example, the nature of the US security relationship with Japan, South Korea, and Saudi Arabia, among others, is such that it is difficult to imagine the recipient country turning to a new supplier even if savings could be achieved by doing so. Similarly, the bilateral arms transfer relationships between Russia and India or Russia and China are partly intended to signal to the United States that there are limits to unipolarity in the international system.

A commitment from the domestic ministry of defence is still the most important consideration for producers deciding whether to develop a large and complex product. However, the European Defence Industries Group (EDIG) has stated that a feeling in industry that permission to export a product to a wide range of markets could be denied may tip the balance in deciding whether or not to develop that product.

Arms export decisions are likely to continue to be on a case-by-case basis, and it is unlikely that any government would commit itself to deregulate arms exports. Nevertheless, the relative weight attached to the impact of licence denial on the industrial base – already an important consideration – is likely to increase in decision-making. This is likely to be specially true for smaller items, such as tactical communication systems or avionics, which are defence-related but not in themselves independent products.

Many of the most important producers of defence equipment are highly dependent on sales of sub-systems in foreign markets. Components of US origin are found in much non-US military equipment, while many US fighter aircraft have flight controls, landing gear, or head-up displays either imported directly from abroad or made by the local subsidiaries of foreign companies (often British or Israeli). Within Western Europe, inter-firm and intra-firm collaboration of various kinds, including a rationalization of the suppliers of components and sub-assemblies, has been observed in recent years.[38]

This section of the international market is less constrained by political factors. Many countries which purchase major platforms from domestic suppliers have already accepted that at the level of sub-systems and components, these end-items will include a significant foreign content. However, governments are sensitive to any effort by a foreign government to exploit such inter-dependencies to bring about changes in foreign or security policy. Increasingly, producers of end-items are seeking guarantees that they will be able to export equipment with significant foreign content according to the national regulations of the country in which final assembly takes place. This is to reduce the extent to which the different national approaches to export licensing and export policy of governments of industrial partners can interfere with the smooth execution of contracts with third parties.

THE NATURE OF THE GLOBAL MARKET FOR MAJOR DEFENCE EQUIPMENT

There is a consensus that the United States is now the predominant supplier of arms and that a stable group of five countries – China, France, Germany, Russia, and the United Kingdom – represent an important second tier of exporters. Among the European countries, other significant arms exporters include the Czech Republic, the Netherlands, Poland, Slovakia, Sweden, and Switzerland.

Table 1.3 indicates the changing shares of the global total accounted for by the major suppliers, according to SIPRI estimates across the period 1986–95. The table highlights the growing dominance of the United States and the dramatic reduction in the volume of arms transfers from Russia and the former Soviet Union.

For the European Union members these data need careful interpretation if they are not to mislead. While the table offers an estimate of changing export volumes, it does not reflect the economic and financial aspects of arms transfers. For these we have no adequate data. Several of the major European producers have published national data on the value of arms exports, but this data is compiled according to specific national definitions and methodologies. Therefore, it cannot be used comparatively. Moreover, there are some major methodological issues associated with the definition and measurement of foreign trade in general which would make it extremely difficult to arrive at such figures even under ideal conditions.

The growing prominence of the European Union as a supplier of major defence equipment largely reflects the scale of the disposal of surplus equipment by Germany, in recent years in particular. The financial flows associated with such transfers have been small. On the other hand, the economic significance of exports for France and the United Kingdom are underestimated in this data because no account is taken of several kinds of transfers which lead to substantial sales. The significance of the Netherlands as a supplier of defence equipment is under-represented for the same methodological reason.

TABLE 1.3
DELIVERIES OF MAJOR CONVENTIONAL WEAPONS BY SELECTED SUPPLIERS AS
A % SHARE OF TOTAL GLOBAL DELIVERIES, 1986–95

	1986	1987	1988	1989	1990	1991	1992	1993	1994	1995
USA	27	28	30	39	35	49	56	52	56	42
USSR/Russia	43	40	38	39	35	18	12	15	4	17
EU	18	15	16	20	20	21	19	21	27	26

Source: SIPRI arms trade database.

The emergence of different forms of internationalization has also had an impact on statistics since not all foreign sales need be exports. For example, UK companies such as the General Electric Company (GEC), the TI Group, Lucas Industries, Rolls-Royce, and Smiths Industries make significant sales in the United States through their local subsidiaries. Within the European Union, the arrival of the single market for many kinds of goods and services has had an impact on the way trade flows are recorded at national borders. The value of transfers in dual-use equipment may no longer be captured in trade statistics. The growth of foreign direct investment by companies may have had an impact on the measurement of trade.

It was noted above that there is still a central politico-military element to arms transfer relations. In recent years this has worked to the advantage of the United States and, to a lesser extent, Britain and France, since these are the only countries that are seen to be capable of offering direct military assistance in a time of crisis. Russia may benefit from the concern of countries which feel that they are or may become the target of US military pressure. While these factors are still very important, the arms market is more flexible than it was during the Cold War, when bloc alignments tended to be very rigid. European producers have a wide range of defence equipment that they can offer to potential customers, and they are trying to establish closer relationships with cash-paying customers of the United States.[39]

In several recent competitions Russia has also demonstrated that it can succeed even in new markets. For example, in Malaysia, Cyprus and the United Arab Emirates, Russian equipment was selected in open competitions. While it is very unlikely that Russian arms will be transferred in the same quantities as before, it is also clear that Russia will remain a significant factor in the international arms market.

Export success also appears to be increasingly dependent on whether a supplier can provide offsetting benefits to the recipient in exchange for a contract award. Both the financing arrangements offered with arms transfers and the various kinds of direct and indirect military and civilian offsets associated with any given deal are acknowledged to be of growing importance.

Finally, recipients want to be reassured that the systems they buy will defeat the forces they are likely to come up against. Therefore, the extent to which equipment is perceived to be at or near the leading edge of performance will also play a role in whether or not its supplier succeeds.

IMPLICATIONS FOR DEFENCE INDUSTRIES

This brief overview suggests some defence industrial trends which are likely to be 'robust'. The first and most obvious is that the combined excess capacity of the defence industry worldwide has not yet been eliminated. In Russia and the former Soviet Union, Central Europe, and, in particular, some Western European countries (notably France), continued contraction seems almost certain. Secondly, the process of concentration on a national basis that is accompanying reduction in capacity will leave a smaller number of companies, but those that remain will be very large and powerful industrial entities.

In terms of patterns of demand, only the United States among the major industrial countries seems likely to experience an upturn in procurement spending between 1997 and the year 2000 (though this upturn is far from certain, depending as it does on many variables related to US domestic politics and economic policy). Therefore, it is predictable that the combination of sustained demand and industrial concentration will consolidate the predominance of the United States as a defence industrial power.

European states, by contrast, have not seen the same levels of concentration in what remains an industry fragmented on national lines. The outcome of the debate on a common foreign and security policy and, subsequently, the elaboration of a common defence policy, seems certain to unfold over many years. In May 1994, reflecting on the need for access to foreign markets and the increasing costs of weapon development, the European Defence Industries Group observed that 'it is highly unlikely that any single [European] nation will be able to contemplate the research and development and production costs of a major item of defence equipment'.[40] However, given the writing on the wall, many of the larger European companies are as likely to explore close partnerships with US or Canadian firms (which enjoy full access to the US market) than with each other.

The Russian defence industry remains in a state of crisis. The size and structure of future demand from the Russian ministry of defence depends on decisions about military reform that have not yet been taken. The growing emphasis placed on exports as a source of revenue for defence enterprises seems likely to be a persistent factor for the foreseeable future. Nevertheless, even after a major contraction, the size of the former Soviet defence industry is such that Russia seems certain to remain a significant global actor, perhaps at a level comparable to the larger West European states.

The future prospects for Central European arms industries – developed to supplement the Soviet industry – seem very limited. While the advantage that they have in terms of price may lead to some successes in the short term, they are unable to offer assurances of security guarantees, and they have few resources that would enable them to stay close to the leading edge in performance or to develop new products. They are also unable to offer financing arrangements or offsets. While political control from the Soviet Union has gone, in many cases producers remain dependent on Russia for some key functions or sub-systems. The smaller central European countries seem more likely to be customers for the larger defence industries than competitors to them.

Defence industries have not been given special treatment by governments negotiating the post-Cold War environment. Some governments have paid lip service to the idea of special measures tailored to the problems of the defence industry – conversion – but few have elaborated systematic programmes. Some of the programmes that did emerge – notably in Russia – were not fully funded. Defence producers have received broadly the same types of support (for example, regional economic support) as those engaged in any economic activity that experiences a sudden and significant reduction in demand.

Governments in general have not given high priority to the formulation of new arms procurement programmes, given the surplus of equipment already in post-Cold War inventories. However, there is some evidence of thinking about a new form of defence industrial policy based on civil–military integration.

The sudden reduction of demand has stimulated producers to look for new markets overseas, but this is not a strategy likely to succeed for more than a small number of companies.

NOTES

1. The global arms industry is surveyed each year in the *Yearbook* of the Stockholm International Peace Research Institute (SIPRI).
2. Bonn International Conversion Centre, *Conversion Survey 1996* (Oxford: Oxford University Press, 1996).
3. M. C. Libicki, *What Makes Industries Strategic?*, National Defense University, McNair Paper no. 5 (Washington DC, November 1989); W. Walker, M. Graham and B. Harbor, 'From components to integrated systems: technological diversity and integrations between the military and civilian sectors', in P. Gummett and J. Reppy (eds), *The Relations between Defence and Civil Technologies*, NATO ASI series (Dordrecht: Kluwer, 1988); and D. Burns, 'What Is The Defence Industrial Base?', *Defence Analysis* 8: 2 (1992), pp. 206–8.
4. For example, the United States has plans to close 275 military bases by the

year 2001. James Murphy, *Military Base and Industry Conversion: The American Approach*, North Atlantic Cooperation Council Symposium on the Possibilities of Harmonizing Conversion Strategies, Budapest, 15–17 November 1995.

5. Among the most important open questions are: will the Commonwealth of Independent States provide a framework for strategic bases and deployment of Russian formations?; will the existing air force and air defence force be combined into a single element?; will the Border Security Force be absorbed into the army?
6. For an overview see S. Kile, 'Military Doctrine in Transition', in Ian Anthony (ed.), *The Future of the Defence Industries in Central and Eastern Europe*, SIPRI Research Report no. 7, 1994.
7. R. Estrella, *After the NATO Summit: New Structures and Modalities for Military Co-operation*, Report to the Defence and Security Committee, AL205, DSC(94)8, North Atlantic Assembly, Brussels, November 1994.
8. For a recent discussion of these themes, see *The Challenges Facing the European Defence-Related Industry: A Contribution for Action at the European Level* (communication from the European Commission to the Council, the European Parliament, the Economic and Social Committee and the Committee of the Regions, Brussels, 25 January 1996).
9. France and Germany have set up a joint armaments agency, but this agency has a management function rather than decision-making authority.
10. D. G. Kiely, *Defence Procurement: The Equipment Buying Process* (London: Tri-Service Press, 1990), p. 45.
11. For a survey of recent take-overs see E. Sköns and B. Gill, 'Arms Production', *SIPRI Yearbook 1996: World Armaments, Disarmament and International Security* (Oxford: Oxford University Press, 1996).
12. C. Gasteyger, 'The Remaking of Eastern Europes Security', *Survival*, 33: 2 (March/April 1991).
13. For example, T. S. Szayna and F. S. Larrabee, *East European Military Reform after the Cold War: Implications for the United States*, RAND study MR-523-OSD (Santa Monica, CA: RAND, 1995); Congressional Budget Office, *The Costs of Expanding the NATO Alliance* (Washington, DC, March 1996).
14. D. J. L. Moore, 'Defence and the Treasury', in *Defence Procurement: Trends and Developments* (London: RUSI, 1993), p. 14.
15. P. G. Kaminsky, 'Building a Ready Force for the 21st Century', *Defence Issues*, 11: 6 (17 January 1996). Kaminsky is Undersecretary of Defense for Acquisition and Technology.
16. United States General Accounting Office, *Deficit Reduction: Experiences of Other Nations*, GAO Report GAO/AIMD-95-30, December 1994.
17. G. Howe, *Conflict of Loyalty* (London: Macmillan, 1994), p. 144.
18. See also J. Rohde and P. Schmidt, 'German Armaments Policy: Its Consequences for the Armaments Industry', *Defence Analysis*, 11: 3 (1995).
19. S. Silvestri, 'Italian Defence Policy', in Trevor Taylor (ed.), *Reshaping European Defence* (London: Royal Institute for International Affairs, 1995); Appendix 8A, *SIPRI Yearbook: World Armaments, Disarmament and International Security* (Oxford: Oxford University Press, 1996).
20. In a separate protocol governments provided their definition of 'excessive' and pledged to adopt national budget procedures consistent with the overall goals laid down in the Treaty.

21. Reduction of Military Budgets: Report of the Secretary-General, UN General Assembly document A/50/277 (20 July 1995).
22. E. Loose-Weintraub, 'Military expenditures in the Central and East European Countries', SIPRI Yearbook 1993: World Armaments and Disarmament (Oxford: Oxford University Press, 1993), and subsections in subsequent SIPRI Yearbooks.
23. Scientific and Technological Developments and Their Impact on International Security, UN doc. A/45/568 (17 October 1990).
24. M. Moodie, The Dreadful Fury: Advanced Military Technology and the Atlantic Alliance, CSIS, Washington Papers no. 136 (Washington, DC, 1989).
25. Y. Boyer, 'Strategic Implications of New Technologies for Conventional Weapons and the European Battlefield', in C. M. Kelleher and G. A. Mattox (eds), Evolving European Defence Policies (Lexington, MA, 1987).
26. M. D. Fry, 'Some Thoughts On The Role Of Military Forces Within A European Security System', in G. Wachter and A. Krohn (eds), Stability and Arms Control in Europe: The Role of Military Forces within a European Security System, SIPRI Research Report no. 1 (1989), p. 83.
27. Scientific and Technological Developments and their Impact on International Security, UN doc. A/45/568 (17 October 1990).
28. Operation Desert Shield – the preparation for the coalition war against Iraq in 1990–91 – demonstrated that moving a large and diverse force at relatively short notice could only be achieved by using civilian infrastructure. See B. R. Posen, 'Military Mobilization in the Persian Gulf Conflict', in SIPRI Yearbook 1991: World Armaments and Disarmament (Oxford: Oxford University Press, 1991). However, this refers to the ability to deploy troops and material to a friendly country in a non-combat environment. It is not as likely that civilian industry would provide technologies and infrastructure to assist in a forced entry, which would require specialist amphibious and/or air mobile forces.
29. P. A. G. Sabin, 'World War 3: A Historical Mirage', Futures (August 1983), 273.
30. C. Johnson, MITI and The Japanese Miracle: The Growth of Industrialized Policy, 1925–75 (Stanford: Stanford University Press, 1982).
31. J. Birkler, J. Large, G. Smith, and F. Timson, Reconstituting a Production Capability: Past Experience, Restart Criteria and Suggested Policies, Report MR-273-ACQ (Santa Monica: RAND, 1993).
32. J. Gansler, 'Industrial Contraction: Facing the Paradoxes of the Post-Cold War', SAIS Review, 13: 1 (Winter-Spring 1993).
33. T. Edwards, 'A Ministry for the Defence Industries?', RUSI Journal (June 1994), p. 30.
34. Committee of Imperial Defence, quoted in G. C. Peden, British Rearmament and the Treasury 1932–39 (Edinburgh: Scottish Academic Press, 1979), p. 6.
35. E. O. Goldman, 'Thinking about Strategy Absent the Enemy', Security Studies 4:1 (Autumn 1994), p. 62.
36. W. H. Gregory, The Price of Peace: The Future of the Defence Industry and High Technology in a Post-Cold War World (New York: Lexington, 1993), pp. 33–4.
37. B. Bond and W. Murray, 'The British Armed Forces 1918–39', in Allen Millett and Williamson Murray (eds), Military Effectiveness: Volume II, The Interwar Period, Mershon Center Series on International Security and Foreign Policy (Boston: Unwin Hyman, 1990), p. 108.

38. Described in E. Sköns, 'Internationalization of the West European Arms Industry', in H. Wulf (ed.), *Arms Industry Limited* (Oxford: Oxford University Press, 1993). The impact on measuring trade flows is discussed in E. Sköns and H. Wulf, 'The Internationalization of the Arms Industry', *The Arms Trade: Problems and Prospects in the Post-Cold War World*, Annals of the American Academy of Political and Social Science, September 1994.
39. Moreover, it is possible that the United States will mismanage its relations with traditional customers in ways that create opportunities for new suppliers.
40. *The European Armaments Agency: Reply to the Thirty-Ninth Annual Report of the Council*, WEU Assembly document 1419 (19 May 1994), p. 15.

2

The Economics of Defence Conversion

MICHAEL D. INTRILIGATOR

INTRODUCTION

The purpose of this chapter is to consider some aspects of the economics of defence conversion as applied to the defence industries in a period of reduced military budgets. Here the 'defence industries' include all entities producing defence material, whether private or public, while 'conversion' refers to the replacement of defence production in the military industries by non-defence civilian production, where those plants that had been producing defence material begin producing civilian goods.[1] By way of an overview, the aspects treated here are: (1) reduced defence budgets; (2) defence conversion; (3) the peace dividend; (4) conversion costs; (5) disarmament as an investment process; (6) arms exports; (7) the economics of conversion in the Western industrialized nations; (8) the economics of conversion in the former socialist nations; (9) the economics of conversion in the rest of the world; and (10) the implications of the discussion for policy.

REDUCED DEFENCE BUDGETS, BUT NOT EVERYWHERE

The end of the Cold War has led to significant reductions in the defence budgets of the United States, of its allies in NATO, and of the successor states of the Soviet Union and its allies in the former Warsaw Pact. For the United States and its allies in NATO, there have been gradual reductions in defence spending, along with the termination of bases and procurement commitments. For the United States in particular, the defence budget that had been some 6 per cent of GNP, peaking at 6.5 per cent of GNP in 1986, has fallen to some 4 per cent or less in the last several years. For Russia, the other successor states of the Soviet Union, and their former allies in the Warsaw Pact, there have been much more substantial reductions or even collapses in defence spending since the breakup of the Soviet Union in December 1991.

The global East–West arms race has wound down with the end of the Cold War. Arms spending in the rest of the world has, however, remained at traditional levels or even increased. In particular, high defence budgets and multiple arms races continue in regions of conflict and warfare. In the Middle East, defence budgets remain high, despite the accords signed by Israel in recent years. These accords have even led to increases in defence spending given the resulting base relocations and the perceived need for building infrastructure and for retraining. Further developments in the peace process, however, could lead to some reductions in military spending both in Israel and in other nations of the region. More generally, defence spending remains high in a broad arc of instability over the globe that ranges from Morocco to Indonesia and covers northern Africa, southeastern Europe, the Caucasus, the Middle East, southwestern Asia, South Asia, and Southeast Asia. This arc of instability includes ongoing conflicts in these regions. There are also ongoing conflicts in various parts of sub-Saharan Africa. Probably the biggest increases in defence budgets, however, are those in East and Southeast Asia, including China, Taiwan, Malaysia, Thailand, Indonesia, and Vietnam. Unlike the Cold War East–West arms race, which at least by some accounts contributed to stability by creating a mutual deterrence regime, these regional arms races will likely lead to instability and further conflict.[2]

The diplomatic historian John Lewis Gaddis has noted several factors that contributed to the 'long peace' of the Cold War period, but most of these were unique to the Cold War and not relevant to current regional conflicts, arms races, and increased military budgets. These factors include the presence of nuclear weapons and their use only as a last resort; the revolution in reconnaissance technology through space-based systems and other systems that lowered the danger of surprise attack; bipolarity and respect for each other's spheres of influence; stable alliance structures; geographic separation and economic independence of the main contenders, the United States and the Soviet Union; domestic influences in these two so-called 'superpowers'; and the ideological moderation of both, whereby each repressed antagonistic ideological interests in favour of the common goal of preserving the international order.[3] All of these factors were important; to the extent that they were unique to the East–West confrontation of the Cold War, arms buildups elsewhere in regions of conflict, including the development of nuclear weapons, would be unlikely to create a comparable 'long peace'. In the Middle East, in particular, the last several factors are missing. Thus further increases in current stockpiles of nuclear and chemical weapons of mass destruction would probably not create a situation of stability and peace, but rather would exacerbate the situation.

THE PROBLEM OF DEFENCE CONVERSION

The problem of defence conversion is that of converting former defence production in the military industries into non-defence civilian production, particularly in those nations with lower military spending. This problem is one of economic reallocation, involving changes in the allocation of resources in the economy and not simply changing a government budget. In particular, converting from military to civilian production is not simply a matter of shifting funds from one category of social spending to another, as suggested by some political leaders. Rather, the process of conversion in the military industries entails a fundamental reallocation of resources in the economy, including retraining soldiers and defence workers; retooling capital;

reprogramming the use of other material and service inputs used in defence production; and, more generally, in developing the capability to produce non-defence goods and services.[4]

The problem of defence conversion in the military industries is a serious one, particularly in those nations that are now reducing their defence budgets. It raises many important issues in nations in all parts of the world that have tried and in many cases failed or only partially succeeded in such conversion, even in countries without an extensive military industrial base. One such issue is that of defence conversion at the plant level in the military industries. Typically, it is not easy to convert plants that produce major military hardware, such as tanks, fighter jets, and missiles, into ones that can produce civilian goods. It is often the case that it is easier and less expensive from the vantage point of the military industries to build a new plant specifically designed for the alternative civilian products that they will be producing than to convert a defence plant that had been specifically designed to produce certain military hardware. Usually conversion at the plant level makes sense only in the case of small products that have similar military and civilian configurations, such as electronics or clothing.

A second issue involves management in the military industries. Managers in these industries typically find it very difficult to change their focus to deal with civilian rather than military production. They become used to a certain military industry culture, and cannot adapt readily to a different culture. Among other complications, these managers become accustomed to dealing with a single customer, with very exacting standards as to quality and delivery. They are not used to the private sector, with many potential customers who are sensitive to factors such as pricing and advertising.

A third issue is that of substantial reductions in the large military research and development budgets of the major powers. These reductions should, in principle, release scientific and technical personnel who could play an important role in promoting future economic growth. In the short term, however, such personnel lose work either in military laboratories or in military industries and, until they are re-hired elsewhere, the effect is not a productive redeployment of scientists and engineers but rather their underemployment or unemployment, as has been witnessed since 1992 in the aerospace industry of southern California.[5]

While potentially there are major gains from disarmament, particularly over the long term, disarmament in the short term can lead to the unemployment of labour and disuse of capital and other resources employed in the military or in the military industries. Policies to deal with the economic aspects of disarmament must take specific account of expected real benefits and costs, particularly the short-term dislocation and unemployment costs and the long-term benefits of alternative production. These policies should be formulated so as to maximize the real benefits and minimize the costs, thereby maximizing the return from disarmament through the productive reallocation of the resources released into alternative uses.

THE PEACE DIVIDEND

Some have argued that the reduction in the monetary costs of defence would yield a peace dividend in the form of resources or social spending that could be used for other purposes.[6] Focusing attention on those regions of the world where defence spending has decreased, in both East and West, we see that there has, in fact, been no automatic peace dividend that can be allocated to alternative uses, and there has been much less discussion as to how to spend such an alleged dividend than during the period when defence budgets started to fall (particularly after the collapse of the Warsaw Pact and the Soviet Union in 1991).

The real benefits of reduced defence spending in the form of a peace dividend are based on the possibility of diverting resources from arms production to other uses in the economy. For labour, there is the real benefit of diverting those serving in the military and those employed in the military industries, or in sectors directly or indirectly supplying these industries, to other socially valuable tasks. For skilled labour, the real benefit lies in using trained personnel, particularly scientists and engineers, for other

33

uses, including civilian research and development. For physical capital, there is the formation and utilization of plant and equipment for civilian purposes. Labour and capital and other inputs into the production process that had been used to produce or to maintain arms as part of the arms race – including energy, material inputs, and services – could, in principle, be reallocated to non-military or civilian uses, resulting in a peace dividend.

The basic economic opportunity stemming from reduced defence budgets is that there can be substantial real economic benefits stemming from the alternative economic use of those resources currently allocated to the arms race. In particular, this could result in the release of resources that can be redirected and used to serve other important tasks. Among many domestic possibilities, these include reducing the size of the government deficit and/or reducing taxes, building or rebuilding infrastructure, funding health or other social services, increasing expenditures on environmental protection, and funding other government programmes. There are many valid uses that have been suggested by various political leaders, each of whom appears to have his or her own favourite plan for the peace dividend.

As to international uses, there are again many possible applications for a peace dividend, including economic development in the third world, the reconstruction of countries devastated by war, support of United Nations peacekeeping or other operations, funding the global war on drugs, assisting nations in the transition to a market economy, protecting and restoring the global environment, and many other clearly worthy causes. The traditional UN position – as formulated since at least 1955 in a series of resolutions unanimously adopted by the General Assembly, conferences, reports, and international commissions – has been that reduced defence spending, especially reductions in military budgets on the east and west sides of the Cold War, should lead to increases in development assistance to developing nations.[7]

Leaders of the former Soviet republics, however, have made the case that some of these resources should be used to provide support in order to prevent conflicts or a recurrence of a new East–West Cold War. They argue that Western assistance derived from the peace dividend could be used to prevent the collapse of their economies that might, in turn, lead to new authoritarian regimes, internal conflicts, and a rekindling of Cold War hostilities. There are clearly many valid alternatives, domestic or international, for the peace dividend, when and if one becomes available.

CONVERSION COSTS

While there are potential benefits from reduced defence spending, it would be a mistake to ignore the related costs. These adjustment costs include, most significantly, potential unemployment of labour, capital, and other resources employed in the military or in the military industries. Defence budget cuts involve such conversion costs, including the direct adjustment costs of retraining defence workers and soldiers, the retooling or building of new capital, and the costs of developing the capability for producing non-defence goods and services. In addition, there are the direct and opportunity costs of not using labour, capital, and other inputs into the production of military goods and services. These are social costs, some of which affect the military industries as costs of retraining workers and retooling plant and equipment, but which, more broadly, affect society as a whole. These conversion costs are incurred over a transition period which may last years or even decades. These costs can ultimately be followed by benefits, provided the factor inputs are reallocated so as to produce civilian goods and services, creating an ultimate peace dividend.

The United Nations studies of disarmament and development mentioned above appear to assume, unrealistically, that reduced defence budgets could be converted at no cost to development assistance. This ignores not only the resource reallocations that would be required and the conversion costs that would have to be incurred, but also the other potential uses of these resources.

The basic economic danger stemming from reduced defence budgets is that they could result in the non-utilization or under-utilization of resources, including labour and capital, thereby leading not only to economic problems but also to potential social and political problems. A particularly important danger is the unemployment of former military officers, soldiers, defence plant workers, and scientists and engineers working in the military or military industries.

DISARMAMENT AS AN INVESTMENT PROCESS

It is useful to analyse the economic effects of disarmament as a type of investment process, where the costs of defence conversion are typically realized in the immediate or short term, while the utilization of resources released by disarmament for other socially useful purposes typically become available only in the medium or long term.[8] The costs of disarmament, including dislocations, unemployment, and adjustment costs, are typically immediate or short term and are usually incurred in the first several years. The benefits of disarmament, based on the utilization of resources released for other socially useful purposes, by contrast, are typically medium- or long-term ones, usually starting after some delay and lasting over many years. This pattern is similar to one resulting from a private or public investment. It involves an initial expenditure or cost, followed by a stream of returns, with initial costs followed by delayed benefits. It is similar to a financial investment, such as the purchase of a bond, that yields some designated return until its maturity, or a capital investment, such as the building of a plant and equipment, that eventually generates a return from the sale of the goods and services it produces with complementary inputs. To compare the costs and benefits occurring at different times requires discounting of their values – typically discounting back to the present time using an appropriate interest rate. The overall net value of disarmament treated as a type of investment process will then depend on the interest rate, where because of the timing of costs and benefits, the higher the interest rate, the lower the overall net value will be.

Looking at the economics of disarmament as an investment process is useful in dispelling two myths which, unfortunately, are frequently held as strong beliefs by their advocates. As concerns defence reductions in developed countries, these myths are the counterparts of the rival views on the relations between military expenditures and economic growth in developing countries. The conventional 'guns versus butter' argument suggests that military expenditures would reduce economic growth, so reduced military expenditures would promote growth.[9] The rival view suggests that military expenditures promote economic growth, so reduced military expenditures would retard growth.[10]

The first myth – that there would be an immediate dividend that could be spent or paid out to the citizens of the disarming country or used in some other way, as discussed in the previous section – is widely held in many nations, including those of the Middle East. Many people, including political elites, expect peace to yield some immediate economic gains. This is a dangerous belief, as it could lead to social strife and instability when such gains do not materialize. The presumption that the reallocation of resources of labour, capital, and other inputs can be implemented instantaneously and free of cost[11] treats military expenditure as a category of social spending that can be simply moved into another category, like shifting money from one pocket to another. It ignores the fact that the process of defence conversion entails a costly reallocation of resources in the economy, with real adjustments to be made in employment patterns, in capital utilization, and in industrial structure in the military industries.[12] It is a mistake to ignore the adjustment costs of disarmament, particularly the potential for unemployment of labour, capital, and other resources stemming from reduced military expenditure, and the secondary consequences in the military industries that supply the defence sector.

The other myth, that disarmament would lead to an economic downturn that would be irreversible, presumes that the economy is completely dependent on military spending. This cynical view ignores past successful conversions following war periods, including, for the United States, conversions after World War II, the Korean War, and the Vietnam War. These past conversions have involved rapid adjustments and have shown that a national economy will eventually recover from disarmament and reap the benefits of greater civilian output. This myth also ignores the fact that, at least for the United States and most Western industrialized market economies, military spending represents a relatively small percentage of output, amounting to less than 5 per cent of GDP, and that this percentage has been declining gradually.

These two myths are mirror images of one another, and both contain some elements of truth. Each has its own set of interest groups that foster it. While the first myth ignores the initial costs of disarmament, the second ignores its eventual benefits. By contrast, interpreting disarmament as an investment process takes a longer-term view of the process of adjustment, allowing explicitly for both the initial conversion costs incurred by the military industries and society as a whole and the ultimate benefits of the peace dividend.

The prospects for the economic effects of disarmament depend greatly on the expected pattern of costs and benefits stemming from defence cuts. Depending on this crucial pattern, the social rate of return from disarmament, treated as an investment process, could range in value from very high to very low or even negative levels. If defence reductions involve relatively low conversion costs, a short transition time from costs to benefits, and relatively high benefits, then the social rate of return is very high, as was the case for the United States after World War II. In the case of moderate conversion costs, a medium transition time from costs to benefits, and relatively modest benefits, then the social rate of return is moderate, as is the case for the United States today in the aftermath of the Cold War. By contrast, if defence reductions involve relatively high conversion costs, a long transition time from costs to benefits, and relatively low benefits, then the social rate of return is very low, or possibly even negative, as appears to be the case in Russia and other nations of the former Soviet Union today. These nations may never be able to recoup the high costs of conversion, contributing to overall economic instability.

ARMS EXPORTS

To avoid the initial problems stemming from disarmament, particularly those of unemployment, some nations have attempted to continue to produce weapons not for domestic use but rather for export. There are tremendous pressures to keep military production lines going and to avoid all the potential short-term problems of disarmament through arms exports. There are also pressures to sell existing weapons to nations involved in regional arms races and to supply equipment, technology, and technical expertise to these nations to earn foreign exchange. Such arms exports and supply of resources serve to intensify the problems of the regional arms races, and they could even lead to the proliferation of weapons of mass destruction and their means of delivery, thereby creating regional and possibly international instabilities and conflicts. A significant challenge to the regions and to the world is that of preventing the exports of both arms and military technologies.

THE UNITED STATES AND OTHER WESTERN INDUSTRIALIZED NATIONS

The Western industrialized nations can probably adjust to the economic problems stemming from disarmament and reap its rewards on the basis of national policy alone, as they did after previous wars. Functioning goods and factor markets in these market economies can play a major role on making the necessary adjustments, as they have in the past. These market adjustments would, however, be substantially assisted by favourable market conditions, including those of an economic expansion, tight labour markets, and substantial sums available for investment in new plants and equipment.

National policies to assist in the process of conversion include initiatives such as personnel retraining programmes, unemployment insurance, job information and job registers, and investment incentives. Given favourable market conditions and such national policies, there would be low conversion costs, a short transition time, and high conversion benefits, resulting in a high 'rate of return' from disarmament.

Historical examples of successful conversions after war periods indicate alternative possibilities for both adjustment costs and the peace dividend.[13] In the United States, there was a very successful conversion from 1945 to 1947, due to many factors, including a pent-up demand for consumer goods, the post-war baby boom, the GI bill, the Marshall Plan, and supportive fiscal and monetary policies. There were also successful conversions after the Korean War, from 1953 to 1956, and after the Vietnam War, from 1970 to 1973. The Korean War involved a significant buildup of defence spending, but not on a scale comparable to that of World War II. As in the earlier conversion, there were initial adjustment costs, with unemployment jumping from 2.8 per cent, to 5.4 per cent in the 1954 recession. There were few programmes introduced to aid in the conversion to a peacetime economy, and fiscal policy was very conservative. The Vietnam War involved an even slower buildup than the Korean War, and the reductions following the war were also quite gradual and long-lasting, resulting in fewer adverse effects on the overall economy than in previous periods. The initial effects of defence cuts can be seen in the fact that the unemployment rate rose to 4.8 per cent in 1970 and 5.8 per cent in 1971, a significant rise from the rates of 1966 and 1969. More expansionary monetary and fiscal policies starting in 1971 led to a recovery in the 1971–73 period. Overall, the macroeconomic effects of the defence reductions were relatively small.

Current reductions in defence spending following the end of the Cold War began in 1989, when real defence outlays reached their peak, amounting to 5.9 per cent of GDP (and down from the high of 6.5 per cent reached in 1986 in the Carter–Reagan buildup). Total defence-related employment rose 27 per cent between 1981 and 1989, but at its peak in 1989 comprised only 5.5 per cent of total United States employment (as compared to 10.3 per cent in 1968). Thus, the defence buildup in the last years of the Cold War was far smaller than the preceding ones relative to the overall economy, and so the macroeconomic effects were likely to be relatively small and concentrated mainly in particular industries and regions. These effects were mitigated by the slow pace of the reductions, with overall macroeconomic indicators reflecting more the state of the overall economy rather than any impacts, positive or negative, of defence cuts. Only relatively small programmes are in place to assist in the conversion process, particularly in the case of base or defence plant closings.

The present defence reductions after the end of the Cold War are starting from a much lower level than those of earlier periods. While the size and pace of the reductions are much more gradual, the current problems of turning defence reductions from costs into benefits stem from modest overall growth, very low rates of domestic savings, jobs being lost as a result of corporate restructuring or shifts to foreign plants, and monetary and fiscal policy being constrained by the continuing international balance of payments deficits and government budget deficits.

These past conversions in the United States have been largely successful, but the potential does exist for a low or even negative return to disarming. Such a negative outcome is more likely if there are short-term episodic reductions in military spending under conditions of economic recession, with high rates of unemployment, with relatively small sums available for investment in new plants and equipment, and with either a lack of governmental action to address these problems or wasteful government 'bail-out' subsidies to unemployed workers or affected industries or regions.

THE FORMER SOCIALIST NATIONS

The ex-socialist nations of the former Soviet Union and Eastern and Central Europe, in contrast to the industrialized nations of the West, have shown that they cannot successfully adjust on the basis of national policy alone to the economic dislocations stemming from disarmament. They lack efficiently functioning goods and factor markets, and they face the challenge of trying simultaneously to convert from military to civilian production and to make the transition from a centrally planned command economy to a market economy. These problems are amplified in the case of the former Soviet Union, especially in Russia and in Ukraine, by the enormous size and influence of the military sector and by the fact that large regions of both nations are devoted exclusively to military production.

These nations have suffered substantial costs as a result of overall reductions in output, including the effects of reduced defence budgets, and they will probably require international support, such as external technical assistance and direct aid in making the needed adjustments in converting from military to civilian production. This assistance and aid can only come from Western nations and from international financial organizations such as the World Bank, the International Monetary Fund, and the European Bank for Reconstruction and Development. The United Nations could also play a valuable role in providing technical assistance by making available methodologies for assessing the economic effects of disarmament and evaluating alternative policies to maximize their benefits and to mitigate their costs. These methodologies should be supplemented by case studies.[14] Even with such international support, there will probably be no available peace dividend in these nations for many years, if ever. They are experiencing massive unemployment or underemployment in their military industries and among former military personnel, and this situation is likely to continue in the future. Some have questioned whether it is wise to aid the former Soviet Union in view of the history of the Cold War, but such aid would be a wise investment to avoid instabilities, particularly in the military and the military industries, that could lead to wider political and social upheaval.

Focusing on the most important case, that of Russia, attempts at conversion from military to civilian production were already being made in the Soviet Union in the late 1980s, under Gorbachev. They were largely unsuccessful. The products that the Soviet military industries tried to produce as alternatives to their military products were largely non-competitive – they included titanium snow shovels, electronic samovars, and machines that were much too complicated to serve their purpose, such as electronic milking machines. Following the dissolution of the Soviet Union, there was an enormous reduction in the military budget and a shift in the allocation of this budget away from procurement of military equipment, the mainstay of military production, toward operations. As a result, the military industries tried with mixed success to continue to produce goods for export rather than for the domestic market, as discussed earlier, building on the traditional role of Russia as a major exporter of military products. The former high levels of military exports have dropped precipitously, however, as these exports have become uncompetitive in terms of performance, service arrangements, spare parts, and so forth, when compared with rival products being exported by Western nations, especially the United States, France, and the United Kingdom. As a result of successive failures, both to convert the military industries and to export arms, there have been massive layoffs and there is widespread underemployment in the Russian military industries, with devastating economic results for huge regions of the country. Even when workers remain employed, they frequently do not have raw materials or resources to work with and, in many cases, they are not paid for months at a time. Where production is still ongoing, it is largely either for inventory or for some remaining exports. It is not clear how, if at all, Russia will be able to dispose of its growing stockpiles of military products in warehouses throughout the country. Clearly, the Russian government should begin long-term restructuring of the military industries, including the development of commercial products both for the internal market and for export. It should also encourage or undertake the retraining of workers and the retooling of plants and equipment in order to start the process of defence conversion to civilian production. At the same time, it should adopt policies that would redeploy its scientific and technical resources to focus on the development of non-military technologies. Such policies, to succeed, will require a successful transition to a growing market economy, but requirements for such a transition include not only the usually recommended policies of privatization, liberalization, and stabilization, but also the development of the institutions of a market economy, the promotion of competition, and an activist government policy.[15]

THE REST OF THE WORLD

The rest of the world, outside the former Western and Eastern blocs, has had various experiences in terms of levels of defence spending and the issues of defence conversion and the peace dividend. In the Middle East, military spending remains at relatively high levels, especially in Israel, Syria, and Egypt, although there could be some reductions in defence spending in the future as a result of the peace process. Israel and Egypt must plan for the conversion of their military industries, but all countries in the region, even those without a military industrial base and reliant on arms imports, such as Syria, must still deal with the problem of converting their military personnel into productive non-military employees. In regions of conflict, military spending continues at high levels. In certain other parts of the world there have been major buildups of defence spending, especially in East Asia and Southeast Asia, where China is modernizing its military forces and building its capabilities for force projection and the surrounding nations to some extent are forced to react by building up their capabilities in response to this Chinese buildup. The problem facing those nations would appear to be the reverse of defence conversion; that is, the mobilization of resources for military production.

As a whole, the rest of the world is where most of the instability lies and where, as in the former Soviet Union, the return from defence conversion is likely to be low, given the relatively high costs and relatively low benefits of such conversion. Thus, the areas of the world outside the former Western and Eastern blocs are those facing the greatest challenges of defence conversion.

POLICY IMPLICATIONS

Looking at the economics of defence conversion as an investment process has several implications for policy, in terms of taking actions in a period of arms reductions so as to reduce social costs and to increase social benefits. The social costs, including unemployment of labour, capital, and other resources, both short term and long term; adjustment costs; and other costs stemming from disarmament are unprecedented since disarmament is occurring without a major prior war (in contrast to disarmament after World War II). In the wake of major war, there is a demand for reconstruction that can provide an impetus to conversion in the military industries. Furthermore, as noted, in several nations, defence conversion is occurring simultaneously with a shift from a centrally planned to a market economy.

Western industrial nations should augment the use of markets to adjust to the economic problems stemming from disarmament and to reap disarmament's rewards, by using initiatives such as retraining programmes, unemployment insurance, job information and job registers, and investment incentives. It is particularly important to develop retraining and other programmes so as to minimize the unemployment of former military officers, soldiers, and defence plant workers. The educational establishment, including high schools, colleges, universities, and trade schools, must play an important role in retraining, which it has not done up to now. The US may need the current equivalent of the GI Bill, which played an important role in the relatively smooth conversion of the military industries after World War II.

The former socialist nations of the former Soviet Union and Central and Eastern Europe, especially Russia and Ukraine, should be assisted in adjusting to the economic dislocations stemming from disarmament by means of international support, including external technical assistance and direct aid from Western nations and from international organizations. The world may need a current equivalent of the Marshall Plan, which played an important role in both European recovery and United States defence conversion after World War II. The current version should be targeted at various international needs for development, conversion, transition, and environmental protection, and it should be supported by all the advanced industrialized nations.

The rest of the world will require new initiatives at the national and regional levels to moderate continuing arms procurement and arms imports and to assist in the process of conversion from military to civilian production. The Middle East may, potentially, provide an example for other regions of how the peace process could ultimately lead to arms reductions, although both defence budgets and levels of imported arms currently remain at high levels. There is also a danger for this region that the hopes for a peace dividend are unrealistically high and do not recognize the costs of conversion in the military industries and the need to reallocate resources to secure the benefits of reduced defence budgets. If there is an ultimate peace dividend for Israel, it could play an important role in the region and set an example for the world by using part of it to help develop a region such as Gaza in a demonstration project of how a relatively rich and industrialized nation can promote economic and social development in a neighbouring poor region. While there have been proposals for a Marshall Plan for the Middle East, the region could establish its own such plan, with Israel in consortium with the wealthy Arab states supporting the economic development of the Palestinian Authority, as an investment in peace.

There is a real danger that arms-producing nations will be tempted to shift into producing arms for export or to export existing weapons, particularly to third world nations involved in regional arms races. Initiatives should be taken and policies should be designed at the national, regional, and international levels to prevent such a development. It is especially important to prevent the export of advanced weapons, the sale of sensitive technologies, and the relocation of technical experts to nations involved in regional arms races, since they could accelerate the problem of the proliferation of weapons of mass destruction.

Overall, the economic effects of disarmament depend on general economic conditions and national, regional, and international policies. With informed national macroeconomic, trade, and other policies, supplemented by new arms control initiatives, particularly those restricting arms exports and preventing the proliferation of weapons of mass destruction, there could be substantial economic returns from disarmament, involving minimum conversion costs to both the military industries and to society as a whole, and maximum eventual benefits.

NOTES

1. See Lloyd J. Dumas, *The Overburdened Economy: Uncovering the Causes of Chronic Unemployment, Inflation, and National Decline* (Berkeley: University,

THE ECONOMICS OF DEFENCE CONVERSION

of California Press, 1986); John E. Lynch (eds), *Economic Adjustment and Conversion of Defence Industries* (Boulder: Westview Press, 1987); Lloyd J. Dumas and Marek Thee (eds), *Making Peace Possible: The Promise of Economic Conversion* (Oxford and New York: Pergamon Press, 1989); Lawrence R. Klein, 'The Economics of Turning Swords into Ploughshares', *Challenge* (March–April 1990), pp. 18–26; Gregory A. Bischak (eds), *Toward a Peace Economy in the United States: Essays on Military Industry, Disarmament, and Economic Conversion* (London: Macmillan 1991); Jürgen Brauer and John Tepper Marlin, 'Converting Resources from Military to Non-Military Use', *Journal of Economic Perspectives*, 6: 4 (Fall 1992), pp. 145–64; Manas Chatterji and Linda Rennie Forcey (eds), *Disarmament, Economic Conversion, and Management of Peace* (New York: Praeger 1992); Congressional Budget Office, 'The Economic Effects of Reduced Defence Spending' (Washington, DC: Congressional Budget Office, February, 1992); Betty Lall and John Tepper Marlin, *Building a Peace Economy: Opportunities and Problems of Post-Cold War Defence Cuts* (Boulder: Westview Press 1992); Ann Markusen and Joel Yudken, *Dismantling the Cold War Economy* (New York: Basic Books, 1992); Office of Technology Assessment, *After the Cold War: Living with Lower Defence Spending* (Washington, DC: US Government Printing Office, February 1992); Michael Renner (ed.), *Economic Adjustment after the Cold War* (Geneva: United Nations Institute for Disarmament Research, and Aldershot, Hants, England and Brookfield, VT: Dartmouth, 1992); US Defence Conversion Commission, *Adjusting to the Drawdown*, Report of the Defence Conversion Commission (December 31, 1992); US Defence Conversion Commission, 'The Economic Effects of Reduced Defence Spending', Supplement to *Adjusting to the Drawdown*, Report of the Defence Conversion Commission (February, 1993); Kevin J. Cassidy and Gregory A. Bischak, *Real Security: Converting the Defence Economy and Building Peace* (Albany: State University of New York Press, 1993); Nancy Ettlinger, 'The Peace Dividend and Defence Conversion in the Context of Corporate Restructuring', *Growth and Change*, 24 (1993), pp. 107–26; Keith Hartley et al., *Economic Aspects of Disarmament: Disarmament as an Investment Process* (New York: United Nations Institute for Disarmament Research [UNIDIR], 1993); J. Davidson Alexander, 'Military Conversion Policies in the USA: 1940s and 1990s', *Journal of Peace Research*, 31: 1 (1994), pp. 19–33; Lloyd J. Dumas (ed.), *The Socio-Economics of Conversion from War to Peace* (Armonk, NY: M. E. Sharpe, 1995).
2. See Michael D. Intriligator and Dagobert L. Brito, 'Can Arms Races Lead to the Outbreak of War?', *Journal of Conflict Resolution*, 28: 1 (March 1984), pp. 63–84; Michael D. Intriligator and Dagobert L. Brito, 'Non-Armageddon Solutions to the Arms Race', *Arms Control*, 6: 1 (May 1985), pp. 41–57; Michael D. Intriligator and Dagobert L. Brito, 'Arms Races and Instability', *Journal of Strategic Studies*, 9:4 (December 1986), pp. 113–31; Michael D. Intriligator, 'On the Nature and Scope of Defence Economics', *Defence Economics*, 1: 1 (1990), pp. 3–11; Michael D. Intriligator and Dagobert L. Brito, 'A Possible Future for the Arms Race', in Nils Petter Gleditsch and Olav Njølstad et al. (eds), *Arms Races: Political and Technological Dynamics* (London: Sage Publications, 1990), reprinted in *Economic Directions*, 3: 4 (1990), pp. 13–18; Dagobert L. Brito and Michael

47

D. Intriligator, 'Arms Races and Proliferation', in Keith Hartley and Todd Sandler (eds), *Handbook of Defence Economics* (Amsterdam: North-Holland Publishing Co., 1995).
3. See John Lewis Gaddis, 'The Long Peace: Elements of Stability in the Postwar International System', *International Security*, 10:4 (Spring 1986), pp. 99–142, reprinted in Sean M. Lynn-Jones and Steven E. Miller (eds), *The Cold War and After: Prospects for Peace*, expanded edition (Cambridge, Mass.: MIT Press, 1993), and John Lewis Gaddis, *The Long Peace* (New York: Oxford University Press, 1987). See also John Lewis Gaddis, 'How the Cold War Might End', *The Atlantic*, 260 (November 1987), pp. 88–100; *The United States and the End of the Cold War: Implications, Reconsiderations, Provocations* (New York: Oxford University Press, 1992); and 'International Relations Theory and the End of the Cold War', *International Security*, 17:3 (Winter 1992/93), reprinted in Lynn-Jones and Miller (eds), *The Cold War and After*. In addition, see John J. Mearsheimer, 'Back to the Future: Instability in Europe After the Cold War', *International Security*, 15:1 (Summer 1990), pp. 5–56, reprinted in Lynn-Jones and Miller (eds.), *The Cold War and After*; Stephen Van Evera, 'Primed for Peace: Europe After the Cold War', *International Security*, 15:3 (Winter 1990/91), reprinted in Lynn-Jones and Miller (eds), *The Cold War and After*; and James Goldgeier and Michael McFaul, 'A Tale of Two Worlds: Core and Periphery in the Post-Cold War Era', *International Organization*, 46:2 (Spring 1992), pp. 467–92.
4. See Michael D. Intriligator and Dagobert L. Brito, 'The Economics of Disarmament, Arms Races, and Arms Control', *Revue d'economie appliquee*, XLVI:3 (1993), pp. 59–76, and Michael D. Intriligator, 'The Peace Dividend: Myth or Reality?', in Nils Petter Gleditsch, Olav Bjerkholt, Odne Cappelen, R. P. Smith, and J. P. Dunne (eds), *The Wages of Peace* (Amsterdam: North-Holland Publishing Co., 1996).
5. See Markusen and Yudken, *Dismantling the Cold War Economy*, and Office of Technology Assessment, *After the Cold War*, op. cit.
6. See Christopher Coker, 'The Myth of the Peace Dividend', *World Today*, 46:7 (1990), pp. 136–8; Deutsche Bank, *The Peace Dividend: How to Pin It Down?* (Frankfurt am Main: Deutsche Bank, Economics Department, 1990); Ettlinger, 'The Peace Dividend and Defence Conversion'; Nils Petter Gleditsch, Adne Cappelen, and Olav Bjerkholt, *The Wages of Peace: Disarmament in a Small Industrialized Economy* (London: Sage Publications, 1994); Nils Petter Gleditsch and Olav Bjerkholt, *et al.* (eds), *The Wages of Peace* (Amsterdam: North-Holland Publishing Co., 1996); and Michael D. Intriligator, chapter in ibid.
7. See Brandt Commission Report [Report of the Independent Commission on International Development Issues], *North–South: A Programme for Survival* (London: Pan Books, 1980); Palme Commission Report [Report of the Independent Commission on Disarmament and Security Issues], *Common Security: A Blueprint for Survival* (New York: Simon and Schuster, 1982); United Nations, 'Final Document' of the International Conference on the Relationship between Disarmament and Development (A/CONF. 130/21) (New York: United Nations, 1987); United Nations Development Programme (UNDP), *Human Development Report 1994* (New York: Oxford University Press, 1994); and Oscar Arias, 'The Arms Bazaar' – the 1995

THE ECONOMICS OF DEFENCE CONVERSION

Paul G. Hoffman speech at the United Nations, presented 11 October 1995.
8. See Michael D. Intriligator, 'The Economics of Disarmament as an Investment Process', *UNIDIR Newsletter* (Geneva: United Nations Institute for Disarmament Research, 19 September 1992); Michael D. Intriligator, 'Economic Aspects of Disarmament: Arms Races and Arms Control Issues', *Defence and Peace Economics*, 5:2 (1994), pp. 121–9; and Michael D. Intriligator, chapter in Nils Petter Gleditsch and Olav Bjerkholt, et al. (eds), *The Wages of Peace* (Amsterdam: North-Holland Publishing Co., 1996). See also Keith Hartley et al., *Economic Aspects of Disarmament* (UNIDIR, 1993).
9. See Wassily Leontief and Fay Duchin, *Military Spending: Facts and Figures* (New York: Oxford University Press, 1983); Saadet Deger, 'Economic Development and Defence Expenditure', *Economic Development and Cultural Change*, 35:1 (1986), pp. 179–96, and *Military Expenditure in Third World Countries* (London: Routledge and Kegan Paul, 1986); Saadet Deger and Robert West (eds), *Defence, Security and Development* (New York: St Martin's Press, 1987); and much subsequent literature.
10. See Emile Benoit, 'Growth Effects of Defence in Developing Countries', *International Development Review*, 14 (January, 1972), pp. 2–10; 'Growth and Defence in Developing Countries', *Economic Development and Cultural Change*, 26:2 (1978), pp. 271–80; and *Defence and Economic Growth in Developing Countries* (Lexington: Lexington Books, 1973); G. Kennedy, *The Military in the Third World* (London: Duckworth, 1974); and much subsequent literature. See, for example, Robert E. Looney, 'Government Expenditures and Third World Economic Growth in the 1980s: The Impact of Defence Expenditures', *Canadian Journal of Development Studies*, 14:1 (1993), pp. 23–42, which identified some five channels through which defence expenditures transmit impacts to the general economy, some of which are positive and some of which are negative, namely, resource allocation effects, resource mobilization effects, spin-off effects, aggregate demand effects, and debt accumulation effects. He concluded that reduced military expenditures in developing countries, unless confined to arms imports, are unlikely in and of themselves to provide much of a peace dividend to stimulate economic growth. An implication is that on strictly economic grounds it might not be beneficial for such countries to reduce defence budgets, although such reductions might be warranted on other grounds, such as promoting peace.
11. See Christopher Coker, 'The Myth of the Peace Dividend', op. cit.
12. See Lloyd J. Dumas, *The Overburdened Economy*, op. cit.
13. See Gregory A. Bischak (ed.), *Real Security*; and Ann Markusen and Joel Yudken, *Dismantling the Cold War Economy*, op. cit.
14. See United Nations Department for Disarmament Affairs, *Disarmament: Topical Papers 5, Conversion: Economic Adjustments in an Era of Arms Reduction*, vol. II (New York: United Nations, 1991), for case studies of the United States, the Soviet Union, China, Japan, Italy, the Federal Republic of Germany, and the German Democratic Republic. This source also includes comparative case studies and special studies of the problems of military personnel, the military industries, the arms trade, and military hardware.
15. See Michael D. Intriligator, 'What is the Future of the Russian Economy?',

49

Business World (Moscow), 17 February 1993 (in Russian); 'The Russian Economy Needs Market Institutions', *Business World* (Moscow), 14 December 1993 (in Russian); 'Reform of the Russian Economy: The Role of Institutions', *Contention*, 3:2 (Winter 1994), pp. 153–70; 'Privatization in Russia Has Led to Criminalization', *Australian Economic Review*, 2:1 (1994), pp. 4–14, reprinted in Russian in *Problems in the Theory and Practice of Management*, 6 (1994), pp. 39–43; 'On the Strategy of Effective Transition to the Market', *Russia and the Contemporary World*, 10:1 (1996), pp. 64–96 (in Russian); 'The Shocking Failure of Shock Therapy', *Russian Magazine*, 30 (September, 1996), pp. 32–33; and 'The Role of Institutions in the Transition to a Market Economy', in Tarmo Haavisto (ed.), *Transition to a Market Economy: Transformation and Reform in the Baltic Countries* (Cheltenham, UK: Edward Elgar, 1996).

3

The Post-Cold War American Defence Industry: Options, Policies and Probable Outcomes

ANN MARKUSEN

INTRODUCTION

This chapter reviews the evidence on American defence industrial firm restructuring in the 1980s and the first half of the 1990s. I argue that the debt-financed buildup of the 1980s deepened firms' defence dependency and heightened the 'wall of separation' between military and civilian markets in many sectors. Confronted with rapidly declinin procurement budgets – of the order of 40 per cent in real terms over a seven-year period – firms have chosen different options, ranging from a rededication of effort toward holding or expanding military market share, often supplemented with redoubled efforts to export, to a commitment of internal resources and organizational overhaul to reposition themselves for civilian markets. I review arguments, both economic and strategic, for and against the current wave of mergers and acquisitions. I suggest that despite a new 'dual-use' posture designed to encourage conversion and dismantle the wall of separation, the United States federal government has devoted too few resources, has been largely ineffective in procurement reforms and planning excercises, and perversely, has offered new incentives that speed consolidation and shore up the wall of separation. I conclude by speculating about the size and composition of the sector over the coming decade.

THE LEGACY OF THE 1980s BUILDUP

The current post-Cold War restructuring of military industrial firms in the US began abruptly, following a decade of unprecedented peacetime buildup. It is generally not well understood how important this previous experience was in deepening the dependency of firms in many sectors on military sales, thereby heightening supply side resistance to cuts, and in undermining the ability of the federal government to use post-Cold War savings to invest in civilian initiatives.

Beginning in 1978 and accelerating up through 1986, the US defence budget rose over 60 per cent in real terms (Table 3.1), to a level well in excess of $300 billion a year. The buildup was almost entirely deficit-financed. By at least one accounting, nearly half the entire national debt accrued by 1986 was attributable to the buildup.[1] The spending hike was devoted disproportionately to private sector procurement, resulting in a dramatic expansion of the contracting sector and the regions hosting it.[2] A number of industries rapidly reoriented themselves to defence markets. Aircraft, for instance, increased its defence sales from around 37 per cent to 66 per cent of output, while military dependency in shipbuilding rose from 61 per cent to 93 per cent (Table 3.1). A number of critical machinery and parts industries dramatically shifted toward defence as well – machine tools, for instance, quadrupled their defence orientation from 8 per cent to 34 per cent.

The impact on individual firms was quite remarkable. Coming as it did when the dollar was overvalued and international competition was on the rise, defence expansion induced many to abandon commercial lines altogether and to concentrate on defence. Bath Iron Works, one of the two major yards building destroyers for the Navy, was balanced about 50/50 between commercial and military shipbuilding projects in the early 1980s, but became 100 per cent defence dependent within a few years.

Many smaller firms similarly lost civilian competence. By the late 1980s, many of the nation's defence contractors were more heavily dependent than they had been in any year since Vietnam.

TABLE 3.1
GROWTH IN MILITARY SALES AND DEPENDENCY, 1980–85 (1977=100)

Industry	Military Output (billion $) 1985	Military 1980	Share of Output (%) 1985
Shipbuilding	5.8	61	93
Ordnance	0.8	79	86
Missiles	5.3	69	84
Tanks	1.1	68	69
Aircraft	11.7	37	66
Communications equipment	15.7	42	50
Machine tools	0.4	8	34
Engineering instruments	0.7	23	28
Optical instruments	0.9	13	24
Electronic components	3.0	16	20
Steel	3.4	6	12
Airlines	3.0	na	10
Oil refining	5.2	4	6
Computers	2.3	5	5
Industrial chemicals	2.0	4	5
Semiconductors	1.6	9	5
Automobiles	6.3	3	3

Source: Markusen and Yudken, compiled from Henry and Oliver, 1987 and unpublished data from the Department of Commerce, 1987.

Cold War defence spending preoccupied not only production lines, but research labs in many corporations. In some sectors, aircraft and electronics pre-eminently, government contracts accounted for large portions of firms' R&D efforts (Table 3.2). More than 80 per cent of the aerospace industries' R&D funds originate in government, accounting for more than 54 per cent of all federal R&D contracted out to the private sector. Elsewhere, we have shown how these skewed patterns of both R&D and procurement spending acted as a quiet industrial policy over the entire Cold War era, helping to construct American comparative advantage in aerospace, communications and electronics sectors.[3] In the 1980s, competition for the nation's scarce science and engineering resources was heightened by disproportionately large increases in military R & D.

Two developments made it inevitable that spending would be cut quite substantially – (1) the end of the Cold War and (2) the growing concern with the US public-sector deficit. The 1980s buildup did not really end until 1989, when defence outlays began to fall in real terms for the first time in over a decade. By then, a select set of US firms, industries, occupations, and regions had become markedly more defence dependent than they had been in the post-Vietnam period. It could be predicted that the leaders of each would resist defence spending cuts and base closures, but they also might act as a constituency for conversion, willing to consider alternative uses, missions and markets. Unfortunately, the budget deficit left little room for elasticity in budgetary allocations. Although the Clinton Administration attempted to mount new infrastructure and environmental programmes linked to capacity redeployment, it was unable to win Congressional support for them. Instead, the peace dividend went largely into deficit reduction.

TABLE 3.2
FEDERAL vs. INDUSTRY FUNDING FOR SELECTED INDUSTRIES, 1989 (millions of dollars)

Industry	Federal Funds	Industry Funds	Total	Federal as % of Total	% of All Federal Funds
Aerospace	15,647	3,511	19,157	81.7	53.5
Electronics, Communications	7,928	10,618	18,546	42.8	27.1
Rubber Products	313	930	1,243	25.2	1.1
Autos, Trucks, RR (inc. Tanks)	1,982	9,431	11,413	17.4	6.8
Scientific Instruments	991	5,531	6,522	15.2	3.4
Machinery (inc. Computers)	1,669	10,457	12,126	13.8	5.7
Fabricated Metals	73	732	805	9.1	0.2
Iron and Steel	21	601	622	3.4	0.1
Chemicals	381	11,134	11,515	3.3	1.3
Petroleum Products	21	2,068	2,089	1.0	0.1
Food and Beverage	0	1,172	1,172	0.0	0.0
Paper/Pulp	0	1,009	1,009	0.0	0.0
Textiles	0	176	176	0.0	0.0
Manufacturing (total)	29,223	59,648	88,871	32.89	100.0

Source: Aerospace Industries Association of America, Aerospace Facts and Figures, 1989–90, Washington, DC: AIA, 1989, p.104, derived from Batelle data.

THE 1990s RETRENCHMENT IN US MILITARY SPENDING

It is not hyperbole to say that military spending in the US has been 'sticky downwards' in the 1990s. It remains, in the mid-1990s, close to the 1970s post-Vietnam trough, despite the cessation of Cold War hostilities. A number of analysts have concluded that US military spending could be substantially cut without threatening US security.[4] Associated budget estimates under various alternative security regimes range from $87 to $246 billion annually.[5]

Nevertheless, cuts from the 1980s high have been relatively deep and rapid from the point of view of firms and communities forced to accommodate them. Overall, defence budgets declined in real terms by 29 per cent from 1987 to 1994, and under Clinton budget projections will decline another 10 per cent between 1995 and 1997 (Table 3.3). Since procurement received disproportionately large hikes in the 1980s, it has declined in like fashion – down 56 per cent through 1994 with more cuts to come. Although the Republican Congress restored some $7 billion in procurement spending to the 1996 budget, further cuts are likely in the second Clinton term.

Employment losses lag budget cuts, because it takes two to three years for appropriations to translate into outlays and because, on the private sector side, a post Gulf War arms export surge helped to keep capacity utilization levels up.[6] Overall, the numbers of Americans employed by the armed services and on military-related contracts fell from 7 million to 5 million through 1994, and are projected to recede to 4.4 million by 1997 (Table 3.4). Industry jobs declined by 32 per cent through 1994, while those in the uniformed services shrank by 25 per cent. Estimating roughly, the US is probably only about two-thirds of the way through this round of budget cuts and their associated impacts.

DEFENCE CONTRACTOR RESPONSES

With $264 billion a year in overall defence spending, about 60 per cent of which are military purchases from the private sector,

TABLE 3.3
CUTS IN MILITARY SPENDING BY CATEGORY, 1987–97 (BUDGET AUTHORITY,
BILLIONS OF 1996 $)

	1987	1994	1997 (planned)	Per cent Change 1987–94	Per cent Change 1995–97
Personnel	97.5	75.0	65.4	–23.1	–12.8
Operations and Maintenance	107.1	92.7	87.7	–13.4	–5.4
Procurement	105.2	46.8	44.4	–55.5	–5.1
RDT&E	47.3	36.6	32.4	–22.6	–11.5
Other	13.2	13.7	9.1	3.8	–33.6
Total	370.3	264.8	239.0	–28.5	–9.7

TABLE 3.4
CUTS IN DEFENCE-RELATED EMPLOYMENT, 1987–97 (MILLIONS OF EMPLOYEES)

	1987	1994	1997 (estimated)	Per cent Change 1987–94	Per cent Change 1995–97
Uniformed DoD	2.24	1.68	1.53	–25.0	–8.9
Non-Uniformed DoD	1.13	0.9	0.8	–20.4	–11.1
Private Defence Industry Employment (direct and indirect)	3.67	2.49	2.03	–32.2	–18.5
Total	7.04	5.07	4.36	–28.0	–14.0

the American government remains a very large market for defence-oriented firms. But the rapid retrenchment in procurement, following the equally rapid upturn of the 1980s, has confronted the industry with an adjustment challenge of crisis proportions. Although this experience is not new – the US steel industry displaced about two-thirds of its workforce over in the 1980s – it is one for which the industry and the regions hosting it were not well prepared. Downsizing has been addressed somewhat differently by the larger firms than the small ones. Each is dealt with in turn in what follows.

Large Defence Contractor Restructuring

Among large firms, three distinct strategies are evident. First, some firms have chosen simply to downsize, in response to cutbacks to the weapons systems in which they specialize, while continuing to compete in markets where they enjoy a competitive advantage. General Dynamics, for instance, stated very early in the post-Cold War period its intentions to 'stick to its knitting'. It aggressively closed down lines, sold off others and used its defence profits and proceeds from the sales of assets to buy back its stock. McDonnell Douglas has similarly focused on lobbying for existing weapons systems, staying aloof from merger activity and more or less eschewing efforts at moving into civilian markets. Other companies, like Honeywell, spun off their defence divisions as stand-alone units (in this case Alliant Systems), preferring to concentrate on their civilian activities.

A second set of firms have chosen to grow aggressively by acquiring and merging with other heavily defence-dependent companies. The recent Lockheed/Martin/Loral merger, which created a company with $30 billion a year in sales, is archetypal but not singular – Northrop Grumman is another. This strategy was motivated by a number of different factors: (1) savings from consolidation of production and research capacity in a shrunken market; (2) savings from the elimination of overhead associated with marketing to and complying with regulations of the Pentagon; and (3) greater market power and leverage with the monopsonistic defence buyer. In a change of practice elaborated upon below, the Pentagon has not only permitted but has actively subsidized these mergers.

A third strategy, chosen by a number of large contractors, is the commitment of internal resources to moving personnel and technologies into civilian markets. Examples include Hughes, Raytheon, Rockwell, and TRW. These firms have selectively resorted to acquisitions, but chiefly for civilian capabilities that will help them become more diversified and bolster their expertise in commercial know-how. Interestingly, each of these firms is the product of an earlier merger between large commercial and defence companies. They demonstrate, as does Boeing and General Electric's long-standing success in commercial as well as military markets, that large defence contractors can bridge the 'wall of separation' successfully, capitalizing on their ability to move resources internally.[7]

The principal factors which appear to account for large

TABLE 3.5
TWENTY-FIVE TOP DEFENCE CONTRACTORS: SALES, EMPLOYMENT, DEFENCE
DEPENDENCE 1989–94

Company:	Sales 1994 (in Millions 1992 Dollars)	Change in Sales 1989–94	Change in Employment 1989–94	Defence/ Total Sales 1989(a)	Defence/ Total Sales 1994(a)
1 McDonnell Douglas	12,549	−16%	−49%	72%	70%
2 Lockheed[1]	12,590	14%	−9%	80%	78%
3 Martin-Marietta[2]	9,404	46%	38%	88%	65%
4 Hughes	13,428	6%	−16%	52%	45%
5 Northrop Grumman[3]	6,391	−35%	−39%	81%	81%
6 Boeing	20,937	−7%	−25%	28%	22%
7 Raytheon[4]	9,536	−3%	−22%	54%	38%
8 United Technologies	19,810	−9%	−15%	24%	18%
9 Litton[5]	3,282	−41%	−43%	60%	92%
10 Loral[6]	3,818	189%	155%	79%	78%
11 General Dynamics[7]	2,912	−74%	−79%	90%	93%
12 Westinghouse	8,427	−41%	−31%	24%	28%
13 Rockwell	10,593	−24%	−34%	28%	21%
14 General Electric	57,247	−6%	−24%	16%	4%
15 Tenneco	11,594	−19%	−39%	15%	15%
16 Texas Instruments	9,824	35%	−24%	33%	17%
17 TRW	8,654	6%	−14%	43%	19%
18 ITT	22,448	1%	−8%	8%	6%
19 Allied Signal	12,207	−8%	−18%	20%	11%
20 Unisys	6,990	−38%	−44%	21%	16%
21 FMC Corporation	3,858	1%	−11%	32%	27%
22 Textron	9,222	11%	−9%	23%	10%
23 GTE Corporation	19,007	−7%	−36%	6%	4%
24 Computer Sciences	2,460	65%	32%	41%	28%
25 Honeywell[8]	5,769	−15%	−22%	21%	7%
Total/Weighted Percentage	302,957	−9.20%	−25%	32.80%	25.00%

Sources: Company Annual Reports, Investment Analysts' Reports, Company Interviews, GAO, Defence Contractors, October 1995, GAO/NSAID–96–19BR, *Defense News*, 'Top 100 Reports', 1990–94.

(a) Estimates from *Defence News*, 'Top 100 Reports', include sales to DoD and estimate of arms export sales. Does not include other government sales such as NASA and DoE.

1. Includes purchase of General Dynamics Military Aircraft, 1994 numbers based on estimate before Martin–Marietta merger
2. Includes acquisition of GE aerospace and GD space systems, 1994 numbers based on estimate before Lockheed merger
3. Data for Northrop Grumman combined in 1989–93
4. Before acquisition of E-Systems by Raytheon
5. Litton spun-off its commercial operations in 1993–94
6. Includes a series of acquisitions prior to purchase by Lockheed/Martin
7. Includes a series of major divestitures
8. Includes the formal separation with Alliant Techsystems

contractor success in diversification include: (1) the potential of a firm's core technologies and product lines; (2) the risk/return opportunities associated with downsizing versus diversification strategies; and (3) the degree to which a company has the institutional capacity and leadership to change its market orientation. Despite Wall Street pressures to divest their military divisions, these firms have ambitiously committed retained earnings and organizational resources to the transferring of aerospace and communications technologies into civilian products for space, automotive, environmental, energy and transportation management markets. In a number of cases, they have constructed innovative organizational structures to facilitate the flow of technologies and personnel. TRW, for instance, set up an Automotive Technology Center in the middle of its California 'Space Park' aerospace operations; the centre hosts dozens of automotive division employees on extended leave each year to explore the potential of aerospace technology applications to automobile problems.[8]

These disparate coping strategies on the part of large contractors have resulted in a substantial shake-out in the ranks of American defence contractors (Table 3.5). The top-ranked contractors are now much larger and more defence dependent, and the gap in defence dependency between these and the more diversified corporations who remain large defence contractors in absolute terms has grown. The largest – Lockheed/Martin, McDonnell Douglas and Northrop Grumman – remain more than 70 per cent defence dependent, while TRW, Hughes and Rockwell have lowered their military sales ratios to less than 40 per cent.[9]

Small Defence Firm Restructuring

Smaller defence firms are not a mirror image of their larger brethren. Most do not weigh in on the radar screen of either the Pentagon or Wall Street in the same way that the top fifty do. Although some have defence profits available for reinvesting in new internal ventures, many have difficulties finding the financial means to move into new markets. Those who have always served both civilian and military markets have a less difficult time surviving,[10] but even these firms have to cope with severe shrinkage in orders without clear alternatives for freed up capacity.[11] One mitigating factor is that intensified outsourcing by larger defence companies has generated additional work for many smaller firms.

Work done by the Project on Regional and Industrial Economics (PRIE) at both regional and national levels in the US suggests remarkable variation in strategy and success on the part of smaller defence contractors. Many have downsized their operations significantly but have simultaneously increased their sales in civilian markets. In Los Angeles, for instance, among a set of 23 firms interviewed, we found average revenue declines of 10 per cent and employment cuts of 36 per cent over the period from 1989 to 1994, a gap which would be somewhat smaller if real rather than nominal sales were taken into account.[12] For these California firms, the differential between sales and employment performance is explained by aggressive, often draconian, pressures to increase productivity in remaining operations, by outsourcing and subcontracting, and by relocation and consolidation at sites outside southern California. However, defence dependency for this set of smaller companies shrank from 75 per cent to 47 per cent from 1989 to 1994, in part from significant expansion in civilian sales. Three out of four of these firms reported sales from new commercial products. In some, sales from new non-DoD (Department of Defense) products have begun to offset defence reductions. Employment has stabilized in a number of firms after several years of job cuts.

These general trends are corroborated by the findings from a large national survey of small and medium-sized defence firms over the period 1989 to 1994.[13] The survey found considerable stability in the universe of smaller defence contracting firms, with real sales and employment increasing modestly and defence dependency decreasing marginally. Since procurement spending plummeted over this period, the survey results strongly suggest that major prime contractors were subcontracting more rather than taking work in-house. Firms in this survey expanded civilian sales on average by about 9 per cent, most commonly into non-DOD government markets (space, transportation, energy, environment).

In addition to the difficult task of developing new products and closing sales in alternative markets, diversifying companies face a number of specific constraints. Companies often lack one or more capabilities in strategic planning, marketing, or operations management necessary to plan and implement market diversification. Firms can benefit, though, from an integrated set of support services to fill crucial gaps. Programmes recently created by state and local governments to provide technical assistance, finance, training and marketing assistance are beginning to improve measurably the performance of a number of diversifying companies.[14]

PRIE research has also investigated spin-off and start up companies that have broken loose from larger defence organizations, be they large defence firms or national laboratories.[15] These companies have successfully entered new commercial markets, although the number of such firms seems to be relatively small given the vastness of the defence technology base. This suggests that federal and regional leaders might put in place mechanisms to increase technology transfer from large defence companies to smaller spin-off companies focusing on new high-growth markets.

THE WALL STREET CONNECTION

Because the Pentagon has no clear vision of a downsized and reorganized defence industrial base, much of the initiative for restructuring has passed by default to Wall Street. Following a decade of 'hands off' posture towards military industrial firms – the GM purchase of Hughes Aircraft was the only major deal of the 1980s involving a large defence contractor, Wall Street investment banking houses have become very active in engineering the large deals like Lockheed/Martin and Northrop Grumman of the 1990s. Their strategy is not only to match up former competitors in either market-deepening or market-widening mergers, but to convince more diversified companies like Rockwell, Texas Instruments and TRW to sell off their military units which would then become available for consolidation with other highly defence-dependent firms.

The Wall Street argument is that the 'wall of separation' is a fact of business life, and that 'pure play' defence companies return better value to their stockholders than do conglomerates who attempt to operate across both types of market. It is difficult to evaluate these claims. 'Pure play' mergers are driven as much by expectations of short term speculative gain as they are by longer-term real returns. Some sceptics see this as simply the Wall Street fad of the mid-decade. In addition, 'pure play' companies of any type may outperform their more diversified competitors on price/earnings ratios. But this may simply be the result of greater transparency of 'pure play' companies and thus of higher bids on their stock.

The evidence is not yet in on whether 'pure play' versus diversified companies are actually more efficient or earn higher returns. Furthermore, if higher returns in the longer run are due to monopolistic profits and market power in defence markets, what is good for stockholders is not equivalent to what is optimal for American taxpayers and citizens. One recent study suggests that large defence contractors who are resisting 'pure play' pressures are investing larger shares of their overall revenues in R&D and are lowering their defence dependency ratios more rapidly than are those who have embraced 'pure play'.[16] These findings suggests that the former group will be better positioned to compete in an economy with a permanently smaller military, and that they will be less apt to be heavily invested in lobbying for maintenance of defence spending levels, arms export permissiveness, and expensive, speculative R&D projects.

PENTAGON INDUSTRIAL BASE MANAGEMENT

In the post-Cold War period, no coherent vision for the future US defence industrial base has emerged from the Pentagon. Early on in the Clinton administration, an Office of Economic Security, with its own undersecretary, was established with the express charge of researching (among other things) defence industrial base issues and charting a policy for the Department of Defense. However, no policy emerged, no reports have been issued, and the Office is in the process of being dismantled. Instead, four different and somewhat contradictory policy initiatives at top levels of the Pentagon have confounded the adjustment process and undermined the speed with which the administration has been able to terminate certain weapons systems and move resources to other priority areas. The four are the following: procurement reform; 'dual-use' technology initiatives; arms export liberalization; and a new permissiveness toward and subsidies for defence corporate mergers. The first two of these act to lower firm 'walls of separation' between operations serving military and civilian markets, while the latter two create incentives for the maintenance of defence-dependent companies.

Procurement reform is a perennial issue which has received renewed attention in the Clinton administration. The reforms are aimed at eliminating or altering onerous and unnecessary military specifications and other regulations which make it difficult for an individual firm to serve both military markets and civilian markets with the same facilities. Success would result in more suppliers, greater price and quality competition and thus lower prices for superior products.[17]

Many smaller businesses are enthusiastic advocates of procurement reform, as are more diversified companies. However, some observers believe the largest, most defence-dependent contractors are resisting procurement reform. In practice, many smaller contractors and would-be suppliers complain that although top Pentagon management is committed to reform, the bureaucracy has been slow to respond, so that gains are disappointing. Some analysts question whether procurement reform can ever work as long as defence production remains high-technology and innovation intensive.[18] Nevertheless, some smaller companies interviewed in PRIE's regional studies have benefited from the ability to sell to the services where previously they were barred by procurement practices.[19]

Dual use technology programmes have served as the major new conversion initiatives of the Clinton administration, commanding more new resources than any other element of the more than $1.7 billion in annual conversion spending. These efforts have been aimed at the R&D and technological capabilities of defence companies and national laboratories, and have consisted of grants (the Technology Reinvestment Program) to consortia of private sector firms, sometimes with university or non-profit partners, and Cooperative Research and Development Agreements (CRADAs) between companies or consortia and government research labs where each partners puts up funds for and/or devotes resources to a joint research effort. The TRP has been managed by the Department of Defense, with other federal agencies involved, while the lion's share of CRADAs have taken place with the nation's nuclear weapons laboratories, overseen by the Department of Energy.

To date, both types have been well-received and heavily subscribed to by the private sector. Although it is too soon to fully evaluate the returns, a number of commercial products have been successfully developed and marketed which would most likely not have emerged without this support.[20] Each has been relatively professionally managed, tailored to avoid charges of pork-barrelling. As a result, each has generated 'losers' whose antagonism has contributed to curbing Congressional enthusiasm.[21] In addition, difficult problems of taxpayer return, proprietary rights and conflict of interest have yet to be worked out.[22] In 1995/96, the Congress gutted many of these programmes, cutting funding for them by more than 50 per cent and instituting strict programme criteria which restricts new agreements and awards to projects which have clear military 'spin-on'.[23]

Arms export policies have been a major target of large weapons systems integrators like McDonnell Douglas, Lockheed/Martin, Northrop Grumman and General Dynamics, and of smaller companies who export leading edge commercial technologies which could be adopted to military uses. Previously restricted from exporting state-of-the-art systems, these contractors have argued that both the trade deficit and the need to keep weapons lines in production are grounds for liberalized trade.[24] The Clinton administration has responded positively to these pressures, overruling the recommendations of some in the armed services and the State Department.[25] Since the Gulf War, American arms exports have soared to more than 45 per cent of the world market (70 per cent by some accounts), and large advanced weapons like F-15 and F-16 fighters have been sold to multiple buyers, often with government marketing and credit assistance.[26] Some production lines are currently supported nearly 100 per cent by arms exports.[27] An escalation of small-arms exports and surplus weapons sales have provided outlets for smaller companies.[28] To the extent that these markets provide profit-earning options for defence contractors, they will be less apt to engage in active efforts to diversify or explore dual use technologies.

The Pentagon's surprising new permissiveness toward mergers among large defence giants is also undermining the 'dual-use', civilian/military integration impetus of the 1990s. In past decades, a concern with multiple sourcing and a desire to use competition as a check on price and quality resulted in what Kurth[29] has called the 'follow-on imperative', whereby the Department of Defense awarded contracts in a sequential fashion that ensured the financial viability of first tier suppliers. In the 1990s, in response to large contractor initiatives, the Pentagon has adopted a passive stance *vis-à-vis* mergers of former competitors. In addition, it has actively subsidized the process by permitting contractors to write-off consolidation costs (golden parachutes for executives, plant closing and severance pay) against existing contracts, on the grounds that these will save taxpayers money in the future. (Similar savings that result when a defence contractor merges with a civilian-oriented firm do not receive equivalent treatment.) Most mergers have not actually eliminated production lines but rather have been of the market-extension type, giving surviving firms a fuller military product line.[30] On balance, this permissiveness and subsidy policy will encourage merger activity to create 'pure play' defence companies rather than diversification efforts.

The US government is thus giving the defence contracting sector a set of mixed messages in the 1990s. While formally committed to dual use and civilian/military integration strategies, it has tolerated and underwritten a remarkably rapid consolidation in the numbers and size of the most critical companies involved in systems integration and future R&D. The largest of these, Lockheed/Martin, will not only dominate design and production of a number of weapons systems but also operate several of the nation's critical national nuclear laboratories – Sandia, Oak Ridge, and the Idaho National Energy Laboratories. Simultaneously, government is downsizing and eliminating its public arsenals faster than those of private-sector capacity. One set of researchers has suggested that the federal government, faced with a growing monopoly over weapons supply, consider treating the complex as a public arsenal once again.[31]

In sum, the Pentagon has no pro-active coherent policy for industrial base management. It has not conducted studies to determine how much capacity the military will require in the coming decades, how many production lines and research labs are amenable to 'dual-use' operation, what the impact on price and quality will be of a dwindling number of suppliers, or the national security risks and/or payoffs of purchasing more internationally.[32] Neither defence contractors nor military base commanders are required to draw up alternative use plans for their facilities, despite the fact that they are asked to plan for many different and highly speculative military contingencies in the future. Much could be done along these lines to render defence armaments and bases more flexible and easier to redeploy.

PROGNOSIS

Decisions by policymakers and defence-firm managers over the coming few years will put in place a defence industry which will likely differ radically from that of the Cold War period. The most likely configuration, if present trends and policies persist, is an industry dominated by a few very large firms with high defence-dependency ratios and market power in major weapons systems final assembly, surrounded by a large pool of contractors who are relatively more diversified and 'dual use' in character. The large contractors will most likely continue to have considerable access to top Pentagon and service decisionmakers, helping to shape evaluations of future weapons needs and receiving favourable treatment on questions of arms-export policy, procurement policy and R&D spending commitments. They may also be increasingly international in purview, with alliances and joint ventures, if not more permanent ties, forged across national borders.[33]

A less likely but more optimal configuration, for both economic and strategic reasons, could be achieved if federal government policymakers were to press aggressively for a more integrated military/civilian industrial base. To do so, they would have to discourage 'pure play' defence firm mergers and reward the acquisition of commercial expertise, reject the rationale of 'keeping the base warm' in fashioning arms export policy, commit strongly to procurement reform aimed at procuring more directly from commercial producers, and offer positive incentives for heavily defence-dependent firms to diversify into civilian markets. The benefit from an industry with greater flexibility and less defence dependency would be lower resistance to defence cuts and less pressure for arms exports. Military spending could come down faster, to match new security realities, and conventional arms proliferation would be slowed down. The American economy and people worldwide would benefit greatly from the rededication of skilled scientific, engineering and blue collar manpower to new challenges on health and environmental fronts and in commercial arenas.

NOTES

1. Michael Oden, *Military Spending, Military Power and US Postwar Economic Performance*, PhD Dissertation, Department of Economics, New School for Social Research, New York, 1992.
2. Ann Markusen and Joel Yudken, *Dismantling the Cold War Economy* (New York: Basic Books, 1992).
3. Ann Markusen, 'Defence Spending: A Successful Industrial Policy?', *International Journal of Urban and Regional Research*, vol. 10, no. 1 (1992), pp. 105–22; Ann Markusen and Joel Yudkin [2]; Candace Howes and Ann Markusen, 'Industrial Strategy and Economic Growth: What the US Can Learn from Japan'. In Steven Ericson and Michael Mastanduno (eds), *A Renewed Partnership? Japan and the United States on the Eve of the Twenty-First Century*, forthcoming.
4. Michael O'Hanlon, *Defence Planning for the Late 1990s: Beyond the Desert Storm Framework* (Washington, DC: The Brookings Institution, 1995); Randall Forsberg, 'Defence Cuts and Cooperative Security in the Post-Cold War World', *Boston Review* (February 1992).

5. Gregory Bischak, 'Contending Security Doctrines and the Military Industrial Base', paper presented to the Council on Foreign Relations, New York, (April 1996).
6. Ann Markusen, 'Mixed Messages: The Effects of the Gulf War and the End of the Cold War on the American Military Industrial Complex', in Thomas Mayer, John O'Loughlin and Edward Greenberg (eds), *War and its Consequences: Lessons from the Persian Gulf Conflict* (New York: HarperCollins, 1994).
7. Michael Oden, 'Cashing-in, Cashing-out and Converting: Restructuring of the Defence Industrial Base in the 1990s', paper presented to the Council on Foreign Relations, New York (February 1996).
8. Michael Oden, Ann Markusen, Dan Flaming, Jonathan Feldman, James Raffel and Catherine Hill, *From Managing Growth to Reversing Decline: Aerospace and the Southern California Economy in the Post Cold War Era* (New Brunswick, NJ: Rutgers University, Project on Regional and Industrial Economics, 1996).
9. Michael Oden [7]; Michael Oden, Ann Markusen, et al. [8].
10. Mary Ellen Kelley and Todd Watkins, 'The Myth of the Specialized Military Contractor' *Technology Review* vol. 98, no. 3 (April 1995), pp. 52–8.
11. Jonathan Feldman, 'Conversion and Diversification after the Cold War: Results from the National Defence Economy Survey', Working Paper, Project on Regional and Industrial Economics, Rutgers University, 1996.
12. Michael Oden, Ann Markusen, et al. [8].
13. Jonathan Feldman [11].
14. Michael Oden, Catherine Hill, Elizabeth Mueller, Jonathan Feldman, and Ann Markusen, *Changing the Future: Converting the St. Louis Economy* (New Brunswick, NJ: Rutgers University, Project on Regional and Industrial Economics, 1993); Michael Oden, Elizabeth J. Mueller, and Judy Goldberg, *Life after Defence: Conversion and Economic Adjustment on Long Island* (New Brunswick, NJ: Rutgers University, Project on Regional and Industrial Economics, 1994).
15. Michael Oden, Ann Markusen, et al. [8]; Ann Markusen and Michael Oden, 'National Laboratories as Business Incubators and Region Builders', *Journal of Technology Transfer* (forthcoming); Ann Markusen, James Raffel, Michael Oden and Marlen Llanes, *Coming in from the Cold: The Future of Los Alamos and Sandia National Laboratories* (New Brunswick, NJ: Rutgers University, Project on Regional and Industrial Economics, 1995).
16. Michael Oden [7].
17. Jacques Gansler, *Defence Conversion: Transforming the Arsenal of Democracy* (Cambridge, MA: MIT Press, 1995); William J. Perry, 'Specifications & Standards – A New Way of Doing Business', Memorandum for Secretaries of the Military Departments, Chairman of the Joint Chiefs of Staff, Undersecretaries of Defense (29 June 1994).
18. Michael Oden, 'The Microeconomics of Defense-Serving Organizations: Implications for Conversion and Adjustment Policy', paper presented at the American Public Policy Association meetings, Chicago (October 1994); Gregory Bischak [5].
19. Michael Oden, Ann Markusen, et al. [8].
20. Michael Oden, Gregory Bischak and Christine Evans-Klock, *The Technology Reinvestment Project: The Limits of Dual-Use Technology Policy* (New

Brunswick, NJ: Rutgers University, Project on Regional and Industrial Economics, 1995); Rose Marie Ham, David Mowery and Hank Chesbrough, 'Managing and Evaluating Single-Firm CRADAs: An Assessment of Five Recent Cases at Lawrence Livermore National Laboratory', Consortium on Competitiveness and Cooperation Working Paper No. 95-7 (Berkeley, CA: Center for Research Management, September 1995).

21. Jay Stowsky, 'America's Technical Fix: The Dual Use Strategy and the Political Economy of US Technology Policy', paper presented to the Council on Foreign Relations, New York (23 February 1996).

22. Ann Markusen, James Raffel, et al. [15].

23. Ann Markusen, 'The Political Economy of Technology Policy in the 1990s', paper presented at the Annual Meetings of the American Association for the Advancement of Science, Baltimore (11 February 1996).

24. William Keller, Arm in Arm: The Political Economy of the Global Arms Trade (New York: Basic Books, 1995); Edward Laurance, The International Arms Trade (New York: Lexington Books, 1992); US Congress, Office of Technology Assessment (OTA), Global Arms Trade: Commerce in Advanced Military Technology and Weapons, OTA-ISC-460 (Washington, DC: US Government Printing Office, 1991).

25. White House, Office of the Press Secretary, 'Conventional Arms Transfer Policy', Fact sheet, 17 February 1995; White House, Office of the Press Secretary, 'Criteria for Decision Making on US Arms Exports', Fact sheet, 17 February 1995.

26. Natalie Goldring, 'Toward Restraint: Controlling the International Arms Trade', Harvard International Review, vol. XVII, no. 1 (1994), pp. 34-7, 78-9; William Hartung, And Weapons for All (New York: Harper Collins, 1994); US Arms Control and Disarmament Agency, World Military Expenditures and Arms Transfers, 1993-94 (Washington, DC: US Government Printing Office, 1995).

27. Randall Forsberg (ed.), The Arms Production Dilemma (Cambridge, MA: MIT Press, 1994).

28. Jefferey Boutwell, Michael Klare, and Laura Reed (eds), Lethal Commerce: The Global Trade in Small Arms and Light Weapons (Cambridge, MA: Committee on International Security Studies, American Academy of Arts and Sciences, 1995); Bonn International Centre for Conversion, Conversion Survey 1996: Global Disarmament, Demilitarization and Demobilization (London: Oxford University Press, 1996).

29. James Kurth, 'The Follow-on Imperative in American Weapons Procurement, 1960-1990', in Jurgen Brauer and Manas Chatterji (eds), The Economics of Disarmament (New York: New York University Press, 1990); James Kurth, 'Aerospace Production Lines and American Defence Spending', in Steven Rosen (ed.), Testing the Theory of the Military-Industrial Complex (Lexington, MA: D.C. Heath, 1973).

30. Michael Oden [7]; Harvey Sapolsky and Eugene Gholz, 'Private Production Lines and Public Arsenals: The Post Cold War Mix', Paper presented to the Council on Foreign Relations (March 1996).

31. Ibid., Harvey Sapolsky and Eugene Gholz.

32. Kenneth Flamm, 'Who and How Much?: A Methodology for a Pro-Active Pentagon Policy for the Defence Industrial Base', paper for presentation to the Council on Foreign Relations (May 1996).

33. Richard A. Bitzinger, 'The Globalization of Arms Industry: The Next Proliferation Challenge', *International Security*, Vol. 19, No. 2 (1994); Michael Brzoska and Peter Lock (eds), *Restructuring of Arms Production in Western Europe* (Oxford: Oxford University Press, 1992); Ethan B. Kapstein, *Global Arms Production: Policy Dilemmas for the 1990s* (Cambridge, MA: Center for International Affairs and University Press of America, 1992); Keith Hartley, 'The Military Industries in the UK', paper presented at the Conference on Politics and Economics of Defence Industries in a Changing World, Bar-Ilan University, Ramat Gan (January 1996), and see his chapter in this volume; John Lovering, 'Restructuring the Global Military Sector: Political, Economic, Social and Institutional Aspects', paper presented at the United Nations' University, Helsinki (10–21 May 1995).

4

Too Small to Vanish, too Large to Flourish: Dilemmas and Practices of Defence Industry Restructuring in West European Countries

MICHAEL BRZOSKA

INTRODUCTION

Combined, Western European countries have formidable defence-industrial capacities. In the European Union (EU) member countries and Norway, the total number of employees in this sector was about 800,000 in 1995. In early 1996, three modern fighter aircraft, four types of main battle tanks and several types of large conventional submarines were in production or in advanced development. This list can easily be extended to demonstrate the technical competence and diversity of West European defence industries.[1]

What may initially appear as strengths, however, are revealed as problems upon closer analysis. The large number of differing types of weapon systems lowers production runs and increases unit costs. Compared to the defence research and the defence budget in the United States, European efforts toward finding and using new technologies are minor. Current changes in military technology may further erode the technological position of industries in Western Europe. Finally, considering post-Cold War procurement levels in Western Europe, the combined defence industries have large overcapacities, and given current procurement planning in Europe and likely exports, they will have to shrink further. Thus, massive restructuring of arms production has occurred since the mid-1980s and more will come about.

Restructuring in Western Europe has taken particular forms, reflecting a peculiar mixture of national and international factors. In general, national governments have hindered rather than helped the necessary restructuring. They have shown little willingness to change outdated procurement patterns, despite frequent proclamations to the contrary. They have given limited support to companies willing to restructure. The European Union, a dominant factor in many economic fields, has no official role in defence production. The EU does run a programme designed to help companies to convert – that is, to find civilian markets, through the extension of existing businesses and new products. On the whole, however, governments provide arms-producing companies with few incentives for change.

Diversity, technological competence, overcapacities, and government inaction are increasingly becoming major problems for defence production in Western Europe. These problems are largely interrelated; a web of dilemmas. The source of these dilemmas, or the ultimate dilemma, is the very familiar one of small states trying to produce a wide range of high technology products. In the West European context, this basic dilemma is modified by the economic integration within the EU and the political integration in NATO.[2]

Five major dilemmas shape the future of the defence industry in Western Europe:

- National autonomy in defence matters versus (West) Europeanization of economies;
- Military alliance with the United States versus (West) European 'defence identity';
- Costs versus sectoral economics (employment, regional economics;
- Technology for the armed forces versus national technology policy;
- Politically motivated arms trade restraint versus export orientation for economic reasons.

These dilemmas are predominantly ones upon which governments and parliaments in Western Europe must act.

Many recommendations for institutional change to cope with the current situation and improve prospects have been made[3]; the more radical ones include creation of a 'defence GATT'; harmonization and ultimate unification of procurement among governments in the Western European Union (WEU); and opening of markets within Western Europe for supply-driven market consolidation.

The institutional arrangements decisively shape the environment for Western European defence companies, including both management and employees. Faced with the decline of procurement in the early 1990s, companies have had to opt for various strategies, ranging from concentration on defence production to abandonment of the sector by decreasing civilian production. Company managers had to act, and many have done so although much remains to be done.

In fact, there remains much overcapacity in arms production in Western European countries, measured against probable longer-term domestic procurement patterns.[4] Company managers are insecure about future defence markets, while conversion into civilian activities is a difficult and not altogether successful endeavour. Lack of government conclusiveness about the future shape of defence production in Western Europe has contributed to the reluctance of companies to downsize.

SMALL MARKETS, LARGE AMBITIONS

In comparison to most other countries in the world, a number of Western European countries have substantial defence industries – measured, for instance, in terms of numbers of persons employed (see Table 4.1). Combined, the defence procurement markets of the member states of the European Union make up the second largest defence procurement market in the world (after the United States). There is not a common Western European defence market, however; rather, markets remain mostly national. Compared to the United States, any single defence procurement market in Western Europe – including the French and the British markets – is small. For most purposes, the comparison with the United States is the appropriate one: US defence companies develop a large range of weaponry, with which West European companies are in actual competition in third markets and in potential competition at home.

TABLE 4.1
ESTIMATED EMPLOYMENT IN ARMS PRODUCTION IN WESTERN EUROPE

Countries	Numbers of direct and indirect employees, in 1,000s										
	1985	1986	1987	1988	1989	1990	1991	1992	1993	1994	1995
UK	470	460	450	490	430	440	380	390	433	310	290
France	340	340	330	320	310	300	290	280	270	260	250
Germany	307	280	260	240	220	200	190	180	160	140	120
Italy	86	80	80	80	80	80	70	60	50	45	40
Spain	66	80	90	100	100	100	80	60	50	40	30
Sweden	35	35	35	30	30	30	30	30	30	30	30
Turkey	20	20	20	25	25	25	25	30	30	30	30
Switzerland	30	30	30	25	25	25	25	25	20	20	15
Netherlands	18	18	18	20	20	20	18	18	18	15	15
Greece	15	15	15	15	15	15	15	15	15	15	15
Belgium	35	35	30	30	25	25	20	15	15	12	10
Finland	10	10	10	10	10	10	10	10	10	10	10
Norway	15	15	15	10	10	10	10	10	10	10	10
Portugal	10	10	10	10	10	10	10	10	10	10	10
Denmark	6	6	6	6	7	7	6	6	5	5	5
Austria	8	8	6	6	5	5	5	4	4	3	3
Sum – W. Europe, in millions	1.47	1.44	1.41	1.42	1.32	1.30	1.18	1.14	1.02	0.96	0.88

Small home markets are of relatively minor importance in the case of free trade. In many civilian commodity markets, companies from small countries are successfully competing in the world market. The situation is different in the defence sector, however, because competition is mainly restricted to markets outside the industrialized world.

Prevalent Procurement Strategies

EU member countries routinely restrict access to their domestic defence markets. This is legitimized by article 223 of the Treaty of Rome, which established the European Economic Community. Other markets that had restrictions – such as non-defence public procurement – have been liberalized, but efforts to do the same for the internal defence market have so far been frustrated.[5]

In the practice of most West European governments, this means that domestic suppliers are chosen whenever possible. Problems arise if there simply is no domestic producer – for instance, in the case of advanced electronics in most of the smaller EU member countries – or when domestic production is too expensive due to a lack of economies of scale.

The traditional 'second-best alternative' preferred by national procurement authorities has been regulated by international collaboration on the basis of what is called the principle of *juste retour*. Through tightly regulated cooperation among partner countries within Western Europe and other NATO member countries, such as the United States, production runs lengthen and unit costs are lowered. International collaboration allows domestic companies to participate in production as partners, in contrast to foreign purchases in which domestic companies may contribute as suppliers of parts at best. *Juste retour* means that work shares are distributed among countries according to shares in financing the project, not according to industrial competition.

These two strategies still cover most purchases of major weapons in Western European countries. Modifications fall into three groups:

- There have been open purchases, especially in the smaller countries – for instance, the air forces of Belgium, the Netherlands and Denmark opted for the F-16 aircraft in the 1970s when they could have been collaborating partners in developing a Mirage fighter plane. Recently, the Dutch and British governments favoured the US Apache attack helicopter over the Franco-German Tigre attack helicopter. The difference between countries with larger defence industries and countries with smaller ones – for instance, in the southern European periphery – is visible in arms export statistics: while there is almost no trade in complete systems among the major producers in Western Europe, the smaller countries are buyers of such weapons systems from the countries with larger defence industries (see Table 4.2).

TABLE 4.2
ARMS TRANSFER DELIVERIES AMONG WESTERN EUROPEAN EXPORTERS

Cumulative values, 1991–93

	Exporter				
	UK	Germany	France	Italy	Other Western Europe
Total exports (in US $m)	13,380	4,555	3,635	1,045	2,800

Importer	Percentage shares of total arms exports to importer				
UK	x	–	–	0	–
Germany	0	x	–	0	1
France	0	–	x	–	2
Italy	0	–	–	x	–
Greece, Portugal, Turkey	0	28	11	3	14
Other Western Europe	2	21	17	22	14

Source: US Arms Control and Disarmament Agency (ACDA), *World Military Expenditures and Arms Transfers, 1993–1994* (Washingon, DC: US Government Printing Office, 1995).

• A major deviation from the traditional pattern was initiated in Britain in the 1980s. The 'Levene' reforms of the early 1980s brought more competition to the procurement process in the United Kingdom, and some foreign systems, such as the Boeing AWACS, were chosen over domestic products. Nevertheless, in the large majority of cases, new systems procured in Britain are also produced in Britain.[6] The British system can probably best be characterized as one of limited competition in a contestable market.[7]

• Shipbuilding has provided something of a special case. While hulls tend to be built domestically, electronics, engines, and weapons are usually an international mix. A large number of ships in Western Europe, and indeed the world, have naval guns from OTO Melara (Italy) and Bofors (Sweden), Exocet missiles from Aerospatiale (France), electronics from Thomson-CSF (France) or Hollandse Signaal (Netherlands), radar from Decca (UK) and diesel engines from MTU (Germany).

Further from national procurement there is more competition. First-tier suppliers are generally encouraged by national procurement authorities to find national second- and third-tier suppliers. Increasingly, however, they are also asked to produce more cheaply, under fixed price contracts and other limitations. No EU member country has a fully diversified lower-tier defence industrial base.[8] Thus, the further down the production chain one looks, the more foreign suppliers one is likely to find. Even systems of national pride, such as the French Rafale fighter or the German U-209 Class submarines, contain a large share of foreign components, mostly electronics.

The Costs and Benefits of Regulated Procurement in Fragmented Markets

The current procurement system has obvious costs compared to other possible procurement systems, such as opening up the West European defence market to competition from other EU member states or the world market. Procurement solely on fiscal cost and technological benefit criteria would most likely result in substantial cost savings.

The first and major cost arises from short production runs. Research and development (R&D) expenditures are large and learning cost curves are typically high in defence production. In a study for the European Commission, Keith Hartley and David Cox have estimated that substantial savings are possible from a less fractured market.[9]

The prevalent form of procurement in fragmented markets – regulated collaboration – does allow savings from larger production runs, but it increases R&D costs. Unfortunately, possible savings from larger production runs are often lowered because governments insist on final assembly lines in their home countries, as is currently the case in the Eurofighter 2000 aircraft programme. Also, regulated collaboration does not necessarily encourage governments to push for the participation of those national companies that are most suited. Gains in technology are larger for less competent firms. The other partners often must accept government decisions even if they lead to sub-optimal forms of collaboration.[10]

The currently dominant procurement system obviously has advantages, or it would not still be in place. There are economic benefits on the national and regional level, such as employment and technology gains. In addition, political advantages, such as stronger influence in international affairs and more autonomy in defence-related decisions, are claimed. There are also benefits for the institutional actors involved in procurement decisions, such as the defence companies and the armed forces.

Without recounting the details of these arguments, one may say that the national-level arguments have lost plausibility due primarily to two factors. One is that with the end of the Cold War, questions of national autonomy in defence procurement seem to have declined in importance for Western European states. The other is that technological gains from defence production seem to be less substantial – in other words, inventions and innovations in the civilian sector are increasingly outpacing the defence.[11] This is partly a result of the relative size of research and development efforts. With the exception of the United States, no government spends as much on military research and development as the world's major companies spend on developing new commercial products.[12]

With respect to defence industry restructuring, the sections below highlight two consequences of regulated procurement in fragmented markets that are of obvious importance, although they are often overlooked in the discussion in Western Europe – namely, the issues of minimum capacities and export pressures.

Small Markets and Minimum Capacity

There is general agreement that in most sectors of the defence industry, barriers to entry are high because of high initial capital costs – in terms of R&D, available labour pools and experience in systems integration. In fact, it is sometimes argued that these barriers to entry are among the defining characteristics of defence industries.[13] Clearly, there are civilian high-tech industries with similar requirements; for defence production, however, they are quite typical – at least for the production of weaponry at the latest level of technology.

From this consideration, it is only a small step to the idea of calculating minimum levels of R&D and production activity in various sectors of defence production. Unfortunately, there are no objective standards of minimum capacity. Many factors influence minimum capacity, such as availability of qualified labour, required depth of production, and required level of technology.

The data in Table 4.3 are derived from a recent German exercise. In 1993–94, representatives of the defence industry and the German Ministry of Defence joined together to do a study on the future structure of the German defence industry.[14] As part of the effort to define an arms industrial policy, minimum order levels were discussed. These were defined as the order levels sufficient to allow production of systems in Germany, either independently or in collaboration with partners within NATO. The numbers may not seem excessively high in the German context, although they exceeded actual R&D and procurement expenditures in a number of categories. Nevertheless, there are obviously large procurements above minimum capacities in some categories. For instance, the Eurofighter 2000 alone will cost about DM 2 billion in annual procurement expenditure when the aircraft is acquired. In any case, these minimum order levels are high for all of the countries in Western Europe with smaller arms industries.

In the fragmented Western European market, governments increasingly tend to be faced with a choice: spend money in order to maintain a minimum capacity or get out of production. As long as the willingness to remain is as great as it has been in the past, production overcapacity will remain a structural feature.

Small Markets and Export Pressures

One of the effects of comparatively small, fractured markets is intense pressure to export to less regulated markets. The relationship between market size and export share is, of course, a general one. For defence markets, however, there is a special attraction. Such exports allow increased production runs and lower unit costs, thus lowering domestic procurement costs. Sometimes they are a necessary precondition for production to occur. Although data is not reliable, it seems likely that some 35 to 40 per cent of all arms produced in Western European countries are exported, mostly to developing countries.[15]

TABLE 4.3
ESTIMATES OF MINIMUM CAPACITY FOR GERMAN DEFENCE INDUSTRY, 1994
in Million DM

	Research & development	Procurement
Armoured vehicles	250	600
– system	200	250
– hull, turret		65
– chain		70
– protection		50
– propulsion		90
– engineering vehicles		60
Artillery, ammunition	170	700
– small calibre, tank cannons, mortars	50	58
– large calibre	62	450
– small calibre	25	45
– training and special ammuntion	22	125
Aircraft	610	1,600
Fighter aircraft	440	1,000
– system	190	350
– propulsion	110	175
– equipment	130	400
Helicopter	140	500
– system	90	250
– propulsion	38	100
– equipment	21	150
UAV	70	85
– system	35	35
– propulsion	9	10
– equipment	26	40
Missiles	310	320
– system	190	150
– C3I	75	90
– warhead	25	30
– propulsion	18	42
Electronics	500	900
– data information	75	120
– communication	125	340
– identification	8	20
– optronics	90	90
– radar	100	160
– ECM	100	100
Sum	1,800	4,500
Actual expenditures, 1994 (including ship building)	2,790	9,620

Source: Wehrdienst, *Nachdruck von Auszuegen des Bericht ueber die Untersuchung zu Wehrtechnischen Mindestkapazitaeten in Deutschland* (Bonn: Griephan Verlag, 1994), and my own estimate.

Economically driven arms export policy is, of course, highly problematic. While there is little doubt that arms exports from Western European countries are economically driven – though to different degrees – all governments insist that they exercise political control over such exports. Governments have also stated their willingness to tightly restrict their arms exports within the framework of international agreements. The absence of such agreements has allowed governments to avoid such possible consequences of their own statements as reduced arms production capacity and employment. The decrease in arms exports in the early 1990s has given some indication of the possible economic effects, although Western European exporters have largely maintained their market shares.

Arms exports are generally portrayed by governments in Western Europe as providing economic gains in terms of employment, foreign exchange and lower procurement costs. Lately, however, academic experts in a number of Western European countries have questioned this assumption – most vocally in France, where the share of exports in production was especially high throughout the 1970s and 1980s.[16] Following are their main arguments:

- Because of intense competition in the international arms market, weapon prices are often set at levels that only cover variable production costs. Fixed costs, such as research and development and tooling, often must be paid by the government of the exporting state. Savings for national procurement, if they occur at all, are limited to the lower production costs resulting from longer production runs.
- Arms exports from West European countries often have a high import content. Even in the French case, in which national autonomy in production is a goal, parts are often imported from other countries – not only in Western Europe, but also the United States.
- Arms exports are subsidized through export promotion, special export guarantees and credit schemes. Probably the most drastic case of export subsidy in Western Europe was that of French arms exports to Iraq in the 1970s and 1980s. Given that repayment of the approximately six billion French

francs is unlikely, these exports ultimately became a large employment programme financed by French taxpayers.

Decreasing domestic budgets have increased export pressures in the early 1990s. Company managers are demanding more support, in both political and economic terms. Efforts in the early 1990s to increase the level of political restraint within the frameworks of the European Union or the Organization for Security and Cooperation in Europe, for example, seem to have fallen victim to these pressures.

On the international arms market, Western European exporters have maintained their market shares mostly due to the collapse of the highly subsidized Soviet export share. In absolute values, there has been a decline. At the same time, compared to the US defence industry, West European industry has not fared well in the 1990s. Interestingly, British industry, which was exposed to more competition at home from the early 1980s, has fared better than other West European states – particularly French industry, which remains highly protected at home. The largest losses in exports can be noted for the Italian and Spanish industries, which, as newcomers in the boom period of the late 1970s and early 1980s, have not been able to withstand the more competitive environment of the early 1990s.

POLICY ALTERNATIVES

As mentioned earlier, several ways to cope with the dilemmas of fragmented defence markets in Western Europe have been proposed. As there is not enough room here to go into the details of a long and tortuous discussion,[17] the sections below focus on the more radical proposals.

The 'Big Brother' Alternative

In most civilian commodity markets, West European governments allow for free competition among the member states of the European Economic Area and for virtually free markets within the framework of the General Agreement on Tariffs and Trade (GATT). Governments generally accept the logic of economic integration in these markets. On the other hand, they have turned a cold shoulder to the frequent proposals from representatives of the US government for a 'defence GATT'.

While it is likely that costs savings would result from open defence procurement, it is also likely that producers from the United States would gain the most. In fact, given the differences in market size and research and development effort, European producers frequently express the fear that only a few of them could survive such competition. The most recent arms trade figures, which show that US companies have gained more than 50 per cent of the world market, provide some support for such claims. This prospect, unwanted by governments and industry alike, is not the only reason why proposals for a 'defence GATT' have little chance. Another reason is the general unwillingness of the US government to open its procurement market to competition.

The 'Close Neighbour' Alternative

Much more likely is a more integrated West European defence procurement market. Proposals for such a market have been made since at least the mid–1970s, when the Independent European Programme Group (IEPG) was founded. They were reiterated in mid-1986 in a famous report to the IEPG by a group of 'wise men' under the chairmanship of former EU commissioner Henk Vredeling[18] and are again being discussed in the mid-1990s in the context of organizing a common defence and foreign policy within the framework of the EU and the WEU.[19]

Two basic approaches have been suggested. The first is demand driven: governments should cooperate and procure jointly whenever possible, choosing among a set of multinational consortia. This approach is similar to regulated collaboration, although it would allow some competition. The other is supply driven: governments should allow competition and procure from whoever offers the best price. While progress within the first approach is likely to come about soon, with the foundation of a European Armaments Agency that will administer collaborative projects, the second, certainly more radical approach does not seem to have advanced in the last decade or so.

There has thus been a significant divergence between words and deeds when it comes to the politics of a more integrated West European defence market. This state of affairs is, of course, not reserved for defence industry issues – it is a more general feature of defence and foreign policy in Western Europe, including the Common Foreign and Security Policy (CFSP) of the European Union member states. As the President of the European Commission, Jacques Santer, has written: 'Described in a recent Commission report as not living up to expectations, the CFSP has suffered, among other things, from a lack of political will, difficulties with the decision-making system, and crippling budgetary procedures.'[20]

EUROPEAN DEFENCE INDUSTRIAL BASE PATCHWORK

The lack of support for a larger defence market has increasingly become a problem for defence production companies in Western Europe. Most of the trends in defence production in the last decade or so have put additional pressure on the fragmented West European producers, for several reasons:

- The pace of technological innovation has been rapid, with the increasing integration of electronics in weapon systems and in intelligence gathering, communication and control and some other major innovations, such as stealth technology.
- Markets have shrunk due to reductions in procurement and exports. As a result, employment in arms production has decreased substantially in a number of Western European countries. While this trend is not much different from the world trend, smaller industries have greater difficulties in remaining competitive.
- The political trend generally favours less government regulation and more open markets. Within the framework of the EU, the defence market is not the last market to be

regulated, but it is the last market to remain within the prerogative of national governments. The 'Levene' reforms in the United Kingdom were a clear signal to defence producers that more competition may ensue. The 1986 Single Act, which established a true common market within the EU, was another such signal. In fact, quite a number of observers and decision-makers, including those in the IEPG, expected the 1990s to be period of much progress toward an integrated European defence market with more competition among producers. This has not come about for reasons that will be briefly reviewed in the final section.

There is only one trend that is countering these disadvantages in part:

• Dual–use technologies have become more important for defence purposes. Particularly in the electronic sector, the difference between civilian and military goods has less and less relevance and there is an increasingly large pool of common civilian and military technologies.[21] The 'Revolution in Military Affairs', about which there is much discussion in the United States, is a revolution in the integration of technologies that are also of great interest for civilian markets. Some of this technology is developed in Europe, often in companies that have little or no defence business. Other dual-use technologies in which Western European companies have competitive positions are new materials and propulsion systems.

Consequently, arms industries in all Western European countries (except Turkey) have shrunk if measured in terms of employment – some, such as the Spanish and Italian industries, dramatically, others substantially (see Table 4.1).

An important element in the discussion of the defence industrial base is the company response to the changes brought about in the late 1980s and early 1990s. In the last ten years, companies have had to cope with dramatic movement with respect to domestic and export demand, technological advances, and military-strategic thinking. Western European companies also had to reckon with the vagaries of the Western European integration process. There were important changes in the approach to arms industrial policies, partly related to world events. As mentioned earlier, in the late 1980s there was much rhetoric about the possible closer integration of the Western European defence market. In the 1990s this trend has reversed; governments and companies have, at least in part, reverted to defining policies in the national context.

Concentration and Internationalization

In the late 1980s, when more competition on a Western European scale seemed imminent, companies reacted in three ways. First, there was concentration on the national level. Second, alliances on the European and sometimes international scale were built. Third, managements in a number of companies, such as Philips of the Netherlands or Krupps of Germany, felt that they would be competitive on the larger, more international market and left the defence business. Concentration led to the creation of national champions in most markets in most countries. This process is not yet fully finished – thus, there are two aircraft manufacturers in France and two major submarine shipyards in Germany – but it has been well advanced in the last decade or so.

From the late 1980s, company managers were also busy creating links among companies in many forms, ranging from equity shares to loose agreements on 'strategic cooperation'. These links were different from the traditional ties within regulated collaboration, as they were neither project oriented nor government instigated.

The increasing trend of unregulated collaboration is clearly demonstrated in the database created by Richard Bitzinger of the Defence Budget Project in the United States, partly on the basis of the SIPRI company data bank (Table 4.4). It is evident from this data that growth of collaboration was most dramatic in the second half of the 1980s, while in the early 1990s it slowed. This may be interpreted as a reaction to the lack of government moves toward greater openness in procurement in the 1990s. Company managers underestimated government inertia, which in some cases led to the break-up of already agreed-on links between companies.

TABLE 4.4
COLLABORATION IN ARMS PRODUCTION AMONG WESTERN EUROPEAN
PRODUCERS

Numbers of Projects

	1991–94	1986–90	1981–85	1976–80	1971–75
Consortia	38	22	20	5	8
Joint ventures	20	8	2	0	1
Mergers and acquisition	12	36	2	0	0
Strategic alliances	10	6	0	0	0

Source: Richard Bitzinger, 'The Globalization of the Arms Industry: The Next
Proliferation Challenge', International Security (Fall 1994).

Civilian and Military Balances and Imbalances

Faced with substantial reductions in domestic procurement and
arms exports in the early 1990s, arms-producing companies have
had to adapt by finding new balances between civilian and
defence markets. Almost all companies tried to expand civilian
business or find new civilian markets, either with existing
company resources such as personnel or by acquisition of existing
civilian businesses.

There are numerous stories of failures as well as partial
successes in finding new civilian production. Unfortunately, good
data on defence industrial conversion are lacking. One data set
that allows some conclusions is the SIPRI company data base of
the top 100 arms-producing companies. Of the 33 Western
European companies among the world's largest defence-
producing companies in 1993 (the latest year for which data was
available), 13 were 'converters' in the sense that they increased
civilian sales while defence sales declined (see Table 4.5). Four
additional companies increased both defence and civilian sales,
in current prices measured in US dollars; three of them also could
be called 'converters' in the sense that they increased the civilian
shares of their businesses. Sixteen companies lost both civilian
and defence business. For 12 of them, defence business decreased
more than the civilian business; for 4 civilian business decreased
more than defence business. None of these companies was able
to expand civilian business to a degree large enough to
compensate for the falling defence demand. The data presented

TABLE 4.5

ECONOMIC PERFORMANCE INDICATORS FOR MAJOR WEST EUROPEAN DEFENCE PRODUCERS, 1990–93

Numbers of companies from among 33 largest defence sellers, 1993:

	with decreasing defence shares in total output	*with increasing defence shares in total output*
'Losers' (decreasing sales both in defence and civilian business)	12, of which: UK 4 France 3 Italy 2 Germany 1 Sweden 1 Switzerland 1	4, of which, UK 3 France 1
'Converters' (decreasing sales in defence; increasing sales in civilian business)	13, of which: Germany 4 France 4 UK 3 Spain 1 Switzerland 1	
'Winners' (increases in both defence and civilian sales)	3, of which: France 2 Germany 1	1, in UK

Source: SIPRI company data base, as published in SIPRI Yearbooks, 1992 and 1995.

here reflect not only efforts to redirect civilian/military balances, but also other factors, such as fluctuations in currency markets and the deep recession in the civilian aerospace industry. The data also reflect some country-specific influences, such as the unification boom in Germany. It reinforces the impression of a mixture of positive and negative experiences in finding more civilian business to compensate for losses in defence demand.

Finding Civilian Markets in Difficult Times

More detailed studies of countries and individual companies indicate that a host of factors are responsible for the mixture of success and failure in finding more civilian business.[22] Prominent among these are the following:

- General economic environment. It is easier to find more civilian business in a growing economy than when demand is declining. Depending on the market reach of relevant producers, the regional, national or international economy may be pertinent. Regional economic health often offers alternatives to company-based approaches, in that resources, such as skilled labour, can be utilized in other companies.[23]
- Industry. Barriers to entry are lower in some industries than in others. There are also differences between civilian and military 'business cultures', and relations between R&D, production and marketing are at least partially specific to industries.[24] In the aerospace industry, for instance, the civil/military balances seem to be less rigid than in the automobile or electronics industries, in which civilian markets are for the most part mass markets.
- Actor activity. The willingness of owners, managers and workers – and in many countries, their unions – to take often-unknown risks is likely to be the crucial factor, according to case studies. Conversion often requires extensive retraining, retooling and reconsideration of management structures. While in our days of 'business re-engineering', thorough business reorganization is rather common, managers in defence companies are often reluctant to pursue this course. From the perspective of owners, managers, and even those

workers remaining employed, a smaller business in traditional defence markets may look more secure than a risky reorganization with the aim of increasing civilian business.

- Earlier civil–military mix. Companies that already have much experience in civilian markets have less difficulty coping than those with a dominating 'defence culture'. German companies were privileged in this sense by the government's earlier decision to insist on a mix of civilian and defence production, while some French companies were hampered by their historic orientation toward defence production.
- Degree of government regulation. This point is closely related to the last one. Enterprises under strict government control, either because they were run as arsenals or due to extensive regulation of arms-production activities, have a more difficult time adjusting to civilian markets than companies already used to more competitive environments.
- Insecurity about defence market decline. Even now, no general agreement exists regarding the mid-term future of defence markets. Companies remain hopeful that a return of these markets will come about. In Western Europe, insecurity is compounded by uncertainty over the development of a possible Western European market, including more common rules on arms exports.
- Ownership. Two-thirds of arms production in Western Europe occurs in private companies. State ownership is still predominant in France, Italy and Spain, however.[25] In addition, defence research and development facilities are predominantly government owned, especially in France and the United Kingdom, where large-scale nuclear research occurs; on the other hand, most work is conducted in private companies in countries such as Sweden and Germany.[26] Government-owned companies often face specific difficulties in expanding civilian business. These difficulties are related to administrative regulation, which limits their access to civilian markets and requires them to behave in certain ways, and to specific company cultures that have developed over time. Regular privatization is therefore considered a necessary step before greater commercialization.

• Government support. This point is not negligible, although it is often given too much weight. Government support for expansion of civilian business has mostly been provided in the form of R&D subsidies. Such subsidies have not been tailored to serve defence conversion, but certain technology lines almost automatically benefit defence industry conversion – including aerospace technologies, certain types of material technology, such as carbon fibre, and certain types of electronics such as fast–switch chips. In the field of R&D subsidies, the European Union is playing an increasingly important role, with the Fourth Framework Programme on Science and Technology running into the tens of billions of dollars; nevertheless, national governments remain the largest spenders. Other types of government assistance benefiting defence conversion are regional and structural assistance programmes – for example, to regions with high rates of unemployment and the shipbuilding industry. This type of support comes from both national governments and the EU. Case studies of such regions as Bremen in Germany[27] and Brest in France[28] demonstrate that integrated regional support has often been fairly effective. The EU is also running a special programme for defence conversion called Konver. The current Konver II programme phase, which is to last from 1995 to 1999, is funded with some US $800 million for all 15 member countries. As it is intended to help not only defence industry conversion but also base closure communities, more than half of the money has been allocated to Germany.

CONCLUSIONS

The adaptation of defence production in Western Europe to the changed circumstances of the 1990s has been rather haphazard. It has resulted neither in a strong European defence sector that can be competitive without extensive government regulation and subsidization in its favour, nor in a large-scale reorientation of defence industries to civilian markets. The dilemmas of defence production in Western Europe thus remain unresolved.

The primary problem is the unwillingness of governments to

pursue in practice courses of action that they all agree to be beneficial in theory. These include greater openness in procurement decisions, at least for competitors from other Western European countries; common guidelines for procurements; common rules for arms exports compatible with the goal of strict political control over such exports; and a more competitive, leaner common defence market.

Although companies began preparations for such a market in the late 1990s, it has only gradually begun to emerge. Indeed, it is far from clear if and when it will come about.

The result of this indecision, which was actually more pronounced in the early 1990s than it was in the 1980s, has been substantial excess capacity in defence production in Western Europe, a fragmented production base, high costs for weapons, and less defence conversion than would have been likely with clear decisions on the future of the West European arms market. Defence production remains one of the last national prerogatives within the member countries and various associates of the European Union.

There are many reasons why progress on the political level has been far slower than that on the company level. Among them are 'Euro–scepticism' in a number of member countries, diverging foreign policy interests, and the special interests of arms producers and procurement authorities. Despite the recent spur in activity – exemplified by the creation of the European Armaments Agency – it is unlikely that enough political will for a more competitive Western European defence market can be amassed in the near future. The end of the Cold War has, at least so far, failed to bring relief to the defence production dilemmas in Western Europe. Rather, it has reinforced existing contradictions.

NOTES

1. Pierre DeVestel, *Defence Markets and Industries in Europe: Time for Political Decisions?*, Chaillot Paper 21 (Paris: Western European Union, November 1995), pp. 26–7.
2. Michael Brzoska and Peter Lock, *Restructuring of Arms Production in Western Europe* (London: Oxford University Press, 1992); DeVestel, *Defence Markets*, 1995; Ian Anthony, 'Defence Industrial Restructuring in Europe', *Peace and Defence Economics*, 6 (1995), pp. 185–205.

3. Brzoska and Lock, *Restructuring, 1992*; Western European Union (WEU) Assembly, *WEAG: The Course to be Followed*, Report Submitted on Behalf of the Technological and Aerospace Committee by Mrs Guirado and Lord Dundee, Western European Union, Document 1483 (6 November 1995).
4. Herbert Wulf (ed.), *Arms Industry Limited* (Oxford: Oxford University Press, 1994); Herbert Wulf, 'Overcapacity in Arms Production', presentation at Conversion Seminar, Monterey Institute for International Studies, Monterey, California, October 1995.
5. WEU, WEAG; Michael Brzoska, 'Prospects for a Common Arms Transfer Policy from the Euopean Union to the Middle East', in Efraim Inbar and Samuel Sandler (eds), *Middle Eastern Security* (London: Frank Cass, 1995).
6. Steven Schofield, 'The Levene Reforms: An Assessment', *Defence Analysis*, 11:2 (1995), pp. 147–74.
7. Simon Webb, *NATO and 1992: Defence Acquisition and Free Markets* (Santa Monica, CA: RAND, 1989); William Baumol et al., *Contestable Markets and the Theory of Industry Structure* (San Diego: Harcourt Brace Jovanovich, 1988).
8. For an overview, see Eurostrategie, 'Dual-Use Industry in Europe', report for the GD III, European Commission (Brussels, 1991).
9. Keith Hartley and Andrew Cox, 'The Costs of Non-Europe in Defence Procurement. Executive Summary', study carried out for the Commission of the European Communities DG III, Brussels, 1992.
10. Webb, *NATO and 1992*; Martin Bittleston, *Co-operation or Competition? Defence Procurement Options for the 1990s*, Adelphi Papers, no. 250 (London: Brassey's/IISS, 1990).
11. John Alic et al., *Beyond Spin-off* (Boston: Harvard Business School Press, 1992); William Walker and Phil Gummett, *Nationalism, Internationalism and the European Defence Market*, Chaillot Paper no. 9 (Paris: Western European Union, 1993); Paul Krugman, *Peddling Prosperity* (New York/London: Norton, 1994); Hans Feddersen, 'The European Defence Firm, National Procurement Policies and the Internationalization of Arms Production', in Andrew Latham and Nicholas Hooper (eds), *The Future of the Defence Firm: New Challenges, New Directions* (Dordrecht: Kluwer Academic Publishers, 1995), pp. 37–43.
12. BICC (Bonn International Centre for Conversion), *Conversion Survey 1996* (Oxford: Oxford University Press, 1996).
13. Alic et al., *Beyond Spin-off*.
14. Wehrdienst, *Nachdruck von Auszuegen des Bericht ueber die Untersuchung zu Wehrtechnischen Mindestkapazitaeten in Deutschland* (Bonn: Griephan Verlag, 1994).
15. DeVestel, *Defence Markets*, p. 49.
16. Francois Chesnais and Claude Serfati, *L'Armement en France: Genese, Ampleur et Cout dune industrie* (Paris: CIRCA-Nathan, 1992); Jean–Paul Hebert, *Production d'Armement. Mutation du Systeme Français* (Paris: Presses Universitaires de France, 1995).
17. Egon Klepsch (rapporteur), 'Report Drawn on Behalf of the Political Affairs Committee on European Cooperation in Arms Procurement', doc. no. 83/78, European Communities, European Parliament (Strasbourg, 8 May 1978); David Greenwood, 'Report on a Policy for Promoting Defence and Technical Co-operation among West European Countries for the

THE POLITICS AND ECONOMICS OF DEFENCE INDUSTRIES

Commission of the European Communities', doc. no. III–1499/80 (Brussels, 1980); Henk Vredeling, et al., *Towards a Stronger Europe*, A Report by an Independent Study Team Established by Defence Ministers of Nations of the Independent European Programme Group to Make Proposals to Improve the Competitiveness of Europe's Defence Equipment Industry (Brussels, 1986); Keith Hartley, 'Public Procurement and Competitiveness: A Community Market of Military Hardware and Technology', *Journal of Common Market Studies*, 25:3 (1987), pp. 237–47; Ian Anthony, A. Courades Allebeck and Herbert Wulf, *West European Arms Production: Structural Changes in the New Political Environment* (Stockholm: SIPRI, 1990); Brzoska and Lock, *Restructuring*; Keith Hartley, 'Crise de lindustrie de armement et reconversion au sein de l'Union Européene', in Roland de Penanros (ed.), *Reconversion des industries d'armament* (Paris: La Documentation Française, 1995), pp. 95–108; DeVestel, *Defence Markets*; WEU, WEAG.

18. Vredeling et al., *Towards a Stronger Europe*.
19. WEU, WEAG.
20. Jacques Santer, 'The European Union's Security and Defence Policy: How to Avoid Missing the 1996 Rendezvous', *Nato Review*, 6 (November 1995), p. 3.
21. Philip Gummett and Judy Reppy (eds), *The Relations between Defence and Civil Technologies* (Utrecht: Kluwer Academic Publishers, 1988); Alic et al., *Beyond Spin-off*; Jacques Gansler, 'The Future of the Defence Firm: Integrating Civil and Military Technologies', in Latham and Hooper (eds), *The Future of the Defence Firm*, pp. 89–96; Daniel S. Gruneberg, 'The Defence Firm and Trends in Civil Military Technologies: Integration versus 'Differentiation', in Latham and Hooper (eds), *The Future of the Defence Firm*, pp. 97–102.
22. Werner Voss, *Die Ruestungsindustrie vor unsicheren Zeiten. Strategien und Diversifikationsbemuehungen ruestungsorientierter Unternehmen* (Bremen: Kooperationsbereich Universitaet Arbeiterkammer, 1992); Nicholas Hooper and Keith Hartley, *UK Defence Contractors: Adjusting to Change*, Centre for Defence Economics, Research Monograph Series 3 (York: University of York, 1993); Martin Grundmann et al., *Ruestungskonversion: Erfolg durch Wandel der Unternehmenskultur* (Muenster/Hamburg: Lit Verlag, 1995); Marie-Noelle Le Nouail, Roland de Penanros and Thierry Sauvin, 'Activites militaires et experience de diversification dans la region brestoise', in de Penanros (ed.), *Reconversion des industries d'armament*, pp. 177–94.
23. Liba Paukert and Peter Richards, *Defence Expenditure, Industrial Conversion and Local Employment* (Geneva: International Labour Office, 1991); Wolfram Elsner, 'Instruments and Institutions of Industrial Policy at the Regional Level in Germany: The Example of Industrial Defence Conversion', *Journal of Economic Issues*, 29:2 (1995), pp. 503–16.
24. David B. Audretsch, *Innovation and Industry Evolution* (Boston: MIT Press, 1995).
25. WEU, WEAG, para. 106.
26. Bonn International Centre for Conversion, 1996.
27. Elsner, 'Instruments and Institutions'.
28. Roland de Penanros (ed.), *Reconversion des industries d armament* (Paris: La Documentation Française, 1995).

94

5

UK Defence Industries

KEITH HARTLEY

INTRODUCTION: THE NEED FOR DIFFICULT CHOICES[1]

Since the early 1980s, the United Kingdom's defence industries have been subject to major changes resulting from a competitive procurement policy, privatization and disarmament following the end of the Cold War. More changes are likely as the UK Ministry of Defence (MoD) and the armed forces face the twin pressures of rising equipment costs and the prospect of further cuts in defence budgets. As a result, the UK will not be able to avoid some difficult choices, one of which concerns the future of its defence industrial base (DIB). The future market environment is likely to be characterized by cancellations, the stretching of programmes (delays) and reduced production quantities. In such a market environment, questions arise about the benefits and costs of the UK's DIB and whether it is worth retaining. These questions also arise at the European level, where there is interest in the creation of a European Armaments Agency, the extension of the Single European Market to embrace defence equipment, and support for the concept of a European DIB. Nor can the threat of international competition be ignored, especially from the large US defence companies seeking to exploit economies of scale and scope.

The chapter is divided into three parts. The first part presents an overview of the UK's DIB; the second part examines definitions and the performance of the UK's defence industries; and the third part considers the prospects for defence equipment becoming part of the Single European Market.

UK DEFENCE INDUSTRIES

The Stylized Facts

Table 5.1 shows some of the recent trends in UK defence spending and employment in the UK's defence industries. The years 1985–86 marked the end of the UK's commitment to NATO to raise defence spending by 3 per cent per annum in real terms; and 1990–91 represents the introduction of a new UK defence policy following the end of the Cold War (known as Options for Change). Between 1985 and 1996, real UK defence spending fell by almost 30 per cent (between 1990–91 and 1995–96 the decline was 22 per cent); the defence burden fell from 5.2 per cent to 3.0 per cent of GDP (and is forecast to fall to 2.8 per cent of GDP by 1997–98); equipment accounted for a falling share of a declining defence budget; and over the period 1985 to 1994, direct and indirect UK employment dependent on defence expenditure declined by almost 40 per cent (over the period 1980–81 to 1993–94, employment in UK defence industries fell by almost 50 per cent).

TABLE 5.1
UK DEFENCE SPENDING AND EMPLOYMENT

	UK defence spending £million (1993–94 prices)	Defence share of GDP (%)	Equipment share of UK defence budget (%)	Employment in UK defence industries (000s)
1985–86	27,976	5.2	45.7	625
1990–91	26,133	4.2	39.6	550
1995–96	20,394	3.0	41.3	395

Note: Employment figures show direct and indirect employment resulting from MoD equipment and non-equipment expenditure plus exports. Employment of 395,000 is for 1993–94.

Source: Ministry of Defence, UK Defence Statistics (London: HMSO, 1995).

The UK DIB is a significant component of the UK economy through its contribution to output, employment, exports and research and development (R&D). For example, over the period 1990–93, the UK defence industry recorded a substantial trade surplus at a time when the UK economy's visible trade balance was in deficit. Some of the key summary statistics for the UK DIB are shown in Table 5.2.

TABLE 5.2
UK DEFENCE INDUSTRIES, 1993

Total Sales of UK Defence Industry	**£14.0 billion**
Comprising: Sales to MoD	£10.6 billion
UK Defence Exports	£ 3.4 billion
Expenditure in UK on Defence R&D	**£ 2.1 billion**
Total Employment in UK Defence Industry	**432,600**
MoD Equipment Purchases in UK and Overseas:	
UK Defence Industry	78%
Collaboration (involving UK Industry)	13%
Imports	9%

$ UK Defence Sales:	= 2.6% of GDP
	= 10% of UK manufacturing output
	= 8% of UK manufacturing industry employment

Source: K. Hartley and N. Hooper, *Study of the Value of the Defence Industry to the UK Economy* (York: Centre for Defence Economics, University of York, 1995).

Role of Government, Strategic Trade Theory, and the DIB

Governments are central to understanding a nation's DIB: they are a major buyer (for some equipment they are a monopsonist) and a regulator of the industry. Government can use its buying power as reflected in procurement policy to determine the size, structure, conduct and performance of the UK DIB. For example, disarmament is leading to smaller defence industries (downsizing: see Table 5.1); governments can also affect industry structure by encouraging and supporting mergers and they can promote entry and prevent exit (by opening up the UK market to foreign firms or by supporting national champions). Furthermore, government can use its buying and regulatory powers to affect industry conduct (e.g., advertising; R&D) and performance through its impact on technical progress, pricing, profitability, and exports.

Defence industries are strategic industries in both a military and economic sense. Militarily, a national DIB offers a source of supply and industrial back-up in conflicts and it offers the

97

capability of meeting unique national requirements. Also, some defence industries have the *economic* characteristics of strategic industries (e.g., aerospace, electronics, nuclear power). These characteristics include high technology and spin-offs; decreasing costs through economies of scale and learning; imperfect competition (monopoly or oligopoly); governments acting anti-competitively in regulated markets with managed competition; and strategic behaviour between governments and companies both within and between different nations.[2]

MoD Competition Policy

In the early 1980s, the MoD adopted a more commercial approach to the procurement of defence equipment. This approach marked the end of the cosy relationship between MoD and UK defence contractors which had been characterized by preferential purchasing ('buy British') and cost-plus contracting, with MoD bearing most, if not all, of the risks. During the 1980s, MoD introduced a more competitive procurement policy by reducing entry barriers for UK and foreign firms, by increasing competition at the sub-contract level, and by allowing the possibility of competition for production work separately from development (thereby making markets more contestable). There was also a greater use of firm and fixed price contracts, with cost-plus contracting used only where unavoidable. Risks were transferred from MoD to industry, and contracts for major projects were awarded to a single prime contractor with responsibility for managing the project. The focus of the 1980s' policy was on *best value for money*, based on narrow defence criteria (performance, cost, delivery of equipment, and the reliability of the estimates), without regard for the longer-term or wider impacts on the UK DIB.[3]

The results of MoD's competition policy appear impressive and offer empirical support for the predicted benefits of the economist's competitive model. There has been a decline in the proportion of cost-plus contracting, from 22 per cent of the total value of MoD contracts in 1980–81 to 1 per cent in each year between 1990 and 1995; at the same time, there has been a rise in the proportion of contracts priced by competition and market forces, from 36 per cent by value in 1980–81 to 73 per cent by value in 1994–95. Not surprisingly, the proportion of defence equipment imported into the UK has increased, from 5 per cent to 9 per cent of MoD's equipment expenditure. As a result of competition, there have been examples of cost-savings of between 10 per cent and 70 per cent, with total savings estimated at over £1 billion per year (1993–94 prices), which is equivalent to some 10 per cent of the annual MoD equipment budget.[4] Competitive contracts for major projects are also characterized by less cost escalation and possibly by fewer time slippages.[5] Furthermore, MoD claims that its competition policy has been a major factor in improving the competitiveness of the UK's defence industry, so enabling it to be more competitive in world markets.

There are, however, problems with MoD's competition policy and claims about its successes. Most of the reported examples of substantial cost savings refer to small equipment and sub-systems (e.g., a saving of almost 70 per cent on Harrier airframe fatigue testing). Nor is it obvious whether the estimated cost savings are genuine savings or the result of poor estimating! Also, vote-sensitive politicians have every incentive to exaggerate the successes of their competition policy, focusing on a few exceptional examples of apparently large savings (e.g., are the estimated savings based on identical equipments?) while ignoring any costs of their policies. The possibility also arises that the major UK defence contractors are protected from competition through their position as domestic monopolies and national champions (would such firms be allowed to exit?) and through their involvement in collaborative projects (where work is allocated on the basis of *juste retour*).

Critics of competition policy claim that it involves substantial transaction costs and that its gains are short term. MoD has to compile tender documents, provide advice to bidders, evaluate tenders, and negotiate and police the contract, all of which will cost the ministry at least 0.5 per cent of the contract value. Industry also incurs costs in preparing and producing tenders and negotiating contracts, with such costs estimated at an average of

3 per cent of the contract value.[6] Concern about these transaction costs led MoD in late 1992 to introduce a number of new measures designed to reduce the number of competitions and the number of firms invited to tender. Normally, no more than six companies are invited to tender (suggesting a numerical rather than a market share definition of competition), and where appropriate MoD will establish long-term partnerships with suppliers. It is also recognized that the trend towards smaller production quantities means that competing for production tranches is less likely to be cost-effective. For some longer duration contracts, target cost incentive contracting will be used to provide efficiency incentives as an alternative to renegotiated or re-competed contracts of shorter duration, and target cost contracts are also used where risk analysis shows that firm or fixed price contracts are inappropriate.

Between 1990 and 1992, MoD awarded some 33,000 contracts worth £4 billion on a non-competitive basis. During this period, an average of 50 per cent of such contracts were priced at the outset, and 61 per cent by the time a quarter of the work was completed, while some 8 per cent were still unpriced when the work was completed. Recognizing that it will never be possible to complete all of its requirements, MoD sought to transfer some of the competitive disciplines to non-competitive contracts. The result was 'no acceptable price, no contract' (NAPNOC), which was introduced for non-competitive contracts in 1992. This initiative was based on the fact that MoD's bargaining position is strongest before a contract is awarded, and the aim is to price 75 per cent by value of all non-competitive contracts at the outset, with the rest priced by the time a quarter of the work is completed.[7]

By the mid-1990s there was increasing concern about the costs to the DIB of MoD's competition policy, reflected in its emphasis on the short-term and narrow interpretation of value for money. In 1996, the Conservative government announced that 'full consideration' will be given to defence industrial factors in procurement decisions.[8] Defence industrial factors embrace 'essential military capabilities' (i.e., technologies), the value to the armed forces of industrial back-up, the contribution of UK defence industries to European collaboration, the avoidance of monopoly or over-dependence on one company or country and the promotion of defence exports. However, 'defence industrial factors' remains a vague, unquantified, and apparently unquantifiable term which will be implemented on a case-by-case basis and not on the basis of general principles. Even where MoD claims that its procurement criteria are defence-based rather than embracing wider industrial and economic objectives, it accepts that account will be taken 'of capabilities in which UK industry has particular expertise or proven strengths'.[9] The government also accepts that it might not be possible to maintain domestic competition in all those sectors of the UK defence industry where it now exists. As a result, the extent to which any loss of domestic competition is acceptable to MoD will depend on the availability and acceptability of overseas suppliers, the importance of maintaining the industrial and technological capabilities in the UK and the strength of MoD's bargaining power as a customer in the relevant market.[10] Regulatory arrangements can also be used to 'police' non-competitive contracts.

The Review Board

The UK Review Board for Government Contracts is a relatively unknown regulatory agency (cf. the regulatory agencies for the UK privatized utilities). It was created in 1968 following two cases of 'excessive profits' on defence contracts, namely, the Ferranti case (1964), with reported profits of 82 per cent on cost and the Bristol Siddeley Engines case (1968), with reported profits on cost of between 74 and 114 per cent. The Review Board focuses on the profit formula used to price non-competitive government contracts, mostly the procurement of defence equipment.

   The Review Board was one result of the 1968 Memorandum of Agreement between the Government and British industry that introduced the following:

• A new profit formula aimed at giving contractors a fair rate of return, equal on average to the overall return earned by British industry (the comparability principle for rate-of-return regulation). Initially, the average rate of return was set at 14 per cent on capital (historic cost basis): this was the average of risk and non-risk work (up to 15 per cent on capital for risk and 8 per cent on capital for non-risk contracts).

- Equality of information which was designed to place both parties in the same position at the point of price fixing (i.e., symmetry of information).
- The post-costing of individual contracts.
- The creation of an independent Review Board with two duties: first, to review the operation of the profit formula every three years; and second, to review contracts where there are believed to be excessive profits or losses (excessive profits were originally defined as more than 27.5 per cent on capital and excessive losses as more than 15 per cent on capital).

The Review Board has no remit to encourage competition: its objective is to give contractors a fair and reasonable profit on non-competitive contracts. In this context its performance has been mixed. During the period 1982–85, contractors earned considerably more than the target rate (7 per cent points above it); but in 1991, when the target rate was 21.2 per cent, the actual rate fell some 5 percentage points below the target rate, so that contractors were not receiving the average return earned by British industry.

Supply Side: UK Defence Industries

Some of the major features of the UK's defence industries are that:

- Ordnance, shipbuilding and aerospace are defence-dependent industries.
- During the 1980s, there was a shift from state to private ownership. Privatization occurred in the aerospace industry (British Aerospace, Rolls-Royce, Shorts); in shipbuilding, involving the warship builders of Cammell Laird (now closed), Swan Hunter, VSEL, Vosper Thornycroft, and Yarrow; and in land equipment, with the sale of Royal Ordnance to British Aerospace (ammunition, guns and missiles) and Vickers (tanks).

- A small number of major companies dominate the UK defence market. In 1993–94 there were more than 500 UK-based contractors paid £1 million or more by MoD, but MoD payments are concentrated on a small group of contractors. The top five prime contractors accounted for some 30 per cent of MoD equipment expenditure. In 1994–95, the major MoD contractors paid £100 million or more were British Aerospace, the General Electric Company (GEC), Hunting, Rolls-Royce and VSEL (each paid over £250 million), together with Babcock, BT, Devonport Management, ICL, LORAL, John Mowlem, Serco, Siemens, Vickers and Westland (each paid £100–250 million).
- Mergers and acquisitions. Examples include the British Aerospace (aircraft and missiles) acquisition of Royal Ordnance; the Vickers (tanks) acquisition of Royal Ordnance tank business; GKN's (armoured fighting vehicles) purchase of Westland (helicopters); and GEC's (electronics) acquisition of Yarrow (frigates), VSEL (submarines) and the defence activities of Ferranti and Plessey.
- The UK domestic market is characterized by domestic monopolies, especially for high technology equipment. Examples include aircraft, missiles, helicopters, aero-engines, frigates, submarines, tanks, torpedoes and defence electronics (e.g., avionics, radars).
- The market testing of activities traditionally undertaken 'in-house' by the armed forces is providing new market opportunities for defence contractors (e.g., the contractorization of management, training, repair, and maintenance functions).

THE UK DEFENCE INDUSTRIAL BASE: PROBLEMS AND PERFORMANCE

Defining the UK DIB

Definitions of the DIB are often vague and difficult to operationalize. Reference is made to key strategic technologies and industrial assets; for example, the 'DIB consists of those industrial assets which provide key elements of military power and national security...'.[11] But key technologies and industrial assets are rarely identified; nor is any indication given as to why certain assets are 'key'; and how much MoD is willing to pay to retain such assets.

The problems of defining the UK DIB make it difficult for policy-makers to accurately estimate its size and to evaluate its economic importance. Data problems abound. Unlike other UK industries, there is no Standard Industrial Classification heading for defence industries. Many UK companies are involved in both defence and civil markets, and there are few companies wholly or almost wholly dependent on defence business (e.g., VSEL arms sales in 1992 accounted for 99 per cent of its total business). Similarly some suppliers might not be aware that they are involved in defence production (e.g., ball-bearing manufacturers). It is also misleading to refer to the DIB as a single, homogeneous entity when it comprises firms of varying sizes, with different combinations of military and civil business, supplying a variety of markets for air, land and sea equipment, with firms involved in one or more of these sectors or in a sub-sector (e.g., components). There is also a lack of satisfactory employment data at the regional and local levels, making it difficult to identify an area's defence dependency and its vulnerability to cuts in defence spending.

Typically, efforts to define the UK DIB focus on its easily identified elements, namely, the prime contractors of specialized defence equipment supplied to MoD (aircraft, helicopters, missiles, tanks and warships). However, this approach neglects the supply chain and the sub-contractors, the suppliers of other goods and services and dual-use items (e.g., food, clothing, construction, vehicles), and the exports of UK defence equipment and services.[12]

Table 5.3 presents a taxonomy for defining the DIB. A distinction is made between dependence on defence sales and the type of defence equipment. In this table, firms in area X (high defence dependency and defence-specific equipment) are clearly in the DIB, but problems of classification arise with movements towards region Y. There are examples of firms in region Y which, during a conflict, become an important element of a nation's defence effort (e.g., civil airliners; merchant shipping).

TABLE 5.3
A TAXONOMY

Type of Defence Equipment	Dependence on Defence Sales (UK and Exports)		
		Low	High
	Dual-Use	Y	
	Defence-Specific		X

Assessing the Performance of the UK DIB

Questions arise as to whether government as a major buyer (and regulator) can determine an industry's performance and whether the performance of the UK DIB is superior to that of other British industries. Two alternative hypotheses were formulated. First, the *beneficial impact* predicts that dependence on government improves competitiveness. This impact operates through the government acting as a competitive buyer, through government support for R&D and innovation, and through government providing a larger home market enabling the exploitation of scale economies. In the UK defence market, for example, MoD has acted as a competitive buyer, opening up the UK market. Second, the *harmful impact* predicts that dependence on government results in an inefficient and uncompetitive industry. This impact reflects a cosy relationship, monopoly markets, cost-based contracts and a culture of dependency resulting in organizational slack (X-inefficiency), low productivity, and poor export performance.

Empirical tests of these hypotheses were based on a study of UK defence, pharmaceutical and medical equipment industries. These three industries are dependent on sales to government (MoD or the National Health Service), they are high technology industries, and they are subject to government regulation. Aerospace, ordnance, and shipbuilding were selected as UK

105

TABLE 5.4
TRADE PERFORMANCE

in percentages

	UK Trade Balance [1,2]	Import Penetration Ratio [1,3]	Export Sales Ratio [1,4]	Degree of Dependency
	1980–91[5]	1980–91[5]	1980–91[5]	1980–91[5]
Ordnance	52.5	10.5	34.5	63.3
Shipbuilding	31.0	6.8	12.2	32.1
Aerospace	19.5	27.6	41.1	30.7
Instrum Eng	–6.8	36.8	32.9	5.4
Mech Eng	13.4	21.4	27.9	2.1
Vehicles	–21.9	32.4	20.7	1.6
Pharmaceutical	36.5	13.8	29.5	44.0
Chemical	9.7	23.3	28.1	(<1.0)
Medical Equip	17.4	29.2	41.3	58.2
Instrum Eng	–12.2	38.4	30.1	(<1.0)

Overall weighted averages[6]

All GDIs	24.8	20.8	34.5	37.7
All NDIs	0.0	26.4	26.3	2.1
Correlation[7]	0.653	–0.472	0.346	

Notes:
1. Imports are valued c.i.f. and exports f.o.b.
2. Trade balance is exports minus imports divided by exports plus imports.
3. Import penetration ratio is imports as a proportion of home demand plus exports.
4. Export sales ratio is exports as a proportion of manufacturers' sales plus imports.
5. Figures are arithmetic averages for the time periods indicated.
6. Weights are based on sales per industry.
7. Degree of dependency is percentage of sales to government (defence and NHS). GDI = government dependent industries; NDI = non-government dependent industries.

defence industries, and a control group of industries not dependent on sales to government was used as a basis for comparison. The study involved a complete set of tests examining the impact of government dependence on industry structure, conduct and performance. An example of the results for various trade performance indicators is shown in Table 5.4. It can be seen that the group of government-dependent industries achieved a superior trade balance, a lower import ratio and a higher export sales ratio than the control group of non-government dependent industries. However, compared to individual defence sectors, some civil industries had a superior performance for certain indicators (e.g., pharmaceuticals, chemicals, mechanical engineering, and vehicles). These results illustrate the opportunities for further research into the impact of government on industry performance and the value to the UK economy of the DIB.

THE SINGLE EUROPEAN DEFENCE MARKET AND DEFENCE PROCUREMENT

The Costs of Non-Europe

Currently, a significant proportion of public-sector procurement in the European Union (EU) is undertaken by defence ministries. Article 223 of the Treaty of Rome means that defence procurement is excluded from the European Commission's directives on public procurement in the Single Market. The result is a set of independent (fragmented) national markets: the costs of non-Europe in defence procurement.

Defence markets in the European Union appear to be inefficient, being characterized by:

- Support for national defence industries. Such support has resulted in the duplication of costly R&D programmes and relatively short production runs reflecting small national orders. For example, in 1996 six European nations were developing three different types of combat aircraft with total production orders of some 1,200 units divided over the three different types (EF 2000, Gripen, and Rafale). US scales of production considerably exceed the scale of output in individual European nations.
- Domestic monopolies (e.g., aerospace; tanks; warships).
- Government-protected markets (e.g., barriers to entry and exit), although some markets, such as the UK, are more open to foreign firms.
- Non-competitive and cost-based contracts.
- State ownership, subsidies and government regulation of profits (e.g., with firms pursuing non-profit objectives: a quiet life in a culture of dependency).

Scenarios

What might a Single European Market for defence equipment and procurement look like and what are its likely economic benefits? Table 5.5 presents three possible scenarios, each of which could be the basis for the creation of a European Armaments Agency. Each scenario assumes a liberalized competitive market restricted to firms in the member states of the European Union or open to firms throughout the world.

Scenario I is a liberalized competitive market with national procurement by national defence ministries. This requires non-discriminatory procurement with national markets opened to firms in either the EU or the whole world. Here, a European Armaments Agency might act as a competition authority focusing on the opening up of national defence markets and ensuring non-discriminatory purchasing.

Scenario II represents centralized procurement of common, standardized equipment with the centralized agency (e.g., a European Armaments Agency) replacing national defence ministries.

Scenario III is the twin-track approach which comprises a mixture of competition and collaboration. Small and medium-sized equipment would be subject to competition (e.g., small arms, electronics, some missiles), while large projects would be undertaken on a collaborative basis (e.g., aerospace equipment; main battle tanks). In this scenario, a European Armaments Agency might promote and manage collaborative programmes.

TABLE 5.5
THE SCENARIOS
ANNUAL SAVINGS (ECU BILLIONS, 1990 PRICES)

Scenario		Liberalized Competitive Market	
		EU	World-wide
I	National procurement in a liberalized competitive market	5.5	7.0
II	A centralized purchasing agency	9.4	10.9
III	The twin-track: competition and collaboration	6.5	9.3

Source: EC, *Aspects of Defence Procurement and Industrial Policy*, memorandum from DG XV, Defence and Trade and Industry Committee, HCP 333 (London: House of Commons, 1995), pp. 99–100.

The extension of the Single Market to defence equipment is expected to produce a variety of economic benefits, which will be reflected in lower prices. These benefits result from: (1) increased competition both within and between nations (the competition effect); (2) savings in costly R&D through reducing 'wasteful duplication'; and (3) economies of scale and learning associated with longer production runs (the scale effect).

While all the scenarios offer improvements in efficiency, economic theory predicts and estimates confirm that Scenario II offers the greatest potential savings (through a combination of both competition and scale effects). There are, however, costs and problems involved in creating a Single Market for defence equipment. Some firms and regions will be losers in a competitive market (and the attendant costs will be in addition to those resulting from disarmament following the end of the Cold War). Difficulties also arise in creating a 'level playing field' and ensuring non-discriminatory procurement. Moreover, if the Market is restricted to firms in the EU, there are dangers of monopoly, cartels and collusive tendering. These dangers might be 'policed' by opening up the Market to firms throughout the world. However, such a solution will mean US competition, with the implications that brings for maintaining a European defence industrial base.

CONCLUSION

The UK and the European Union countries cannot avoid some difficult choices about defence procurement and their defence industries. For these nations, independence through supporting a domestic DIB is costly. The alternatives are importing foreign equipment (usually American), possibly with some form of work-sharing (offsets; licensed production), or collaborative pro-grammes. Collaboration with or among European nations involves substantial transaction costs resulting from elaborate international management and policing arrangements and work-sharing requirements (*juste retour*).[13] And while reference is often made to a European DIB, the concept remains vague and ill-defined. There are also genuine concerns that powerful producer groups will seek the creation of Fortress Europe with all the worst features of protectionism: no competition, subsidies and inefficiencies.

NOTES

1. This paper is based on research funded by the ESRC as part of its Contracts and Competition and Single European Market Programmes (nos L114251031 and W113251009).
2. P. Krugman (ed.), *Strategic Trade Policy and the New International Economics* (Cambridge, MA: MIT Press, 1986).
3. National Audit Office, *Ministry of Defence: Initiatives in Defence Procurement*, HCP 189 (London: HMSO, 1991).
4. National Audit Office, *Ministry of Defence: Defence Procurement in the 1990s*, HCP 390 (London: HMSO, 1994).
5. National Audit Office, *Ministry of Defence: Major Projects Report 1994*, HCP 436 (London: HMSO, 1995).
6. HCP 390, 1994, p. 19.
7. HCP 390, 1994, p. 21.
8. The UK Labour Party is committed to developing a long-term strategy for a 'strong' DIB which is of 'vital importance to the nation's economic performance' with defence companies recognized as world-class competitors in a high-technology sector with high value-added processes and skills. Labour will not leave the DIB to market forces; and they will create a Defence Diversification Agency funded from the defence budget to assist defence firms to enter civil markets; *Strategy for a Secure Future: Labour's Approach to the Defence Industry* (London: Labour Party, 1995).
9. *Government Reply to the First Reports from the Defence and Trade and Industry Committees Session 1995–96 on Aspects of Defence Procurement and Industrial Policy*, HCP 209, 210 (London: HMSO, 1996), p. vi.
10. HCP 209, 210, 1996, p. v.
11. Defence Committee, House of Commons, *The Defence Implications of the Future of Westland plc*, HCP 578 (London: HMSO, 1986), p. xxxvii.
12. P. Dunne, 'The Defence Industrial Base', in K. Hartley and T. Sandler (eds), *Handbook of Defence Economics* (Amsterdam: North Holland, 1995); K. Hartley and N. Hooper, *Study of the Value of the Defence Industry to the UK Economy* (York: Centre for Defence Economics, University of York, 1995); T. Sandler and K. Hartley, *The Economics of Defence: Surveys of Economic Literature* (Cambridge: Cambridge University Press, 1995).
13. Sandler and Hartley, *The Economics of Defence.*

6

Adapting to a Shrinking Market: The Israeli Case

AHARON KLIEMAN

There is at presently sufficient credible statistical evidence to confirm the two most basic verities governing today's international arms trade. First, it is patently clear by now that we are in the midst of an extended era of shrinking markets rather than a temporary interlude, as arms analysts thought originally. Military transfers worldwide averaged $51 billion per annum between 1985 and 1989, whereas in the years 1991–93 they fell by 50 per cent to a mean of only $26 billion.[1] Secondly, conventional weapons flows are becoming increasingly dominated by an hegemonic supplier, the United States, which already accounts today for half if not more of total global defence sales.[2]

THE ARMS MARKET AND THE SUPPLIER PYRAMID

Reflecting these predominant trends, the hierarchy of arms suppliers has been undergoing a major restructuring. The changes are most pronounced at three different distinct levels of this export pyramid.

At its apex, the United States threatens to leave the competition behind, using its comparative political and commercial advantages to pull further ahead, thus distancing itself even more from its closest rivals, the secondary country suppliers. Unofficial sources for 1990–94 show the US holding an approximate 47 per cent market share, followed by: Britain with 16 per cent; France, 14 per cent; Russia, declining dramatically to less than 10 per cent; and 'the rest of the world', perhaps 11–12 per cent, down from a high of almost 28 per cent in the previous comparable four-year period, 1985–89.[3]

Not unrelated is the fact that, at the opposite extreme, the base of the pyramid is also narrowing. In an unsparing competitive selection process, it is only logical to expect that the smallest arms exporters and what are basically fringe suppliers will quietly fall by the wayside. (For them, this is a boon in disguise according to economic theorists. Those forced to drop out of the arms sales race – a race that in any case has become one of the less remunerative branches of international commerce owing to reduced profit margins – are then able to begin recouping lost social and developmental 'opportunity costs' through accelerated economic growth spearheaded by civilian rather than military industrialization.)

Where the sense of alarm is felt most acutely, however, is among perhaps some ten weapons-trafficking states clustered at the third focal point located somewhere midway down the narrowing arms pyramid. Their shared plight is quite simple and straightforward. No longer are they assured, on the one hand, of being able to improve upon their previous arms sales position and annual performance to any appreciable degree. They are, on the other hand, too deeply committed by now to arms transfers to simply desist, abruptly and irrevocably – whether their commitment is for reasons of prestige, national security, diplomatic ties, or the logic of commercial gain (in first retrieving initial 'start-up' costs incurred by those huge outlays of previous R&D capital investment sunk into their own indigenous military industry infrastructure, and in then turning a profit).

A partial roster of countries entrapped at the middle range of the supplier scale includes Brazil, Italy, the two Koreas, the Netherlands, Pakistan, South Africa, Spain, Sweden, and even Russia. But first and foremost in this category is Israel. As is true of these other middle-tier arms-manufacturing and arms-exporting states, their governments, and their weapons industries, the resulting dilemma for Israel is two-fold: whether to redouble the national commitment and resolutely to stay the course, and if so what competitive survival strategy to adopt that might offer a better-than-average fighting chance at surviving in a troubled and shrinking defence market.

Israel: Staying Viable

Logic dictates Israel be among the sharply receding number of exporters, given its comparative disadvantages, which are readily observable. The principal constraints include:

- An almost total lack of the strategic and industrial raw materials vital for arms production.
- A small domestic base, in light of reduced defence military expenditure at home, plus at this point a built-in preference by now among Israel Defence Force arms procurement officials for buying American even at the expense of the local industries. Thus, local weapons purchases by the IDF in 1995 were 23 per cent lower than they had been in 1984, constituting only 17 per cent of the defence budget – in contrast to 40 per cent a decade earlier.[4]
- Israel's exclusion for reasons of politics from bidding on lucrative contracts in the large Arab–Middle East defence market.
- Preemption by the larger and more politically influential exporters (France, Germany, Great Britain), or by regional suppliers enjoying easier entrée to local markets (South Korea, Singapore, Australia in the Far East; South Africa to its neighbours; China to third countries).
- Especially in the 1990s, preemption by a private American defence sector pursuing an aggressive marketing drive supported by US administration officials assertively claiming for the country the role of 'global security manager'.

To these constraints can be added the mounting insistence on transparency through such treaty mechanisms instruments as the UN Register of Conventional Arms, which poses yet a further restriction on countries such as Israel, whose principal patterns for redirecting defence aid have traditionally included discreet back-channels.[5] Data from within Israel all but confirm that as a direct consequence of the above-mentioned market pressures and recent trends, the indigenous arms sector is indeed experiencing serious dislocation.

With the Israel weapons industry as a whole in the throes of a painful, extended process of contraction, the number of employees has declined sharply: from the benchmark figure of perhaps 80,000 or more in the peak years of the early 1980s to some 40,000 in 1990, 24,000 in 1994, and 18,000 by the close of 1996.[6] Despite laying off personnel and other steps at economizing, individual companies continue to threaten factory closures and to report annual losses. Of particular concern is the financial plight of Israel's three flagship arms corporations. In 1994 the Israel Aircraft Industries (IAI) marked a deficit of $450 million for the previous year, and the Israel Military Industries (IMI) indicated losses of $70 million in 1994 and $85 million in 1995.[7] Meanwhile, the very fate of Rafael, the national weapons development authority, remains up in the air; never a commercially viable enterprise, it is criticized for becoming a losing proposition – over $100 million in 1995 alone – and a mounting burden upon the government budget.[8]

And yet, the weight of such evidence notwithstanding, there is room for a counter-thesis: namely, that Israel just possibly may be weathering the storm. Mid-decade finds it still a viable contender, and in fact one of the few international defence suppliers of significance. Consider, for instance, the following fragmentary yet illuminating piece of evidence.

On one of those infrequent occasions when government spokesmen were willing to speak for the record about military exports – in a July 1994 briefing – unnamed defence officials volunteered that during the course of 1993 actual weapons deliveries amounted to $1.3 billion – the same as in 1992. Moreover, overseas defence orders scheduled for future delivery, rather than decreasing, had increased by a full 20 per cent.[9] To place this performance in a wider perspective, those sources maintained that in the very same period between 1975 and 1992 that saw arms transactions worldwide plummet by 45 per cent,

Israeli military sales had actually had actually grown by 75 per cent.

Let us leave aside for the moment the questionable accuracy of arms-related data everywhere. We may simply assume the self-serving nature of all such statistics, which can be manipulated in either direction: upward, to mask any decline in most recent years, or downward, to deflect attention from domestic critics and foreign competitors alike. Yet should the data even come close to approximating the actual recent trade performance of Israel's defence exports sector, then the country's merely holding its own is an impressive achievement. This is true all the more in that Israel is not engaged in selling major weapons systems, nor is it a principal supplier to Saudi Arabia or any other of the really big arms-importing countries.

Assuming that Israel has managed more or less to retain its overall ranking and share of the market, the operative question is: for how long? All that can be said with any degree of confidence is that the answer will be a function of only two factors. The first factor is global, political and market forces well beyond Israel's sole or immediate control. These systemic and independent variables include UN transparency measures and any other negotiated multilateral arms controls; the pace-setting US arms policy; and New World Order successes – or setbacks – in peaceful conflict resolution and in reinforcing the democratic peace. The second factor is a dependent variable, however: unilateral steps, representing more a matter of will than the dictate of outside forces, that fall largely under Israel's own control.

The Makings of an Improvised Survival Strategy

To Israel's credit, some notable errors of the past in administering foreign military assistance, which helped to convey the distinct impression of policy disarray, have been rectified – some consciously, others by default. And there is an approach, albeit as yet insufficiently rationalized, purposeful, or comprehensive enough to be honoured as a full-fledged strategy, that does at least suggest outlines and guidelines for an integrated arms sales policy. If assigned a name, this policy would perhaps best be termed 'downsizing without downgrading.'

The current approach is decidedly more prudent than in former years. Previously, indiscriminate arms links produced a string of diplomatic embarrassments and commercial setbacks, some of the more prominent and best-known including the fall of the Shah and the sudden loss of the Iranian market military ties with South Africa; the Falklands contretemps; the even more unfortunate Irangate episode; and association with Somoza in Nicaragua, as well as with a number of equally disreputable regimes in Africa, the Americas and Asia during most of the 1960s, 1970s and 1980s.

There is similarly a far better 'mix' between military and non-military trade in the 1990s. Arms exports presently constitute a declining percentage – in the neighbourhood of 10 per cent – of both industrial and total exports. These are estimated to have reached a respectable $19 billion in 1995.[10] In itself this is not only healthy but encouraging, for it means the national economy is moving away from excessive dependence upon this singularly unstable trade component (in the early 1980s believed to have been as high as one-quarter or one-fifth of exports). On the other hand, there should be no doubt that foreign defence assistance continues to be a high priority in Israel's 'triad' of military, commercial and political statecraft.

Additional factors working in Israel's favour can be enumerated. For purposes of discussion, six assets are especially worthy of note, starting with the Jewish state's newly acquired international respectability.

Political Entrée: Israel's external affairs have experienced a dramatic turn-about since the start of the decade. In brief, it has gone from being a pariah and international outcast to being a country whose emissaries find nearly all doors are open. For our purposes, this implies that military and commercial interests, rather than conflicting with diplomatic ones, actually complement them. In other words, arms sales have become fully integrated within Israeli foreign policy, instead of serving as a substitute for it. At least for the moment, 'politics and economics' – the central theme of this book – dovetail.

Policy Concert: This fundamental pro-arms rationale is, in turn, having a four-fold positive effect at home. It has made for consensual decision-making. It has enabled greater bureaucratic accountability, as well as coordination along the internal chain of policy command and execution in Tel Aviv and Jerusalem. It has made Israel somewhat more circumspect as a supplier and also more discerning in its choice of recipients. The impression, at least, is of clearer policy guidelines and export controls – so-called 'red lines' concerning exactly whom to supply, with what forms of military aid, and under what terms. This would reduce the future likelihood of unauthorized 'rogue operations', and also of undue influence exercised by private arms dealers. Fourthly, cabinet ministers and other top state officials are much more openly supportive of the external marketing effort. Acting in their official capacity and not hesitating to utilize personal contacts, they serve as effective defence promoters in their own right, as an integral part of the intensive 'forward press' worldwide military sales campaign orchestrated during the last decade by David Ivri, director-general of the defence ministry.

The American Connection: Although not without its problematic side, the close working defence relationship that presently exists between Israel and the United States must be counted as a definite advantage. Here, the salient operative figure is the $1.8 billion in sustained annual assistance intended for military purchases in the US, but close to one-third of which Israel, by special congressional permission, may spend at its discretion on defence locally.[11]

In addition to this direct support, supplemental defence aid comes through buy-back arrangements as well as in other inventive forms such as draw-downs from NATO surplus, leasing, and pre-positioning.[12] Nor do friendly arms ties stop here. Further significant yet indirect benefits include: (1) preferential access to American weapons systems and technologies; (2) Israel's slow but steady entry as a foreign supplier in the US arms market over the last decade; (3) government-to-government project collaboration that now extends to joint weapons research and development between defence agencies and individual military industries in the two countries; and (4) subsequently, Washington's consent (never automatic, subject to veto on a case-by-case basis, and often frustrated because of bureaucratic delay) to Israel's re-exporting to acceptable third parties US equipment refurbished by Israeli defence companies or Israeli products containing American components.

Dependability: From the standpoint of Israeli's foreign competitiveness, the fact that that the Pentagon endorses Israeli-manufactured military goods as meeting strict American defence standards can only enhance Israel's credibility elsewhere. Part of this reputation has come to rest upon the calibre of 'made-in-Israel' (known as 'blue & white') military products; part, upon the ability of Israel to maintain utmost discretion no less than prompt delivery timetables. Considerations of trustworthiness may have been decisive, for instance, in the unpublicized decision early in 1996 to go ahead with promised delivery of four US-approved 'Kfir' planes to Ecuador, suggested caution by Washington and opposition from Peru notwithstanding.

Of critical importance are two final assets: greater specialization and selectivity concerning both Israel's product offerings and its targeted clients.

Niche Specialization

During the 1980s, Israeli political, industrial and defence strategists had to be coerced kicking and screaming into coming to grips with their own national limitations as well as with objective limits to what was physically and politically possible in future weapons development. In this larger sense, forced cancellation of the ambitious Lavi fighter project in 1987 due to prohibitive costs and American opposition needs to be seen as a blessing in disguise. With hindsight, that agonized decision is working to Israel's longer-term advantage, for no matter how painful, it signalled an early end to Israeli pretensions about the sky literally being the limit in contemplating further generations of indigenous major weapons systems. A full decade later, by comparison, other competitors with similar aspirations – most particularly Sweden, Japan, Sweden, France, and some of the other Western European countries – have still to learn the lesson.

That disillusioning experience with mainframe and platform design came at about the same time as the emergence of possibly a dozen smaller arms-producing countries. On the scale of Brazil, Pakistan, Singapore, and Spain, these newer entrants as a rule tend to be better positioned to offer neighbouring or affiliate countries low-tech equipment and standard arms comparable to what Israel has to sell, and at far cheaper prices.

The nineties, in effect, find Israel squeezed from both ends of the weapons defence inventory scale: major weaponry and also small arms. True, Israel continues to market a full catalogue of products from the Uzi and the Galil rifles to Nesher trainers and Arava transport planes. But that is not where its future lies.

The main thrust of the national armaments effort is being led, almost as if it compelled, to concentrate on a most promising upper level of defence design and production. Defying any single, hard or fast definition, this special category nonetheless in itself covers a fairly extensive range of sophisticated arms activity, extending to the following principal classifications of both military goods and services:

- The complex sub-systems and specialized components (more than the actual mainframes or platforms themselves) – on the scale of fire-control and navigating systems – that ultimately go into armoured vehicles, naval vessels and jet aircraft.
- 'Smart weapons': electronics, computers and software devices for coding and deciphering; lasers and infra-red sensors; night vision optics; C3I communications equipment; remote-sensing satellites; avionics; diagnostic systems; simulators; homing devices; and precision-guided delivery systems that military planners are convinced will provide the qualitative cutting edge needed for surviving and even mastering the emerging electronic battlefield. Force multiplying and integrating technologies of this sort are precisely those areas in which local medium-sized companies such as Elbit, El-Op, Elta, and Tadiran have been concentrating their high-tech weapons development efforts for a number of years already. Not coincidentally, their marketing performance during this time has also been impressive, enabling them to take up a good deal of the slack caused by depressed sales on the part of the larger conglomerates, IAI and IMI.

- Missiles: Ever since the 1960s Israel's defence industries have laboured to stay at the cutting edge of missile warfare. As a result, its latest sales directories offer an assortment of ballistic missile delivery systems suitable for every conceivable arena of air-to-air, sea-to-sea and ground-to-ground combat. In this category the indigenous Gabriel low-level sea-skimming missile enjoys the greatest name recognition. Employed by a number of the world's navies, it has earned an international reputation, not to mention more than a billion dollars in aggregate sales over the years.

- Design and multi-purpose use of RPVs or pilotless drones, with such names as Ranger, Hunter, Harpie and Searcher, to monitor enemy troop deployment, relay photographs of military installations, and perform any number of other real-time intelligence-gathering functions. Israel was one of fewer than a handful of countries pioneering the early development and integration of these items, and therefore it still retains an important head-start over the competition. Moreover, since the age of unmanned RPVs is only now beginning, there is a potentially vast market for future generations of such extremely cost-effective and dual-use that have important civilian applications as well.

- Last, although certainly not least in importance, are the Israeli-designed upgrading and retrofit data packages that Israel has put out for sale on the open market. The principle calls for extending the shelf-life and combat effectiveness of ageing or otherwise obsolete generations of major weapons systems by inserting sophisticated sub-systems. This form of assistance is becoming increasingly attractive for a great many armed forces that have to confront security threats with dwindling defence procurement budgets. Unable to afford the prohibitive costs of the latest state-of-the-art equipment, and forced to make do with less, they are finding an acceptable, cost-effective alternative in opting to refurbish existing stocks. Not only does Israel offer such technical know-how and packages, but it does so with an impressive array of models; from American Phantom jets to eastern bloc MiG fighter craft and a Falcon early-warning reconnaissance plane capable of performing many of the same airborne monitoring functions of the higher calibre (but also far more costly) AWACS; and from Soviet T-sequence armour to British Centurion and US Patton tanks.

Supplementing this extensive category of intermediate-level military goods and advanced, higher-grade technologies is another form of foreign defence assistance rendered by Israel: Israeli advisers who contract to provide specialized services. These extend from training foreign personnel in the maintenance, repair, storage and actual combat use of the weaponry acquired from Israel, to overseeing the licensed manufacture overseas of such purchased components, missiles or sub-systems. These technical, service-oriented activities are all too easily underestimated or entirely overlooked in academic studies narrowly preoccupied with tangible arms deliveries, and yet they deserve to be factored into Israel's diversified military export programme.

An expanded definition of military links includes the transfer of aviation and production technology to aerospace industries in friendly countries. By way of illustration, in February 1996 the Singapore defence ministry for the first time officially acknowledged Israel's aid in helping set up a modern defence establishment and industrial complex aimed at giving Singapore greater military self-sufficiency.[13] In today's world, what is often referred to in the literature as 'the invisible arms trade' can even encompass technical assistance to Russia and former Soviet republics in the important area of defence conversion or aiding former war-torn countries such as Cambodia and Mozambique in dismantling anti-personnel and anti-tank land mines.

Preferential Customers

The sixth and final pillar of Israel's survival strategy also underscores the central theme of specialization. My point here is that the shift to top-of-the-line quality products is also indirectly having a profound – and much-to-be-desired – effect upon the other side of the arms equation: the prospective clientele for Israeli defence aid.

During the many years when Israel was trying to break into the international defence market and to establish itself as a competitive supplier, there was a strong inclination on the part of pro-arms government officials, backed by defence personnel and even more enthusiastic arms merchants, to give virtual blanket endorsement for weapons contracts solicited from almost any quarter. Today the indications are of greater circumspection in the choice of partners.

The mere fact that, at a conservative estimate, more than over seventy countries are reliably believed to be recipients of military aid from Israel is proof enough of the arms diplomacy's success. Based upon previous experience, however, there are at least two essentially diplomatic drawbacks in casting so extensive a net and in attempting to maintain so many relationships simultaneously. Firstly, Israel risks entanglement in local disputes between two clients, or between its arms customer and another politically neutral or even friendly country: Britain and Argentina in 1982; China and Taiwan periodically; Peru and Ecuador of late. Secondly, pursuing too indiscriminate a sales campaign by giving greater and usually decisive weight to commercial or military considerations over political sensitivity more often than not has earned Israel international opprobrium for being either too frequently or too prominently associated with questionable clients.

Here, in my view, lies the subtle and yet quite marked change in the profile of Israel's preferred arms importers. Leading manufacturers, IDF war games planners and the scientific research community have elected, each for their own reasons and self-interest, to focus uncoordinated individual efforts primarily, if not exclusively, on the upper rung of military and dual-use technologies. Again, for emphasis, this fortuitous set of circumstances derives more from a series of decentralized, largely incremental and non-governmental decisions than any overarching strategic game plan. Nevertheless, the effect is a positive one in helping to direct national efforts at mapping out prospects for new relationships. What it means in the larger sense is a marked lessening of dependence upon marginal third world countries, military dictatorships and underdeveloped economies

– those arms users who, with few exceptions, in any event lack the financial resources and technical skills necessary for integrating advanced weapons inventories.

The corollary to this argument is that in their stead, the industrializing democracies of North America, Western Europe and Southeast Asia assume pride of position as natural and desirable arms consumers. It is no accident that in recent years Israeli arms strategists have targeted the Far East, and the Pacific Basin in particular, as a primary area for expanding defence ties. The reasoning is fairly obvious. That part of the world is in the grips of a classic security dilemma. The region contains a number of nations – many of them members of ASEAN and often referred to by the media as the Asian 'dragons' or 'tigers' – best characterized as prosperous, liberalizing, and hewing to a conservative, *status quo* orientation in their foreign policies. Nevertheless, they find themselves increasingly caught up in a fluid and unstable regional balance of power which, in turn, is generating a renewed arms-racing dynamic fuelled by an unprecedented arms buildup and military modernization. In 1995 alone, Asian-Pacific countries reportedly spent $130 billion or more on defence, with virtually every country in the area bent upon acquiring advanced fighter planes, warships, and missiles with increased accuracy, potency and range.[14] Their rates of strong and sustained economic growth, their levels of industrial and technological skill, and monetary resources also provide them with the financial means to afford, for example, some of the more expensive hardware put on display by some 200 firms from Israel and the other leading weapons-manufacturing countries in February, 1996 at the Asian defence exhibition in Singapore.

With its network of political and trade relationships spreading across the region, and established military ties already in place, Israel is favourably positioned to compete for a not-inconsequential share of the Asian defence business. Defence ministry spokesmen in Tel-Aviv acknowledge that in 1995 no fewer than 40 per cent of new defence orders originated in the Far East.[15] One final 'sweetener' or incentive for Israel: short of terminating arms trading entirely, the readiness to assist these types of countries in meeting their defence needs is far less objectionable on ethical as well as political grounds, in terms of Israel's own self-image as well as its international standing.

A selective listing of current partnerships and principal arms recipients perhaps best captures the transformation taking place in Israel's pattern of military relationships. In 1976, Iran, South Africa and the Latin American republics were among the largest clients. In 1996, by contrast, the United States, its NATO allies and other members of the European Union, and the Asian democracies headed the roster.

With specific reference to the US, a few recent signposts suffice to illustrate the first fruits of initiatives on Israel's part to convert the special bilateral strategic military relationship into a two-way street and to gain a foothold into the American arms market.

- During 1995 TAAS (IMI) and McDonnell Douglas reached an agreement on future joint marketing of Delilah and Light Defender missile systems.
- At year's end the Congress approved further bilateral project collaboration, earmarking $38 million to buy Popeye missiles (from Rafael), $14 million for armour protective plating, and an additional $56.4 million in Arrow missile development, as well as funding for the Nautilus laser system, designed to intercept Katyusha rockets, a longer-range Delilah RPV detector, and Israeli-manufactured fuel tanks for the F-16 fighter.[16]
- In January 1996 McDonnell Douglas pledged to make purchases worth $750 million from Israeli defence firms under a buy-back programme involving acquisition by Israel of 25 F-15I aircraft costing more than $2 billion.[17]
- That same month an Elbit Defence Systems subsidiary, Elbit Fort Worth, won a contract to develop and manufacture the positioning interface box for the Bradley A3 armoured personnel carrier.

The important point to bear in mind is that while selling just a single component to the American armed forces might seem to many observers as dealing in bits and pieces, nonetheless, for Israel, these project links today add up to millions of dollars annually in defence business.

The circle of democratic customers extends beyond North America to the Western European countries. There the list of patrons includes Germany, with which Israel has a very close defence relationship dating back to the 1950s and extending to two-way arms deals. The same is true for Switzerland, whose army signed a contract in December 1995 for Israeli Ranger RPVs and other electronic equipment totalling $85 million.[18] Symptomatic of the improved political climate are the revised arms policies of Britain and France. For decades both had assiduously boycotted Israeli military products as a sign of their displeasure at Jerusalem's stand on the Arab–Israel conflict, but also in bidding fiercely for lucrative weapons contracts of their own throughout the Arab Middle East. Breaking with established policy, Paris resumed defence ties in 1993, and early in 1996 defence officials finally authorized consummation of a pledge made the previous June to Prime Minister Yitzhak Rabin for French acquisition of five Hunter pilotless RPV units.[19]

Many of the former Warsaw Pact countries of central and eastern Europe now opening themselves to liberalization are recent newcomers to Israel's list of clients. Among them: the Czech republic, Hungary, Poland, and the Baltic states, which have sought Israel's advice in upgrading earlier stocks of Soviet-designed tanks and fighter planes as part of an attempt at modernizing their armies while moving closer to inter-operability with NATO equipment. By the early 1990s Elbit negotiated two breakthrough contracts with Romania: one, a tender received for refurbishing older, Western European consortium Puma 330 helicopters; the other, a $300 million contract to upgrade a fleet of MiG 21 aircraft.[20]

To continue eastward, Israel and Russia lately have also reportedly begun efforts at selling weapons jointly to third countries, under an agreement on expanding military and technical cooperation signed in Moscow in April, 1994.[21] While it remains to be seen whether anything of real substance will come from this signed paper, the mere fact that it could be negotiated attests to the transformed post-Cold War climate and Israel's improved standing as well as to prospects for doing business with Russia even in the sensitive defence sector.

Interesting in this respect is unconfirmed evidence that Israeli and Russian passengers killed in November 1996 when a hijacked plane crashed into the sea off the coast of the Comoro Islands, were part of a joint project team working on upgrading the Ethiopian air force. Following in Russia's wake, many of the Confederation of Independent States that once comprised a hostile and undemocratic Soviet Union – such as the Ukraine, Azerbaijan and Kazakhstan – similarly have moved toward establishing bilateral military relationships with Israel and Israeli companies.

Another interesting 'northern tier' relationship with a full member of NATO: the case of Turkey. Featuring the exchange of formal state visits by political, military and business delegations, the relationship was marked by an order placed by Ankara in 1995 for 54 Phantom-2000 upgrading technology packages.[22] The successful bid provides for much of the work to be carried out in Turkey – itself a boost for the budding indigenous Turkish arms industry – but with high-tech upgrading kits from Israel. The potential for arms cooperation to fuel an Israeli–Turkish security regime was signalled by the bilateral defence pact announced in February 1996. The one serious drawback, however, is on the Turkish domestic front. While Turkey's military élite are enthusiastic supporters of expanded arms ties, the political ascendancy of Turkish Islamists of late necessarily dampens Israeli enthusiasm for sharing sensitive military technologies.

Moving still further eastward, a fascinating defence collaboration is now opening up with India, the world's largest democracy, and Asia's third biggest economy. On the Asian mainland, an Israeli military mission has been functioning in China since 1994, effectively signalling the importance assigned that country and its monumental efforts at transforming a backward people's army into a more streamlined and efficient fighting force. This complicates, but at least thus far has not precluded, a concurrent supply relationship with Taiwan, as indicated by Israel's help in co-developing the Sky Sword II air-to-air missile.[23] Other noteworthy regional customers include South Korea, Thailand, the aforementioned Singapore, and the Philippines.

Future Prospects – Good and Bad

This survey has sought to analyse the ways in which Israel as a smaller, secondary or middle-tier supplier is attempting to retain a niche for itself in a global arms market that is both dwindling and reconfiguring. In keeping with this approach, the main thrust of the presentation has been upon Israel's own room for manoeuvre and freedom of independent action, within given constraints imposed on it by the international market for conventional arms and military technologies.

Yet precisely because of the changes taking place in the flow of conventional weapons, however, no combination of past achievement and recent success in holding the line will suffice to guarantee future survival. For Israel to stay the course and contend into the twenty-first century under the shadow of the really big exporters, still further proof of adaptability and flexibility are called for, as well as additional sacrifice. And required before anything else is realism. The balance sheet indicates definite strengths, but also weaknesses.

By way of conclusion, therefore, and as a brake against either undue or excessive optimism, four cautionary signals must be sounded. That they need to be openly stated for the record as prejudicing Israeli global arms diplomacy prospects derives from basically three considerations, detailed below. None of the warnings are theoretical or abstract academic exercises. On the contrary, they already address a present if not entirely clear danger. And yet, thirdly, there is a certain reluctance among policy makers to acknowledge their existence, their immediacy, or their severity; or to chance dealing with them early, or head-on.

The first cautionary note refers back to the American connection treated earlier as a definite asset for Israel. It is an asset, but not an undiluted one. Given the acknowledged paramountcy of the United States in almost every aspect of world affairs, no arms-exporting country can blithely afford to defy America's will with full immunity. In this narrow sense, Israel is unexceptional. Where it differs from other suppliers is in Washington's double-veto hold over most weapons transfers by Israel. The first veto owes to strategic reliance upon the US for economic support, qualitative military superiority, and close political concert. The second choke-point stems from the presence of US-supplied components in so many of the defence items Israel offers for sale or resale abroad, thereby warranting prior American approval.

The potential for friction is even greater when one adds still another set of arms-related irritants. In no sphere of international business is there much room for sentiment; least of all in the exceptionally competitive defence bazaar, where tension is heightened by the threatened loss to would-be competitors of existing or prospective contracts. For example, glaring disparities between these two supplier countries aside, American weapons salesmen have not for the first time perceived of Israel as a serious, if scrappy rival in bidding for tenders put out by the Philippine air force, or when Eastern European defence ministries narrow the choice to buying either older models of the American F-16 or Israeli-improved Phantoms or Kfirs.

What compounds this ever-present commercial rivalry is that the global politics of arms sales might easily find Israel and the United States on opposite sides of a regional contest. Jerusalem's strategic assessment underscores relations with China, whereas mid-decade finds serious policy differences between Beijing and Washington. Another example is Israel's expanding military assistance to India, in direct contrast to the US–Pakistan supply relationship. This dependence *vis-à-vis* the United States, in short, under certain circumstances poses the first limitation on further arms activity by Israel.

A second limitation, already alluded to, is the danger always lurking in the background that by pushing defence trade into such regions of great political uncertainty as central and east Asia, Israel could find itself unexpectedly caught up in latent regional power struggles. In such an eventuality, Israel also opens itself to the charge of exacerbating local tensions and serving as a destabilizing influence because of its arms inflows. Going through with promised delivery of Kfir jets to Ecuador at the height of Ecuador–Peru border strife in late 1995 and early 1996 is one such case in point; potentially there are countless others, from Bosnia and the eastern Mediterranean, through the

Caucasus and the Indian subcontinent, all the way to Formosa, the South China Sea, and the contested Spratly islands. The main point, however, is that any such arms notoriety runs counter to the primary diplomatic goal being pursued by Jerusalem of cultivating world opinion and reasserting Israel to be a member in good standing within the international community.

A third problem for Israel with arms diplomacy at a time of great political disorder both within and between states is client unreliability. Throughout most of the 1980s this found monetary expression in the tendency of third world debtor nations to default on scheduled arms payments. Arguably, for Israel this type of hazard should be all but eliminated by the updated policy of singling out those preferred customers that have not only the appetite and talent for absorbing advanced military technologies but also the economic and financial wherewithal to be able to pay for them. Today the greater danger lies in sudden and radical shifts in a particular country's diplomatic posture – from defensive to irredentist – or in its ideological alignment, from liberal to reactionary.

With the national experience of the Iranian revolution etched in collective bureaucratic memory, the abrupt turn in Turkey's domestic politics toward the close of 1995, for example, must surely give Israeli arms administrators deep cause for concern. Until Turkish national election results exposed the rapid ascendancy and surprising grassroots political strength of Islamic fundamentalist elements in that pro-Western country, every optimistic forecast for sustained defence exports emanating from Tel Aviv and Jerusalem pointed with satisfaction to deepening cooperation with Ankara. And justifiably so, since Turkey was as reliable and politically correct an arms client as Israel could possibly expect: a moderate, pro-American, secular Middle Eastern state intimately affiliated with NATO, and solidly bent on a rapid course of industrialization, democratization, and military modernization, while also supportive of the regional peace process and relied upon as an effective counter to Khomeinism. Turkey was, for good measure, keenly interested in cultivating closer security ties with Israel. Literally overnight, all such calculations have had to be revised, for fear that Turkey's temporary tilt to the Islamic east might become permanent, and extravagant plans for intimate cooperation in the foreseeable future on joint weapons projects have been suspended indefinitely pending clarification of the Turkish republic's true political course. Clarifications notwithstanding, it would be folly for Israel to continue counting on Turkey as a safe and dependable arms ally.

Doing the Doable

We end with our fourth, and final caveat. To some extent it is the most serious; but the problem it addresses is also the one that most lends itself to correction and adjustment by Israel acting alone.

Arms transfers by their very nature are dyadic, meaning that they involve a two-player supplier–client relationship, or, in situations of collaboration among equals, at least a joint partnership. Hence, American primacy, the contingency and element of surprise always present in world affairs, and customer unreliability are three given determinants of the conventional arms trade that, as the saying goes, come with the territory.

Not dyadic is the capacity that every arms competitor, big or small, retains for adjusting as early, as quickly and as comprehensively as possible to changing conditions – a capacity which it must demonstrate if indeed it is to continue being a respected player. Conversely, any refusal to make those adjustments called for by market realities – regardless of the reason or reasons – is tantamount to fighting, and competing, with one hand tied.

It is on this count that Israel and its arms policy-makers are vulnerable to criticism. The fault does not lie not in not doing *enough* – after all, the military industry survives – but in not doing *more* to maximize the country's competitiveness. For there remains a strong, entrenched institutional resistance to drawing the necessary conclusions from dominant market trends.

To be more specific: at this late date, those in charge of directing foreign arms sales have yet to put an end to the intolerable situation of Israeli companies competing against sister firms for foreign contracts by actually outbidding and even discrediting each other. This happened several years ago in Romania, reaching the point that negotiators in Bucharest predisposed to buying from Israel had to insist Israeli government leaders abandon their Olympian detachment and intervene to put a halt to the embarrassing situation. Rather than drawing the necessary conclusions, an almost identical situation was allowed to recur in January 1996, when two subsidiary electronics companies, Elta (IAI) and Elisra (Koor), succeeded so effectively in outbidding each other for a tender put out by India, that the eventual winning bid, by Elta, was so low as to virtually preclude any profit from the transaction.[24] Only then did representatives of the leading electronics manufacturers belatedly reach an accord that aims at regulating the competition among themselves for foreign military contracts, and it still remains to be implemented in actual practice.[25]

Another equally serious, but far more 'expensive' impediment is also self-inflicted: Israel's declining cost-effectiveness against rival suppliers. Here the argument attributing lost contracts or exclusion from markets to international politics discriminating against Israel no longer holds, and is really mostly a pretext for evading the actual causes, which are internal. Overpriced and therefore uncompetitive defence items are chiefly attributable to domestic conditions; in particular, the spiral of inflated labour costs and exaggerated wage agreements resulting from pressures applied against government ministries by powerful labour unions in the defence sector.

I submit that tolerating both inter-company back-stabbing and prohibitive price tags, even while attempting to vie against other smaller, comparable or larger foreign arms suppliers, is merely the manifestation of a larger problem at home. Arguably, the single greatest challenge before Israel, as it strains to cross into the twenty-first century as one of the few remaining long-distance defence survivors, is the unfinished business of consolidation among the local defence military industries. There are simply too many inefficiencies and too much unacceptable duplication within the existing framework for Israel, already labouring under its objective disadvantages, to stay in the bidding if this continues. This is reason enough for giving serious and urgent consideration to a major restructuring of what has become over five decades a sprawling, decentralized arms-manufacturing complex.

A second line of argumentation rests on what in any event is already taking place outside, around and independent of Israel. Richard Bitzinger and others cite the inexorable 'globalization' of the international arms industry, driven by economic realities.[26] This internationalization of the development, production, and marketing of arms is moving forward on two separate tracks. It is marked at one level by domestic mergers and buyouts, and at another by increased multinational co-development and co-production.

In a society and country which tends to measure itself by American standards there may be some wisdom in counselling, 'What's good for America is good for Israel'. For the US defence sector, even with the impressive lead the country already enjoys, is itself moving slowly but surely to assure greater 'efficiencies of scale' in struggling to further enhance the country's international competitiveness, through such means as pooling resources, product specialization and corporate consolidation. Witness the dramatic announcement in 1996 that Westinghouse Electric Corporation had agreed to sell its defence electronic systems to Northrop Grumman. Meanwhile, Lockheed/Martin has bought the Loral Corporation's defence electronics business. Similarly, McDonnell Douglas, refusing to be left behind, is active in achieving its own 'critical mass'. A similar trend is concurrently underway in Europe, with steps taken to increase arms cooperation between EU members.

Therefore, drastic steps by Israel to put its own house in order – including structural adjustments – are becoming increasingly imperative if the country is to keep pace with American, European and even Asian consolidation. This is where the critical question of setting national priorities comes to the fore. But formulating and then actually carrying out a national arms competitiveness policy will require considerable political courage, going up against the forces of institutional conservatism and inertia, and, to be sure, vested bureaucratic as well as corporate interests. Still, it is the national interest that must prevail. For, in the last analysis, this courage and industriousness and dedication inside Israel are going to be no less a determinant of its staying power as a middle-range military exporter than alertness in keeping step with changing external diplomatic realignments, defence economics, and security threats.

NOTES

1. Stephanie G. Neuman, 'The Arms Trade, Military Assistance, and Recent Wars: Change and Continuity', *The Annals of The American Academy of Political and Social Science*, 541 (September 1995), p. 54.
2. Congressional Research Service, 'Conventional Arms Transfers to Developing Nations, 1987–1994', Library of Congress CRS Report 95-862F (Washington, DC, August 1995). The trend favouring US arms superiority was already underway toward the end of the previous decade, and before the exhibition of American arms prowess during the 1991 Kuwait crisis, as predicted in an earlier piece by Stephanie Neuman, entitled 'The Arms Market: Who's on Top?', *Orbis* 33:4 (Fall 1989), pp. 509–29.
3. *The Economist*, 28 October 1995, p. 27
4. *Ha'aretz*, 16 January 1996.
5. Aaron S. Klieman, *Israel's Global Reach: Arms Sales as Diplomacy* (New York and London: Pergamon-Brassey's, 1985).
6. Klieman, *Israel's Global Reach*, pp. 56–7; more recent figures are in *Ha'aretz*, 4 January 1995.
7. *Jerusalem Post*, 2 February 1996, and *Ha'aretz*, 11 February 1996.
8. *Ha'aretz*, 16 January 1996.
9. Export disclosures by official government spokesmen were published in the *Ha'aretz*, 15 July 1994.
10. Relying upon the base figure of $19 billion given by the Israeli Export Institute and reported in *Ha'aretz* on 19 September 1995.
11. About $1.325 billion in American military aid to Israel is used for military acquisition in the US, with the balance of $475 million spent in Israel. *Jerusalem Post*, 2 February 1996.
12. According to the *Jerusalem Post* of 2 February 1996, the US is believed to be stockpiling $300 million worth of military equipment in Israel.
13. A correspondent for *Ha'aretz*, quoting military sources in the defence ministry of Singapore, 9 February 1996.
14. *International Herald Tribune*, 'East Asian Nations Race to Stock Up on an Array of High-Tech Weaponry', 13 October 1995.
15. Israeli defence ministry sources in *Ha'aretz*, 8 February 1996.
16. *Ha'aretz*, 12 December 1995 and 22 January 1996.
17. *Jerusalem Post*, 12 January 1996.
18. *Ha'aretz*, 21 December 1995.
19. Ibid., 8 February 1996.
20. *Jerusalem Post* magazine, 2 September 1994.

21. *IHT*, 2–3 December 1995.
22. *Ha'aretz*, 3 and 18 September 1995; 6 December 1995.
23. *IHT*, 3–4 February 1996.
24. *Ha'aretz*, 10 January 1996.
25. Ibid., 7 February 1996.
26. For a good description of what has been transpiring in the area of multinational collaboration, see Richard A. Bitzinger, 'The Globalization of the Arms Industry', *International Security* 19: 2 (Fall 1994), pp. 170–98.

7

Conversion and Diversion: The Politics of China's Military Industry after Mao

YITZHAK SHICHOR

INTRODUCTION

Since the death of Mao Zedong in September 1976, China's military industry, like so many other aspects of its economy, society, culture, politics and international relations, has undergone a series of comprehensive reforms.[1] Most important among these developments is the conversion from military to civilian industrial capacity. Beginning in the late 1970s in an experimental and unofficial way, this policy has been approved formally and applied extensively since the mid-1980s. Indeed, by the mid-1990s, the Chinese had proclaimed their conversion to be an incredible success, with more than 76 per cent of China's total military-industrial production value consisting of civilian goods. In some industries, the share of civilian production has topped the 80 and even 90 per cent levels, while the electronics industry, traditionally an integral part of China's military production complex, is reported to have been completely civilianized. This achievement has been widely acclaimed, and is even regarded as an international model by countries whose conversion efforts have by and large failed.[2]

There is no doubt that China's 'defence industry', a term that calls for a more precise definition, has indeed increased its civilian production dramatically. Yet there is some doubt as to the extent to which this increase constitutes 'conversion', at least in the *Western* sense of the term. To understand the *Chinese* conception of conversion, many questions should be raised regarding the nature of China's pre-reform defence industry; the origins, incentives, and motivations behind its conversion policy; its short- and long-term objectives; the unique features of China's conversion decision-making, processes, and achievements; the reasons for its 'success'; and the civilian as well as the military implications of conversion.

Economics, the discipline most commonly used for studying military-to-civilian conversion, provides only partial answers to these questions, at least in the China case. This bold statement does not only reflect the fact that I am not an economist, and the fact that Chinese data are often insufficient and too unreliable to allow a proper economic analysis of military-to-civilian conversion. It does reflect the fact that most if not all Chinese initiatives are driven primarily by political considerations, cultural and behavioural norms, collective historical memories, and a dialectical philosophical bent. These, to my mind, are essential for understanding the realities of Chinese phenomena, including the so-called conversion of China's military-industrial capacity to civilian use. The origins of the conversion can be traced back to the historical development of China's military industry.

Military industry was one of the earliest industries in modern China. Traditional China had invented gunpowder and designed and produced a large variety of weapons, including swords, spears and halberds, sophisticated crossbows, chariots, incendiary weapons, and firearms, as well as armoured cars, rockets and ballistic weapons, and, with Jesuit help, cannons. Yet these were no match for the Western advanced military technology when these two civilizations collided in the mid-nineteenth century. One of the most important lessons of the humiliation China had suffered was the need to launch modern military industry. A score of military factories built since the early 1860s survived to the turn of the century. Some of them are still operative under different names or in different locations, for example the Chongqing Chang'an Machinery Plant, built in 1862, and the Jianshe Machine Tools Plant, which was founded in 1889 as the Hubei Guns and Cannons Manufacturing Factory in Hanyang and then moved to Chongqing during the Sino-Japanese war.[3]

Following the 1911 revolution, both the nationalist Guomindang government, and the warlords who controlled the northern parts of China set up their own military factories. Production capacity was limited in quantity and quality. Quite a few of these factories, such as the Shenyang Wusan Complex, founded in 1920, are still active. Later, the Chinese Communist Party (CCP) built its own military production facilities, usually in isolated and remote base areas (setting up a precedent to be revived in the 1960s and 1970s) in north and northeast China where, after 1945, it also succeeded in taking over a small number of abandoned Japanese military plants, such as the Northeast Machinery Plant in Shenyang and the Qingyang Chemical Plant (later renamed the Liaoning Qingyang Chemical Industrial Corporation), both built in 1937. The remaining military factories, built by the Japanese beginning in the early 1930s, were dismantled and removed by the Soviet Union following Japan's surrender in the summer of 1945.

On the eve of its victory, the CCP controlled approximately 100 military factories, 72 of which had been abandoned, and occasionally sabotaged, by the retreating Nationalists. Expecting the end of the civil war, the beginning of economic construction and, perhaps, Soviet military support, the CCP began to *convert* some of these rather backward military plants to civilian use in such fields as farm machinery, light industry, machine-building, and metallurgy, even before the inauguration of the People's Republic of China (PRC) in October 1949. Consequently, by the end of the year, no more than 76 defence enterprises remained, mostly for ordnance (45), but also for aircraft (6), radio equipment (17), and shipbuilding (8), with over 100,000 employees. Under Mao, these became the four main branches of China's military-industrial sector. Two additional main branches – space (missiles and satellites) and nuclear weapons – were added later.

MILITARY INDUSTRY UNDER MAO

Mao's China, seeking peace and stability, very soon after its inauguration found itself involved or implicated in domestic, regional, and even global conflicts. These conflicts, and China's ambitions of becoming a great power, called for a considerable investment in the reconstruction and expansion of its military-industrial infrastructure. For almost three decades, the development and nature of China's military industry were shaped by Mao's revolutionary legacy and ideological militancy; by frequent political upheavals, centralized control and constant bureaucratic interference, economic difficulties, and techno-logical backwardness; by overwhelming dependence on massive Soviet support in the 1950s; and, not less important, by Beijing's high threat perceptions and constant security concerns both within and without its borders.[4]

One of the problems that complicated military production in Mao's China (and in post-Mao China as well) was frequent reorganizations. Initially, no distinction was made between military and civilian production, and both were handled by the Ministry of Heavy Industry, through specialized commissions and bureaus. In August 1952, this ministry became the First Ministry of Machine Building (MMB) responsible for civilian production (including shipbuilding); in turn, a Second MMB was established to take charge of ordnance and aviation industries. The Bureau of Telecommunications was transferred from the First MMB to the Second MMB in March 1953. Recombined in February 1958, the two MMBs were separated yet again in September 1960, when the Third MMB was set up to supervise all aspects of conventional military production. Non-conventional military production (nuclear weapons) had become the sole concern of the Second MMB.

By then, research and development (R&D) related to military production had been coordinated by the Commission of Science and Technology for National Defence (COSTND), created in October 1958 under the Ministry of National Defence. In November 1959, the CCP Central Military Commission (CMC) decided to establish a Defence Industry Commission under Marshal He Long, which merged with the Third MMB in January 1961. In November 1961, an Office of Industry of National Defence (OIND) was set up by the State Council and the CMC to coordinate military-industrial production.

The growth and diversification of China's defence industry finally called for a major reform of the entire military MMB system. In February 1963, radio (later called electronics) was removed from the Third MMB to form the Fourth MMB. Ordnance and shipbuilding industries were taken from the Third MMB in September to become the Fifth and Sixth MMBs. Now responsible for aviation and missiles alone, the Third MMB was dismembered yet again in November 1964, when a Seventh MMB was set up to control all aspects of missile industry. In sum, by the mid-1960s China's defence-industrial complex consisted of six MMBs: the Second (nuclear weapons); the Third (aircraft); the Fourth (electronics); the Fifth (ordnance); the Sixth (shipbuilding); and the Seventh (missiles). While during the Cultural Revolution, from the mid-1960s to the mid-1970s, there were many changes in the over-arching organization of the Chinese military-industry sector, this ministerial structure remained virtually unchanged until the early 1980s.

Creating a good deal of confusion in the policy-making process, in control and coordination, in R&D, and in production, these frequent reorganizations reflected domestic political and bureaucratic tendencies, China's international relations, and economic and technological shortages. China's military-industrial production was given a boost in the early 1950s by the Korean War, which led to an immediate *demand* for arms and arms production, and by the Sino-Soviet alliance, which provided for the *supply*. Indeed, the First Five-Year Plan (1953–57) included 44 new big military-industrial projects, and 51 medium-to-big projects for the reconstruction or expansion of old military factories. Owing to economic difficulties, in 1956–57 Beijing decided to slow down the construction of defence industries and to shift (or convert) funds for economic construction.

Still, by the late 1950s China's military industry had made much progress. Of the 156 major national construction projects built with Soviet assistance, 41 were in the defence industry, including ordnance (15), aircraft (13), radio and electronics (8) and shipbuilding (5). Fifty were 'closely related' to it. An additional 44 defence-industry projects were included in the Second Five-Year Plan (1958–62). By the end of 1959, ten years after the establishment of the PRC, its defence industrial complex consisted of more than 100 major enterprises, with 700,000 employees. This expansion had been made possible, since the early 1950s, by the transfer of manpower, facilities, and resources from civilian enterprises and departments to reinforce defence industries – an inversion of conversion. Ultimately, however, the Soviet aid was said to have 'played an important role in the early days of the Chinese defence industry, meeting the urgent needs of national defence construction and the preparation for war'.[5] Despite its rapid progress during the First Five-Year Plan, China's defence industry managed to maintain good productivity and good investment return, and to turn out quality products. This period was called 'one of the best periods in the defence industry construction in New China'.[6]

The next period was one of the worst. In 1958, soon after the beginning of the Second Five-Year Plan, the PRC was facing simultaneous domestic and international crises. American involvement in the Middle East and the Taiwan Straits was perceived as a threat to the PRC, stimulated by, yet also stimulating, the radicalization at home. The Great Leap Forward seriously disrupted the original defence industry construction plan. Too many new projects were launched; capital construction investment increased without proportion; over-anxiety about achieving quick results led to the setting of impractically high targets, putting speed above quality, and grossly exaggerating output data; normal procedures of work, production, and management collapsed – all leading to great losses and blunders which have taken years of recovery.

This situation deteriorated in the summer of 1960, with the sudden withdrawal of all Soviet assistance and advisers due to serious disagreements with Beijing. Left on its own and cut off from alternative sources of supply, China's military industry was facing an enormous challenge. Mostly preoccupied with copy-producing a variety of Soviet weapons, the Chinese managed to quickly digest advanced design, technology, and production techniques and skills, and to gain a good deal of experience and training. Yet, dependence on Soviet materials, tools, and guidance was so widespread that little room, if any, was left for industrial creativity and innovation. Integral to the traditional

Chinese education system, this predisposition to imitate, emulate and duplicate external models – as well as the failure to apply and adapt theories and ideas to practical use and mass production – has been one of the main reasons for China's agonies and frustrations in undertaking independent military production – and remains so to this very day.

Self-reliance, perhaps a long-term blessing but a short-term curse, was not only inevitable and expedient but also revolutionary. To cope with its growing isolation and perceived threats, Beijing has since the early 1960s adopted two fundamental policies that also affected its military industry in two major ways. One policy was to concentrate its military doctrine on the two extreme and opposite ends of the strategic spectrum: the most primitive (people's war), and the most advanced (nuclear war), in order to achieve quick and credible deterrence. Consequently, the midway option (conventional war; also the most dependent on the Soviet Union) was downgraded. It was only after Mao's death that the State Council and the CMC decided, in December 1977, to give priority to the development and production of conventional weapons and equipment. By that time China's conventional military-industrial infrastructure had accumulated an enormous surplus of under-utilized human and material capacity and relatively low and outdated technology. This surplus is an essential component in understanding China's later military-to-civilian conversion 'success'.

The other fundamental policy was Beijing's strategic decision in May–June 1964 to move many defence industries to remote and sometimes inaccessible inland areas to protect them in view of the 'serious international situation'. In retrospect, this is regarded as one of China's colossal mistakes. In the words of one source, 'Errors such as excessively large scale, too wide an area, dispersed distribution of bases, incomplete projects and the improper moving into mountainous areas and caves ... caused extreme difficulties to production, research and people's lives.'[7] These difficulties were further exacerbated by the turmoil caused by the Cultural Revolution that erupted two years later and disrupted all aspects of life in China, not sparing its conventional military industry. Leading managers, engineers, and technicians were attacked and persecuted; R&D was paralysed; established rules and regulations were abolished; production, particularly quality production, decreased and deteriorated; supply and transportation arteries were clogged; valuable equipment was demolished; and numerous accidents (especially involving aircraft) occurred.[8]

Much of this disruption was over by the late 1960s, when the violent phase of the Cultural Revolution ended. Yet, military production continued to be undermined by radical politics, first by 'serious obstructions from the Lin Biao clique' and, after his downfall, by the Gang of Four. The former pushed for accelerated development of all weapons based on 'crazy plans', 'fantastic imaginations', and 'haunting targets which were far beyond reach'. Consequently, in China's words, capital investment plans were inflated, investments escalated, and plans overran the national resources, leaving defence science, technology, and production in a state of a serious disorder – at a time when the national economy was already lagging. The Gang of Four used whatever means available to frustrate the efforts of China's more moderate leaders – Zhou Enlai, Deng Xiaoping, Ye Jianying, and others – to readjust and stabilize military production.[9] These efforts were aborted with the death of Zhou Enlai in January 1976 and the (second) purge of Deng Xiaoping shortly afterwards, but not for long. On 6 September Mao Zedong died and precisely a month later, on 6 October, the Gang of Four was smashed, thus ending ten years of turmoil.

To be sure, by 1976 China's *conventional* military industry had still managed to move on from copy-production to independent design and development of a variety of weapons, including aircraft, tanks, and guns. However, most of these weapons, sometimes hand-made, were no more than endlessly improved and upgraded versions of obsolete Soviet hardware rather than original high-tech Chinese creations. It was primarily in the *non-conventional* field and its related technologies – atomic and hydrogen bombs, missiles, satellites and nuclear submarines – that China made its most remarkable achievements in the 1960s and 1970s. Needless to say, in those militant and turbulent years, China's defence industry, controlled for a while by soldiers rather than officials, catered almost exclusively to military needs, ignoring civilian ones almost completely.

This had not always been the case. In the early 1950s both revolutionary values and economic shortages encouraged China's infant defence industry to produce civilian goods. In May 1952, for example, the Central Ordnance Commission pointed out that every military factory should select at least one civilian product for production. In his well-known April 1956 speech, 'On the Ten Major Relationships', Mao Zedong dealt with this issue, in the third section, 'The Relationship Between Economic Construction and Defence Construction'. Addressing the Supreme State Conference, he went on urging defence industries to adopt two sets of technologies for the production of both military and civilian goods.[10] Marshal Zhu De, vice-chairman of the PRC and its greatest military leader, underlined this suggestion in his report to the CCP Central Committee in April 1957. Based on these convictions, the defence industry was instructed to implement the policy of 'Dual Duty, Dual Skills Combination of Peace and War Production', entailing 'production of both military and civilian products simultaneously on the basis of ensuring the fulfillment of military production and gradually raising the level of technology'.[11]

Indeed, this policy was implemented very quickly by the military MMBs, which, undoubtedly, used existing civilian production facilities and experience, under civilian production management organizations. In 1959 the value of the civilian output produced by defence industries reached 52 per cent of their total production value. Yet beginning in the early 1960s, with the growing political radicalization and the increased threat perception, civilian production by defence industries was criticized as 'unprofessional' by 'leftists' who blamed military enterprises for 'not attending to their proper duties' (bu wu zhengye). Calling on these enterprises to mind their own business (namely, to engage in military production), these radicals caused a sharp decline in civilian output.

An initiative by Premier Zhou Enlai to revive the policy of combined military-civilian production, expressed in his report to the Third National People's Congress (NPC) in late 1964, failed.

Before long the Cultural Revolution erupted and civilian production by military enterprises practically came to a standstill. In 1978, on the eve of China's post-Mao reforms, the share of civilian products in the total defence industrial output was 6 to 8 per cent. This share began to increase gradually yet consistently only after Mao's successors reintroduced the policy of converting military production capacity to civilian use, as a part of the long-overdue Four Modernizations programme.

MILITARY-INDUSTRIAL CONVERSION AFTER MAO: ORIGINS

Although there are many varieties of military-to-civilian conversion, reflecting different political, ideological, and economic systems, different circumstances and motivations, and different sources of initiative, they all boil down to two fundamental types. The most common, which can be called *negative conversion*, is based on lack of choice as a result of the termination of war and conflict, the signing of a peace treaty, a considerable relaxation of tension, a disintegration of the political system or a territorial division, the downfall of military regimes or leaders, economic crisis, or the shrinking of demand by arms consumers at home and abroad. Such situations can make governments, military-industrial enterprises, or individuals realize that continued large-scale military output is not only counter-productive, useless, wasteful, senseless and unnecessary, but often simply impossible. Much less common, the other type can be called *positive conversion*, since it is based more on moral grounds and the pursuit of peace, stability and international cooperation, as well as on the realization that military production comes at the expense of economic development and the people's welfare.[12] The Chinese case combines both types, in a traditional dialectical way.

To begin with, the conversion of China's defence industries to civilian use has been determined by domestic preconditions and incentives, primarily political. Among these, the most significant were the death of Mao, the arrest of the radical Gang of Four, and the gradual demotion and removal of the neo-radicals led by Hua Guofeng. With this major source of opposition gone, China's reformist leaders, headed by Deng Xiaoping, slowly consolidated their power. Based on their twenty-year-old belief that economic backwardness is the most serious obstacle on China's way to socialism, they revived the mid-1960s and mid-1970s modernization agenda (which could not be implemented due to radical obstruction), according the highest priority to the reform of agriculture, industry, and science and technology – and the lowest to national defence.

Scaling down the place of military reform in the Four Modernizations programme and, consequently, launching the conversion of military production capacity to civilian use, could not have been achieved without political stability and CCP control of the PLA. Eroded during the Cultural Revolution when the PLA had become not only the main surviving organization but also the main power-broker, civilian control over the military was gradually restored after the fall of Lin Biao and his supporters in the early 1970s. Reluctantly, the reshuffled, purged and submissive PLA high command was convinced that military modernization should be based on a strong economy and should, therefore, be postponed until prosperity was achieved. Under these circumstances, and in view of the fact that the PLA was allegedly cut by 25 per cent, the military could by no means oppose conversion: China's defence industries kept turning out obsolete and low-technology weapons that even the PLA rejected. The considerable reduction in domestic orders further underscored the main drawback of China's military industry, namely, a huge under-utilized production capacity of low-technology weapons as well as a substantial workforce surplus, typical of all inefficient Chinese state-owned enterprises.

Yet, this drawback of over-capacity still had many potential advantages: skilled manpower; the best scientists; relatively easy accessibility to raw materials and energy resources, capital, transportation networks and to the policy-makers; relatively advanced facilities and machinery; discipline and the *esprit de corps* fed by prestigious military R&D and production affecting national security. All these could be mobilized to serve economic growth and civilian ends under a proper leadership. Successful conversion, especially in authoritarian societies and socialist command economies such as the PRC, calls for a determined leadership, committed to modernization and development, self-confident in its policies and achievements, and relatively stable. While China has been fortunate enough to have such leadership, as well as the other domestic prerequisites for military-to-civilian conversion, these might have been of little consequence had China been facing external threats and hostility. As it turned out, it has not been.

Though fundamentally exogenous phenomena, threats and hostility are also a function of endogenous circumstances. Domestic radicalization breeds potential threats abroad and perceived threats at home. Whether actual or imagined, external threats are detrimental to the conversion of military-industrial production capacity to civilian use, and vice-versa. China's earlier experience confirms these correlation cycles. Its initial conversion endeavour in the mid-1950s reflected the leadership's self-confidence, a product of domestic political stability; firm civilian control over the military; concentration on economic development; and reduced threat perception, following the relative international relaxation, the settlement of the wars in Korea and Indochina, the alliance with the Soviet Bloc, and China's own policy of peaceful coexistence. Later, all these elements vanished. An exaggerated emphasis on socio-political transformation created economic blunders and undermined political stability and the leadership's cohesion and self-confidence. Military considerations assumed greater importance as the Sino-Soviet split left China isolated and encircled from practically all sides. Under these threatening circumstances, peaceful coexistence was abandoned, and so was conversion.

Since the late 1970s, however, the correlation between internal and external relaxation has re-emerged. Already begun in the early 1970s, the expansion of China's diplomatic relations network was given a boost in January 1979 with the establishment of full official links with Washington. Within the next couple of years, relations with Moscow began to improve, gradually removing the most serious and immediate threat to China's security. These developments led to a thaw in the PRC's relations with Vietnam and India and then with ASEAN (the

Association of South East Asian Nations) and South Korea. Moreover, China's post-Mao leaders, primarily Deng Xiaoping, began to suggest that the danger of a global confrontation, in which China could become entangled, had diminished considerably. In fact, China's post-Mao foreign policy has been oriented toward the preservation of the global *status quo* and international peace and stability, as conducive to economic growth and modernization.

Anticipating at least a decade or two of peace, China could afford to downplay military modernization in the short run and concentrate on economic development, so as to lay the foundations for military modernization in the long run. In this strategy the Chinese have been consciously or subconsciously following the Japanese example of creating a huge GDP, based on market economy and extensive international economic relations, only a fraction of which could provide ample resources for modernizing the military system. In sum, a combination of internal and external incentives has provided an opportunity for converting useless military-industrial production capacity to useful civilian ends.

MILITARY-INDUSTRIAL CONVERSION AFTER MAO: PROCESS

Attempts at converting surplus military production capacity to civilian use began, like so many other policy changes in China, long before they became official. Perhaps foreshadowing the coming demise of radicalism, some military-industrial enterprises had started to produce civilian goods as early as 1977, immediately after Mao's death and the arrest of the Gang of Four. Yet it was only after the well-known December 1978 Third Plenum of the Eleventh CCP Central Committee had triggered the overall reform drive, that the forsaken policy of integrating military and civilian production 'was once more placed on the agenda for discussion'. Experiments could then be safely carried out, and indeed, many military factories launched civilian production, beginning in 1979. This 'spontaneous production stage' lasted until the mid-1980s.[13]

To start implementing the trial integration of military and civilian production, the OIND issued a 'Management Method for Civilian Production by Military Industry' in May 1980, and it urged defence industry ministries to work out development plans for civilian products. By then CMC chairman and China's uncrowned leader, Deng Xiaoping endorsed this drive in January 1982, with his policy known as the 16-character instruction 'to combine military with civilian, peacetime with wartime, give priority to military products, [and] use the civilian to provide for the military' (*junmin jiehe, pingzhan jiehe, junpin youxian, yimin yangjun*). 'National defence industries', he stressed, 'should combine military and civilian work, and make civilian products to finance the military.' He urged the industries to research, develop, and produce civilian goods – apart from fulfilling their assignments for weapons and military equipment.[14] It was agreed that these assignments should be accomplished gradually on the basis of self-reliance, importing no more than a few critical technologies. Deng reiterated that, in the period of national economic construction, expenses for military equipment and investment in defence industries are 'impossible to increase greatly'. Therefore, major projects were to be undertaken very carefully and selectively, or not at all. He called instead for the development of modern weapons and military equipment to 'concentrate on R&D by every possible means, including *reducing weapon systems production*'.[15]

To adapt to the new situation, a major reorganization was started in 1982, after a few years of preparation. In May of that year, the CCP, CMC, and the State Council created the Commission of Science, Technology and Industry for National Defence (COSTIND) which superseded COSTND, OIND, and other organizations, to become the leading management board of all national defence R&D and production. Also in May, the NPC decided to replace the Sixth MMB with the China Shipbuilding Corporation, thus giving it more flexibility to adjust to an embryonic market economy. Meanwhile, the Second, Third, Fourth, Fifth, and Seventh MMBs were respectively renamed the ministries of Nuclear Industry, Aviation Industry, Electronics Industry, Ordnance Industry, and Space Industry.

In November 1982, after this reorganization and the beginning of experimental military-civilian integration, the State Planning Commission (SPC), the State Economic Commission, and COSTIND jointly worked out long-range development plans for 275 types of civilian products in all industrial fields. Military and civilian ministries held coordination meetings and workshops throughout 1983 on practical issues involved in conversion. Some military leaders must have been concerned about the harmful effects of conversion of China's defence capability, because in 1984 Deng told the CMC that using defence industry facilities and manpower to civilian ends would support not only national economic construction but also national defence: 'This will produce a hundred advantages and not one disadvantage.'[16] It was his insistence that finally paved the ground for a strategic transition gradually undertaken by China's military industry.

The timing of this transition reflected a re-evaluation, or reconfirmation, of the domestic and the international situation in the mid-1980s. After concentrating for five years, with incredible and unprecedented success, on reform in agriculture and foreign economic relations, Beijing felt confident enough to embark on urban-industrial reform in September 1984. This reform has affected defence industry not only directly but also indirectly, by deliberately expanding the market for consumer goods. To reactivate idle military industries, a series of defence conversion technology exchange conferences were held in major Chinese cities in early 1985, launching a campaign for the wide-ranging transfer of military technology and products for civilian use. This marked the beginning of the second stage. Given a green light, the conversion of China's defence industry accelerated and intensified, merging with, and even outrunning the growth of China's national economy.

Turning these experiments into officially approved policy by mid-1985 reflected not only their initial success but also China's domestic social and political stability, the remarkable achievements of the economic reforms, and the considerably reduced threat perception. Self-confident, enjoying more international respect than ever before, and yielding to Deng's prognosis,

China's post-Mao civilian as well as military leadership was ready to take bold measures. In May–June 1985, a crucial enlarged CMC meeting finally made some far-reaching decisions that included the demobilization of 25 per cent of the PLA and conversion. In November, the CMC instructed all military production organizations to adjust, prepare, and deliver their reports and opinions on the feasibility of conversion. It had taken some three years for the military-industrial ministries to finally submit their respective production adjustment schemes in 1988. The outstanding conclusion was that 'roughly one-third' of their total production capacity was enough to cover military production, while the other two-thirds could be 'switched over to the support of the national economic construction sector'.[17]

This conclusion entailed further reorganization. In July 1986, four former military-industrial ministries (Nuclear, Aviation, Ordnance and Space) were placed directly under the State Council, while COSTIND continued to control their military aspects, a major reform of the national defence industries. 'By placing the development of military industry manufacture of civilian goods within state planning and within the plan for national economic development, it created favourable conditions for resolving the problem of separation of military and civilian production, which had existed for a long time in the upper management levels of national defence scientific and technical industries.'[18] Reorganization continued.

In December, the Ministry of Ordnance and the (civilian) Ministry of Machine Building were temporarily combined into the State Commission of Machinery (SCM). The new Ministry of Aerospace Industry was created in April 1988 after the Ministry of Aviation Industry merged with the Ministry of Space Industry. Then the new Ministry of Machinery and Electronics Industry (MMEI) emerged, combining the recently formed SCM and the Ministry of Electronics Industry. The Ministry of Nuclear Industry was turned into the Nuclear Energy General Corporation, controlled by the (civilian) Ministry of Energy Resources, while the China Shipbuilding Corporation became part of the MMEI in May. In August, the MMEI also incorporated the China Northern Industries (Group)

Corporation, a newly established ordnance conglomerate. Indeed, to further knock down time-honoured inter-organizational bureaucratic barriers, Beijing created 55 trial enterprise groups, a new form of joint cooperation at multiple levels centring around well-known products. In the military-industrial field, these included the Jialing Group, the Hubei Aviation Group, the Xi'an Aircraft Industries Group, the Guizhou Aviation Group, the Shanghai Aviation Group, and the Southern Powered Machinery Group.

Reorganization, however, could not in itself promote conversion. It also called for huge investments. Indeed, during the Seventh Five-Year Plan (1986–90), Beijing provided China's defence industry with nearly RMB 4 billion in loans to construct 450 civilian production lines, which enabled almost 50 per cent of the enterprises to produce 'mainstay' (zhizhu) civilian products. State conversion loans during the Eighth Five-Year Plan (1991–95) totalled RMB 6.3 billion, which enabled all military enterprises to produce civilian goods. To make a more efficient and economic use of these funds, allocation according to plan has been replaced since early 1987, following two to three years of study and trial, with a contract system according to instructions. These new appropriation provisions applied primarily in R&D, which received priority over the production of equipment. One result was 'Plan 863', a high-tech research and development project that combines military and civilian science and technology in bio-technology, energy resources, space, information, laser, automation, and new material technology.

To promote conversion and make even better use of the existing military and civilian production potential of China's defence industry, two additional policies have been adopted. To begin with, as early as 1980 the expansion of trade was authorized. Consequently, China's military-industrial ministries and organizations successively set up their trading arms, such as the New Era Corporation (Xinshidai), under the OIND; China Nuclear Energy Industry Corporation (CNEIC), under the Second MMB; China Aero-Technology Import–Export Corporation (CATIC), under the Third MMB; China Electronic Technology Import–Export Corporation (CEIEC), under the

Fourth MMB; and China Northern Industries Corporation (NORINCO), under the Fifth MMB. 'The existing facts proved that developing export trade of military products is an efficient way for keeping up defence R&D and production capabilities, stabilizing and training defence science and technical forces, accumulating development capital, and realizing the nurturing of import by export in peace time.'[19] Along with their growing military exports, China's defence industries have considerably increased their civilian exports, whose value in 1989 was 16 times their 1979 value.

The second measure, part and parcel of China's Open Door policy, has been to encourage defence (especially Third Line) enterprises, not only to establish 'windows' (chuangkou) in the more prosperous coastal cities, but to seek joint ventures and sign cooperation agreements with foreign companies.

Initially, China's military industries civilian production consisted mostly of light consumer goods and electrical appliances, such as cameras, bicycles, sewing machines, refrigerators, and motorcycles. Based, however, on its 'technological superiority', the defence industry gradually began developing more advanced products. China's nuclear establishment, for example, has produced mini-reactors, nuclear medical instruments, automatic fire warning systems, nuclear power valves, radiation immune medical packs, and nuclear radiation detection devices. Moreover, in October 1985 Beijing decided to assign to the (still military) Ministry of Nuclear Industry the responsibility for building the two civilian nuclear power stations, Qinshan, near Shanghai, and Daya Bay in Shenzhen.

In addition to producing a variety of civilian aircraft such as the Yun series (5, 7, 8, 11, and 12), helicopters such as the Zhi series (5 and 9), and ultralight agricultural aircraft, China's Aerospace Industry has also produced textile machinery, refrigeration equipment, industrial robots, and satellite communications and remote sensing systems. Shrinking military orders have forced ordnance factories to produce cars, special heavy duty trucks and minibuses (whose share in the total national output volume was 50 per cent by the late 1980s), underwater electric pumps, coal mining excavators, oil rigs, and other non-military goods. While undertaking their own civilian production, China's defence industries have provided the civilian industries with tens of thousands of technical sets, facilities, equipment, and technologies. This process has been given a boost since the mid-1980s. The number of contracts for transferring military technology to civilian usage increased from 416 in 1983 to almost 20,000 in 1985 and nearly 30,000 by the end of the 1980s.

The Chinese provide long lists of examples of civilian goods produced by the defence industry. Within ten years, from 1979 to 1988, their value kept a steady annual growth of more than 20 per cent, or an 11.6-fold overall increase. To hail these achievements and to sum up ten years of experience, an 'All-China Work Conference on Combining Military and Civilian Production' was held in October 1989.[20] Some 30 per cent of all colour television sets produced in China and almost 20 per cent of those exported came from military electronics enterprises. More than 50 per cent of China's motorcycles and 11 per cent of China's vehicles (in 1991) were produced by defence industries.

DIVERSION: MILITARY BUILDUP AFTER MAO

Following ten years of accelerated growth, especially in the latter half of the 1980s, the process of military-industrial conversion began to slow, reflecting changes in the domestic, regional and international situation. To some extent, this slowdown has been determined by problems within the industry (to be dealt with in more detail below). For example, many military enterprises have met serious difficulties of quality production, costs, marketing, technology, and investment, and some have reached saturation in their civilian output. However, the newly emerging balance in China's military industry (and defence policy in general) has derived much more from problems outside the industry.

To begin with, by the late 1980s certain domestic developments began to erode the leadership's self-confidence, built up in the early part of the decade. These developments included economic, social and political problems, such as accelerating inflation, growing regional gaps and social inequalities, widespread corruption, religious and national minority grievances, rural dislocations, and political unrest. All these problems converged in the April–June 1989 Tiananmen demonstrations, which exposed Beijing's weaknesses and anxieties to the outside world. Indeed, the hostile Western reaction and its consequent political, economic, and military sanctions have revived bitter Chinese memories of earlier years, decades, and centuries, supposed to have been forgotten by then. Concerned about the unstable internal situation, suspicious about the intimidating external messages, and aware of their edge over the state and the party, a few Chinese military leaders must have begun to argue (probably in private at that stage) that, following ten years of relative neglect, it was about time that China's military system be given a higher priority.

Nothing much was done about it for more than a year. On the contrary, because of the PLA's initial reluctance to suppress the Tiananmen demonstrators by force, Beijing muffled any mention of professional military modernization, concentrating instead on an extensive political and ideological indoctrination campaign among servicemen. This campaign faded, and military modernization was resurrected, against the background of the Gulf War. It taught Beijing three crucial lessons: (1) that although the prospects of a global conflict have indeed diminished, the prospects of regional and local conflicts have increased; (2) that a militarily weak state would remain vulnerable to pressure, intimidation, and ultimately, to aggression; and (3) that conventional military power, still the predominant component of 'comprehensive national strength' in the emerging New World Order, is a function of superior technology.[21]

An additional incentive for a military buildup has paradoxically emerged in the disintegration of the Soviet Union. Apparently it has removed the immediate and most serious threat to China's security, thus justifying Beijing's downgraded defence reform and its military-to-civilian conversion policy. At the same time, however, the Soviet collapse and Moscow's shrinking presence in central, southeast, and northeast Asia have stimulated greater Chinese military vigilance, for two reasons. On the negative side, new potential risks to Chinese security were created and must be dealt with. On the positive side, also created were new potential opportunities for Beijing to restore its long abandoned traditional role as the central and most important regional power in East Asia (as implied by its name: *Zhongguo*, the Middle Kingdom).[22]

Finally, China's brisk economic growth (an annual average of nearly 10 per cent from 1979 to 1995) has affected its military theory and practice in several respects. For one, it has induced Beijing to reinforce its military monopoly, while the phenomenal economic growth of its southeastern provinces has increased their political leverage to the extent that some people, both in and out of China, anticipate a breakup in the future. Economic growth has also made the Chinese leadership aware of the long-term need to protect its ambitious modernization and development drive on land, in the air, and at sea. Finally, this impressive growth has for the first time created (and, if sustained, would continue to create) enough resources for the reactivation and upgrading of arms production by defence industries and for an advanced military buildup in the future. In sum, domestic developments (a weakening centre, a strengthening periphery, a more prominent PLA, socio-political instability, and successful economic drive), as well as increased perceptions of threat and new opportunities abroad, have begun to change the balance between civilian and military modernization, tipping the scale in favour of the latter.

Indeed, since the early 1990s there have been indications that China's military doctrine and strategic ideology are undergoing a subtle, yet very significant, change. Whereas in the 1980s the Chinese decided to downplay and, in fact, delay defence modernization as dependent on, and a function of, economic growth, now some high-ranking PLA officers suggest (still unofficially) that it is the other way around: continued economic growth is dependent on, and a function of, defence modernization. This argument, that 'without a strong national defence, there will be neither security nor development to speak of', emerged as early as January 1991, in the wake of the Western offensive in the Gulf,[23] and has been reiterated by China's military leadership. Yang Baibing, now out of favour but then vice-chairman of the CMC and director of the PLA General Political Department, indicated that China's modernization drive should be guaranteed by a powerful army: 'Only when we have boosted the economy and built a powerful army and a firm national defence can we acquire the proper position of a big country in the international community.'[24]

Liu Huaqing, his successor as the senior CMC vice-chairman and, moreover, a member of the Politburo Standing Committee, has reinforced these views as a part of his efforts to promote defence modernization. Indirectly disapproving Deng's doctrine, he said: 'It takes a long period to carry out research on weapons and equipment and to manufacture them. Therefore, the thinking that the Army should be modernized only after the economy becomes rich is one-sided. If we do that, the gap between us and the advanced standard in the world will become bigger and bigger.'[25] Therefore, he advocates that military equipment and weapons should be developed as much and as soon as possible.

The most obvious indication of this change has been the consistent increase in China's defence expenditures since 1990, more than doubling within five years (though in nominal terms), while the PLA manpower was reduced by a quarter. In real terms, to be sure, military expenditures have increased at a considerably lower rate, if inflation is taken into account. Still, however we look at it, China's *official* defence outlays have increased and, according to several respectable intelligence and academic estimates, *unofficial* defence appropriations have increased even more. Such increase by no means conforms to a military-to-civilian conversion policy, which usually derives from a reduction in defence expenditures or entails such reduction. Where, then, do these additional military appropriations go?

Beijing claims that most, if not all of them have been used to upgrade the long-neglected PLA serviceman standard of living, by raising salaries and improving food supplies, housing conditions, the quality of uniforms, and other conditions. Yet China's claims that these expenses absorb one-third of its national defence budget seem grossly exaggerated. Apparently, some of the additional funds finance China's growing *military import* of technologies and complete weapon systems, particularly from Russia since the Soviet collapse. Likewise, the additional funds go to defence industries to beef up their *military export* potential. For, while the Chinese justify the need to convert their defence industrial capacity to civilian use by the 'sharp reduction of armament demand in a peaceful environment',[26] there was in fact an unprecedented increase in Chinese arms sales in the 1980s and even the early 1990s.[27] Indeed, some of China's underutilized military production lines have been reactivated, expanded and even modernized, to cater not so much to the shrinking domestic arms market, let alone to civilian production, as to satisfying the endless third world, and primarily Middle Eastern, hunger for arms.

There are indications, however, that a large portion of the additional funds are invested in research, design, development, and future production of a new generation of weapons. Especially since the mid-1980s – and even more so since the late 1980s – Chinese leaders have pointed out that the economy should be developed alongside, rather than at the expense of defence industry. The CMC confirmed that attention should still be paid to the development of conventional weapons, to close the gap with advanced international standards, and with 'appropriate' development of strategic nuclear weapons. Indeed, during the Seventh Five-Year Plan (1986–90), the proportion of funds for the development of conventional weapons increased. Priority has been given by the CMC to urgently needed air defence and anti-tank weapons, but suppression weapons, tanks and armoured vehicles, and light weapons have also been developed, as well as new and upgraded versions of military aircraft, vessels, missiles, electronic equipment, strategic missiles, and nuclear weapons.[28]

While most of these achievements have pure military value, some have civilian applications as well. For example, China's re-entry remote sensing satellites, launched since August 1987, provide valuable information related to national territorial surveys, crop harvest estimation, oil exploration, railway line surveys, oceanic and coastline investigations, power station site selection, earthquake forecast and warning, grassland and forest investigation, historical relics and archaeological studies, map production, and more. Also, since February 1986 China has launched a series of telecommunications and broadcast satellites and, since September 1988, test weather satellites.

CONVERSION AND DIVERSION: A BALANCE SHEET

Compared not only to the agonies of other countries involved in conversion attempts, but also to its own attempts to reform its state-owned industrial sector, China's policy of converting defence industrial capacity to civilian production can be considered as an outstanding success, at least according to Chinese claims. This 'success' derives from the unique features of China's military industry.

To begin with, China's definition of 'defence industry' is vague. In spite of the Chinese claims that, prior to its conversion policy, military production was totally separated from civilian production, defence industries had often combined both. This is occasionally admitted by Chinese sources: 'The military electronics industry and the shipping industry have always been both military and civilian industries.'[29] Thus, even if we accept the Chinese claim that on the eve of reform, in the late 1970s, the share of civilian output in the total production value of China's defence industry was as low as 6.5 per cent, much of this industry retained a huge unutilized or under-utilized production capacity and infrastructure, both military and civilian, which could rather easily be simply reactivated, not necessarily 'converted'. While this situation is typical of the Chinese defence industrial sector, most of the Chinese state-owned enterprises (SOEs) have a surplus unemployed or underemployed workforce which may reach one half or even two-thirds of their total manpower. Defence industries, a mainstay of China's SOEs, can divert their surplus workforce to civilian purposes without affecting military production, if and when conversion is undertaken.

Other reasons for the 'success' of China's military-to-civilian conversion have to do with the fact that military production lines have not really been 'converted' in the sense of being 'transformed'. Most examples of China's military conversion, and definitely the best ones, represent an addition of turnkey civilian production lines that are imported from abroad, usually from Japan, and set up alongside, rather than instead of, idle or active military production lines. In fact, although China is steadily crawling in the direction of market economy, these civilian production lines, still part of military SOEs, are subject to the rules of the centralized socialist command economy. Therefore they enjoy huge subsidies, have privileged use of transportation and communication networks, and have easier access to energy resources, raw materials, advanced technologies, and, last but not least, the decision-makers. In short, their 'success' is an outcome of, among other things, unfair competition. The priority given to the defence industry's civilian production lines is evident in their high annual growth rates of about 20, or even 30 per cent, compared to annual growth rates of the entire SOEs sector, which are the lowest and slowest of China's industrial economy.

Finally, much of the 'success' of China's conversion policy is based on claimed production data (mostly given in relative rather than absolute terms), only one aspect of military-to-civilian conversion. Data on other aspects, such as marketing and sales, costs, prices and profits, taxes, investment, and so on, are limited or missing. It seems, for example, that some of the defence industry's civilian products (such as televisions, refrigerators, washing machines, air-conditioners, and even cars and trucks) cannot be marketed and are being kept in warehouses due to poor quality, lack of demand, high prices, and saturation of the market. Despite Beijing's claim, China's military industries do not have a technological edge over civilian industries, as do those in the West, first and foremost because from 1960, for 30 years, they were cut off from external sources of advanced science and technology. In fact, some civilian industries that had formed relations with non-socialist countries, primarily Japan (already in the 1960s), do have relatively more advanced technology compared to military industries, which, for obvious reasons remained isolated. Beijing admits that no more than one-third of its defence enterprises make money; one-third break even; and one-third acquire losses.

While it is unthinkable that China's defence industries would be privatized as in Russia, the Eastern European countries, and the West, one way to resolve some of their problems is through external cooperation. This is not only a fundamental component of China's international economic relations policy, but also one of the main incentives for its conversion policy. It is much easier, especially after the Tiananmen massacre, to mobilize foreign technology and capital for civilian purposes than for military ones. Yet many advanced civilian technologies could not only contribute to raising the standard of military R&D, but could be also be applied directly to military production. This is one reason why Beijing has been so insistent in the last few years on luring foreign companies into providing the civilian production lines of China's defence industry with capital, technology, equipment, know-how, and expertise, through joint ventures and other forms of partnership and investment. This, in addition to marketing both civilian and military products, has been the main target of the many international conferences and exhibitions organized by the Chinese in recent years.

Moreover, even without direct or indirect military application, civilian products could provide defence industries with additional funds for military R&D, despite repeated Chinese denials. In fact, one of the earliest incentives for military-to-civilian conversion has been that the increased income from the sale of civilian products by military enterprises should supplement the decreased appropriation of resources by the state. Though muted and denied by the authorities, this policy is still effective. It is, however, disliked by the defence industries managers who have come to prefer civilian production which is more profitable and free from tight central bureaucratic control to military production, which is far less profitable and still subject to supervision. In this respect, the conversion of China's defence industry to civilian use has some long-term political and ideological implications. Encouraged by Beijing to become involved in civilian production according to the rules of market economy and through increased participation of foreign companies, military industries, part and parcel of China's SOEs system, could paradoxically contribute to the further erosion of socialist values and the state control of the economy.

In sum, there is no doubt that China's military-industrial sector has increased its civilian production dramatically, yet there is more than a doubt whether this reportedly successful policy can be considered as 'conversion' in the western sense. It is a unique Chinese process, with typical, even traditional, dialectical dimensions, whereby military resources are being 'converted' to civilian use at the same time as civilian resources are being converted to military use. Absolute figures may change but not necessarily the proportions. Especially since the early 1990s, Beijing has been committed to making China a great power, economically *and* militarily, by the first quarter of the next century, which is also the beginning of the third millennium. Power will be needed not only to protect the fast-growing modernization processes and to deter external hostile adversaries, but also as a symbol of greatness.

NOTES

1. The best analysis is Paul Humes Folta's *From Swords to Plowshares? Defense Industry Reform in the PRC* (Boulder: Westview Press, 1992); see also John Frankenstein, 'The People's Republic of China: Arms Production, Industrial Strategy and Problems of History', in Herbert Wulf (ed.), *Arms Industry Limited* (Oxford: Oxford University Press, for SIPRI, 1993), pp. 271–319.
2. See, for example, Jean-Claude Berthelemy and Saadet Deger, *Conversion of Military Industries to Civilian Production in China: Prospects, Problems and Policies*, OECD Development Centre Report (May, 1995).
3. Much of this and the following information is based on *China Today: Defence Science and Technology*, 2 vols (Beijing National Defence Industry Press, 1993), hereafter: CTDST; Jin Zhude (ed.), *Guide to International Cooperation and Investment with Enterprises of China Defence Industry* (Beijing: The China Association for Peaceful Use of Military Industrial Technology, 1993); and the various volumes on China's defence industries in the *Dangdai Zhongguo* [China today] series. On the early development of China's military enterprises, see Thomas L. Kennedy, *The Arms of Kiangnan: Modernization in the Chinese Ordnance Industry, 1860–1895* (Boulder: Westview, 1978) and Wang Ermin, *Qing ji binggongye de xingqi* [The rise of the armaments industry in the late Qing period] (Taipei: Academic Sinica, Institute of Modern History, 1963).
4. For earlier studies of China's defence industry, see James R. Blaker, 'The Production of Conventional Weapons', in William W. Whitson (ed.), *The*

Military and Political Power in China in the 1970s (New York: Praeger, 1972), pp. 215–27; Parris H. Chang, 'China's Military-Industrial Complex: Its Influence on National Security Policy', *Asian Affairs* (January–February 1975), pp. 145–54; Harlan W. Jencks, 'The Chinese "Military-Industrial Complex" and Defence Modernization', *Asian Survey*, 20:10 (October 1980), pp. 965–89; Harlan W. Jencks, *From Muskets to Missiles: Politics and Professionalism in the Chinese Army, 1945–1981* (Boulder: Westview, 1982), pp. 189–221; Sydney Jammes, 'China', in Nicole Ball and Milton Leitenberg (eds), *The Structure of the Defence Industry* (London: Croom Helm, 1983), pp. 257–77; Sydney Jammes, 'Military Industry', in Gerald Segal and William T. Tow (eds), *Chinese Defence Policy* (London: Macmillan, 1984), pp. 117–32; John Frankenstein, 'People's Republic of China: Defence Industry, Diplomacy, and Trade', in James Everett Katz (ed.), *Arms Production in Developing Countries: An Analysis of Decision Making* (Lexington, MA: Lexington, 1984), pp. 89–122; Joseph P. Gallagher, 'China's Military Industrial Complex: Its Approach to the Acquisition of Modern Military Technology', *Asian Survey*, 27:9 (September 1987), pp. 991–1002.

5. *CTDST*, vol. I, p. 18.
6. Ibid.
7. *CTDST*, vol. I, p. 58. See also Barry Naughton, 'The Third Front: Defence Industrialization in the Chinese Interior', *The China Quarterly*, No. 115 (September 1988), pp. 351–86, and his 'Industrial Policy during the Cultural Revolution: Military Preparation, Decentralization, and Leaps Forward', in William A. Joseph, Christine P.W. Wong and David Zweig (eds), *New Perspectives on the Cultural Revolution* (Cambridge, MA: Harvard University Press, 1991), pp. 153–81.
8. See a reference by Deng Xiaoping, 'On Consolidating National Defence Enterprises' (3 August 1975), in *Selected Works of Deng Xiaoping (1975–1982)* (Beijing: Foreign Languages Press, 1984), p. 40 (hereafter: *SWDXP*, vol. I).
9. These accusations and terminology can be found in *CTDST*, vol. I, pp. 78–90; see also 'On Consolidating National Defence Enterprises' (3 August 1975), a speech at a conference on key enterprises of the national defence industries, in *Selected Works of Deng Xiaoping (1975–1982)* (Beijing: Foreign Languages Press, 1984), pp. 39–42.
10. Michael Y.M. Kau and John K. Leung (eds), *The Writings of Mao Zedong 1949–1976*, vol. I (Armonk, NY: Sharpe, 1986), pp. 49–50, and *CTDST*, vol. I, p. 159; see also Cao Shixin (ed.), *Zhongguo junzhuanmin* [China's military-to-civilian conversion] (Beijing: Zhongguo Jingji Chubanshe, 1994), p. 11 (hereafter: *ZGJZM*). For a translation, see Foreign Broadcast Information Service, *Daily Report: China (Supplement)*, 27 July 1995 (hereafter: *FBIS-CHI*).
11. Duan Zijun (ed.), *China Today: Aviation Industry* (Beijing: The China Aviation Industry Press, 1989), p. 42.
12. There is by now a considerable amount of literature on various aspects of conversion; see, for example, Lloyd J. Dumas (ed.), *The Socio-Economics of Conversion from War to Peace* (Armonk, NY: M.E. Sharpe, 1995); Jacques S. Gansler, *Defence Conversion: Transforming the Arsenal of Democracy* (Cambridge, MA: The MIT Press, 1995); United Nations, Department of

Disarmament Affairs, *Conversion: Economic Adjustments in an Era of Arms Reduction*, Disarmament Topical Papers 5, 2 vols (New York: United Nations, 1991) (an extensive bibliography on pp. 285–305).
13. ZGJZM, pp. 11–12.
14. Ibid., and *Beijing Review*, 13 (1994), pp. 8–11.
15. CTDST, vol. I, p. 120.
16. ZGJZM, p. 12.
17. CTDST, vol. I, pp. 146–7.
18. ZGJZM, p. 14.
19. CTDST, vol. I, p. 157.
20. CTDST, vol. I, pp. 165–6.
21. On the concept of 'comprehensive national strength', see Yitzhak Shichor, 'Defence Policy Reform', in Gerald Segal (ed.), *Chinese Politics and Foreign Policy Reform* (London: Kegan Paul International, 1990), pp. 77–99.
22. Yitzhak Shichor, 'China's Defence in a Changing World', in Kevin P. Clements (ed.), *Peace and Security in the Asia Pacific Region: Post Cold War Problems and Prospects* (Dunmore and United Nations University, 1992), pp. 183–203.
23. For example, Sa Benwang, in *JFJB*, in *FBIS-CHI*, 11 January 1991, pp. 1–2; Luo Xiaobing, 'Strengthening National Defence Building is an Important Guarantee for Economic Development', *JFJB*, 6 February 1991, in *FBIS-CHI*, 1 March 1991, pp. 33–5.
24. Yang Baibing, 'Shouldering the Lofty Mission of Escorting and Protecting China's Reform and Construction', *Renmin Ribao*, 19 July 1992, pp. 1, 3, in *FBIS-CHI*, 5 August 1992, pp. 29–35.
25. Liu Huaqing, 'Unswervingly Advance Along the Road of Building a Modern Army with Chinese Characteristics', *Qiushi* [seeking truth], 15 (1993), and *JFJB*, 6 August 1993, pp. 1–2, in *FBIS-CHI*, 18 August 1993, p. 18.
26. CTDST, vol. I, p. 146, for example.
27. There is a good deal of literature on this subject. For the best summary and analysis, see R. Bates Gill, *Chinese Arms Tranfers: Purposes, Patterns, and Prospects in the New World Order* (Westport: Praeger, 1992); see also Yitzhak Shichor, 'Unfolded Arms: Beijing's Recent Military Sales Offensive', *The Pacific Review*, 1: 3 (October 1988), pp. 320–30.
28. CTDST, vol. I, pp. 167–76.
29. ZGJZM, p. 17.

8

The Military Industries of the Arab World in the 1990s

GIL FEILER

INTRODUCTION

This chapter deals with the development of arms industries in the Arab states during the 1990s. After considering the characteristics of the munitions industry at the state level, the research includes an outline of attempts to divert some production lines to the civilian sector, going on to a description of inter-Arab efforts at joint manufacture of military products. The research also deals with the positions of Arab policy-makers, as voiced in Arab strategic journals, in relation to the future development of the Arab arms industry.

In general, the Arab states are industrially underdeveloped. Despite the fact that the industrial sector in some Arab states employs 20–25 per cent of the overall workforce, the overwhelming majority work at small concerns with 20 employees or fewer,[1] reflecting the slow pace of industrial development in those countries. Table 8.1 exhibits the percentage of industrial employees in the Arab states under study and Iran.

Despite the development and progress they have undergone in recent years, the Arab states still lag far behind international standards in science and technology. Overall expenditure on research and development in the Arab states is low in relation to the world's industrialized countries. Table 8.2 presents data on research and development in the Arab states.

TABLE 8.1
PERCENTAGE EMPLOYED IN INDUSTRY, 1990

State	Percentage of employees*
Saudi Arabia	20
Egypt	22
Iraq	18
Syria	24
Iran	23

* including employees of the oil industry

Source: UNDP (1996)

TABLE 8.2
RESEARCH AND DEVELOPMENT SCIENTISTS AND TECHNICIANS
PER POPULATION OF 1,000, 1988–92

State	Per 1,000 persons
Iran	0.1
Jordan	0.1
Tunisia	0.5
Lebanon	0.1
Egypt	0.8

Source: UNDP (1996)

Such a lack of an adequate industrial base has hampered Arab efforts to develop an advanced munitions industry. In consequence, foreign manufacturers of arms and munitions have targeted the Middle East as an attractive market, as illustrated, inter alia, by the striking turnout of arms manufacturers at the International Defence Exhibition (IDEX) held in 1995 in the United Arab Emirates. Apart from importing munitions, the Arab states also buy advanced manufacturing technologies and foster the human resources required for their exploitation.

Its lack of industrialization notwithstanding, munitions plants are among the longest-established industries in the Arab states. In Egypt, such plants were functioning at the beginning of the nineteenth century. A modern arms industry has continued to evolve in Egypt over the years, with development spurred by an enlarged stream of investments prompted by armed conflicts with Israel and elsewhere (Yemen for example). However, despite close to two centuries of arms production, Egyptian weaponry has not been of the highest quality. Alongside Egypt, other Arab states have developed military industries; notably, Iraq, Saudi Arabia and Syria deserve mention in this category.

Iraq's invasion of Kuwait, and the ensuing Gulf War, altered the status of the region's munitions industries. In the first place, Iraq, hitherto possessing one of the region's most advanced military industries, was compelled to halt its manufacturing endeavours and open up its military installations to UN inspectors. The latter uncovered Iraq's capability in the manufacture of weapons, conventional and non-conventional, the findings highlighting the fact, already familiar to intelligence agencies the world over, that Iraq was well along the road towards its goal of manufacturing nuclear weapons.

In addition to revealing Iraq's capability, the Gulf war also convinced the countries of the region to alter their strategic concepts, a decision with effects that extended to their arms industries. Heads of defence establishments in the Arab countries, Egypt and Syria principally, undertook a thorough study of the campaign, evidently learning lessons with significant impact on the character of military production. Accordingly, since the early nineties, the trend has been towards manufacture, actual or attempted, of advanced weaponry of combat-proven effectiveness (accurate guided missiles, for example) or weapons of mass destruction. The effects of the long-range surface-to-surface missiles targeted at population centres in Israel and Saudi Arabia also appear to have been studied thoroughly by the leaders of the region. This background explains the efforts of some Arab states, such as Syria, to step up their capability in the manufacture of long-range missiles, and biological and chemical weapons.

Altered overall strategic concepts extended to a further aspect linked to the arms industry and stemming from the economic standing of the Arab states, and the decline in oil prices. With the aim of alleviating the economic travails plaguing many Arab states in recent years, their governments have been obliged to introduce a degree of reform – under the pressure and guidance of global institutions like the International Monetary Fund (IMF), as well as the real necessity of responding to their economic predicament. Furthermore, oil revenues in the eighties and nineties have been lower in real terms than they were in the seventies and early eighties. In consequence, national governments balk at allotting large sums to the conventional arms industry and simultaneously, for development of non-conventional armament; accordingly, they elect to focus on developing non-conventional weaponry, regarding an enhanced capability in biological and chemical weaponry, and nuclear arms too to a degree, as a response to Israel's nuclear edge.

EGYPT

In the extent and variety of its output of conventional weaponry and military equipment, Egypt is the most experienced and prominent of the Arab states. At the end of the eighties, the Egyptian arms industry's capital totalled $1.5 billion; its output of military products was estimated at $400 million, the goods produced for the civilian market earning a further $400 million. In all, Egypt's munitions industry has 30 functioning plants. Correct to the mid-eighties, the number of workers employed reached 100,000.[2] With that, some plants do not operate at full capacity; since the late eighties, there has been a marked and growing trend to divert production lines to the civilian market.[3]

Conventional weaponry

Background

Egypt's munitions industry was founded under Muhammed Ali, but its modern successor has developed progressively from the early fifties onwards. Significant expansion commenced as far back as the late monarchical period, following charges that the faulty weapons supplied to the Egyptian forces in the 1948 war were the cause of their debacle. Two factories were built in 1950: the aerodynamics plant in Helwan and the 'Qader' factory. The officers' coup of 1952 gave the armaments industry a further boost. The 'Saqr' factory was built in 1953 and a further plant was erected at Helwan in 1960. At the time, Egypt drew upon the assistance of experts from Europe – West Germany principally – and India. The plants manufactured, *inter alia*, training planes, aircraft parts, surface-to-surface and surface-to-air missiles, and explosives.

The factories' operations were curtailed when the Soviet experts left Egypt in the mid-sixties. In consequence, several plants were closed down in the late sixties, the rest engaging in production of light arms, and repair and maintenance of imported weaponry. An attempt launched in 1970 to extend Soviet–Egyptian cooperation in the manufacture of military equipment did not work out, due equally to the Soviet refusal to supply Egypt with technology, and President Sadat's growing propensity to closer links with the West.

In 1975, Egypt attempted to promote its military industry by inter-Arab cooperation, through establishment of the Arab Organization for Industrialization. Egypt sought the lead role in the Organization, whose factories were mostly built on its territory. The Organization survived as a joint body till 1979, when its three Gulf partners pulled out. Ever since conclusion of the peace treaty with Israel, the United States has become Egypt's principal partner in munitions industry and arms manufacture, giving Egypt an edge over other Arab states interested in developing their own munitions industries.[4]

Production and its organization

Egypt's munitions industry is controlled by the ministry for military production, and the supreme armaments commission whose members are the president, the vice-president, and the ministers of defence, foreign affairs, finance and military production. As of October 1993, the ministry of military production has been directly subject to the defence ministry. The plants of the munitions industry function under two organizations: the Arab Organization for Military Industry, and the National Organization for Military Production. The two bodies are expected to secure Egypt's own supply of light arms and ammunition, and other military equipment.

The National Organization for Military Production is charged with running the companies manufacturing weapons and ammunition for the ground forces; the companies' plants are fully state owned.[5]

The Organization for Military Industry is responsible for the companies engaging in production of aircraft, missiles, engineering and electronics. In 1990, the Organization ran nine companies: five fully state owned, the rest joint projects with Western multi-nationals. In theory, the projects are also open to Egypt's private sector, but this is not effected extensively. Egyptian businessmen are generally wary of the enormous financial investment required, and the bureaucratic red-tape characterizing the domain. For its part, the state offers few investment opportunities, out of considerations of secrecy.

TABLE 8.3
FACTORIES OF THE NATIONAL ORGANIZATION FOR MILITARY PRODUCTION

Name of plant	Est.	No. of Employees	Products
Abu Za'abal Co. of industrial engineering (Plant 100)	1976		Anti-aircraft guns, artillery pieces, tank cannon, development of Soviet weapons, manufacture of integrated systems and munitions production under licence.
Ma'adi Co. of development of engineering (Plant 54)	1949		Light arms, industrial Soviet pistols, production of locally designed pistols
Helwan Co. for Mechanical Instruments			Telescopic equipment spares, 60/82/120 mm calibre mortars, barrels for 122 mm. shells, range-finding systems
Helwan Co. for industrial engineering (Plant 99)			Metal components, protective coating for medium and heavy ammunition, development and manufacture of anti-armour warheads and projectiles, stealth bombs, artillery shells, anti-tank shells, rockets and bombs
Heliopolis Co. for chemical industries (Plant 81)			Ammunition for medium and heavy arms, 105 mm tank shells, mortar shells, non-guided artillery rockets, mines, smoke and illumination shells, naval mines, guided anti-aircraft weapons, etc.
Shubra Co. for engineering industries (Plant 27)	1953		Light arms ammunition

TABLE 8.3 (continued)

Name of plant	Est.	No. of Employees	Products
Abu Qir Co. for engineering industries (Plant 10)	1952	1,630	Ammunition for assault rifles, smoke bombs, mortar shells, rifle cleaning equipment
Al-Ma'ashara Co. for engineering industries (Plant 45)	1956		Ammunition for medium-calibre machine-guns, anti-personnel mines, hand-grenades etc.
Abu Za'abel Co. for special chemicals (Plant 18)	1950	4,000	Explosives and gunpowder (began for light, medium and production heavy arms, for Swingfire in 1957) anti-tank missiles, for mines, bombs and rockets; various types of fuel
Kaha Co. for chemical industries (Plant 207)		1,500	Training ammunition, tracer bullets, grenades, military batteries and chargers
Helwan Co. for metal industries (Plant 63)	1963	4,000	Alloys for cartridges for light and heavy arms
Helwan Co. for Ferric Products (Plant 9)			Iron casings for military installations, motors, mechanical devices, electronic motor-bodies and associated components
Benha Co. for electronic industries (Plant 144)		3,000	A variety of transmitters and receivers for military telephones and radios, timers, delayed action fuses, explosive devices, etc. Manufacture of tank and squad radios in association with the British Plessey company, licensed manufacture of AN/TPS 63 radar under supervision of the Westinghouse Corp. (US)
Helwan Co. for diesel engines (Plant 909)	1964		Various engines, 8 to 150 h.p. Aims to expand to produce engines up to 500 h.p.
Abu-Za'abal Co. for tank repair			Maintenance of US-made tanks, and plans to produce spares for them in future.

Source: *Al-Difa' al Arabi* (Lebanon) and Yezid Sayigh

Beyond the diverse products specified in Table 8.3, Egyptian industry also manufactures airplanes, spares, components and engines for airplanes, military vehicles, ballistic missiles, guided missiles and naval vessels. Airplane production, the most developed sector, is largely confined to licensed production of Western-designed aircraft. The naval vessel sector is least developed, but nevertheless considered the most advanced of its kind in the Arab world.

In the domain of conventional weaponry, the most outstanding project is the joint production with the US of the M1A1 tank, currently in train at an estimated cost of $2.4 billion. Most of the work on mounting the project is carried out by American companies. Thus, General Dynamics for instance won a $150 million contract for designing and equipping the Helwan plant. A memorandum of understanding relating to the project was signed in 1989, providing for production of 540 tanks of this model. Production commenced two years later; in 1993, the project's first 31 tanks went into service with Egypt's armour units.

Egypt's gain in technology transfer is rather limited as most of the project's advanced components are manufactured by the Americans; i.e. finished parts are shipped to Egypt for final assembly. Accordingly, the technology transferred to Egypt is confined to welding armour, mechanization, assembly and inspection. Under Egypt's agreement with the US, the project is scheduled for completion in 1997; its future beyond that has yet to be settled. In late 1995, talks on the matter between the Egyptian defence minister and senior US officials yielded no practical results.[6] Leaks from the talks revealed that the US side, with General Dynamics support, urged the Egyptians to convert the project to production of another type of armoured combat vehicle. *Inter alia* the Egyptians were advised to manufacture armoured troop carriers of the Bradley and Warrior types; or alternatively, military and commercial trucks, and spares for them.[7]

In the field of tactical ballistic missiles, in the years to come Egypt is to embark upon production of Scud C missiles, employing North Korean equipment.[8] It was reported in June 1996 that North Korea had conveyed the necessary equipment to Egypt some months previously, delivered in seven large shipments, including steel plate designated for manufacture of Scud missiles and other auxiliary equipment.[9] It should be recalled that Egypt had formerly shared in a joint project with Iraq and Argentina for development of the 1,000-km range Condor 2 missile. Egypt withdrew from the project in 1989, but is presently applying Condor technology to develop the Vector missile, whose range exceeds 1,000 km.

The electronics sector of the Egyptian munitions industry is as yet undeveloped. However, in the early nineties, Benha – one of the leading companies in the field[10] – signed contracts with the British companies Plessey and Racal for manufacture of communications systems. By means of these contracts, the company intends to boost its exports to the Arab states. There are also a number of private companies active in electronics, notably the 'Arab International Optronics Company'.

'Optronics' is a joint project, with 51 per cent held by an affiliate of the Egyptian defence ministry and the UK United Scientific Holdings company owning the remaining 49 per cent. The presence of such a partner grants the company use of progressive technology to manufacture advanced systems. Founded in 1982 in a Cairo suburb, 'Optronics' specializes in producing fire-control systems and equipment from ordinary optical equipment, as well as manufacture of electro-optical systems including night-vision systems and laser-based range-finding systems. The company also produces electronic equipment for surveillance, fire-coordination and control by day and night and a variety of weapons such as machine-guns, artillery, projectile-launchers in service with units of infantry, armour, artillery, anti-air defence and reconnaissance, as well as the airforce and navy. The company hopes to commence manufacture of fire-control systems, infra-red night-vision systems, systems operating on solar energy, systems for establishing geographical location, and guidance systems operated by infra-red rays.[11]

The arms industry's difficulties and ways of handling them

Overall, Egypt's munitions industry still depends to a marked degree on imported technology, principally Western. A primary factor that impedes its growth is, of course, a lack of capital. Egypt's foreign debt and the difficulty of raising loans are factors hampering the development of the munitions industry.

A further difficulty facing Egypt's munitions industry is marketing. Manufacture of military products becomes financially viable when pursued on a large scale, for only thus can Egypt exploit the relative advantage represented by its cheap work force. This is the context for the words of Egyptian commander-in-chief Safi ad-Din abu Shanaf, who argued that 'due to the high costs of military production, the arms market must be large for the plants of the munitions industry to continue their operations'.[12] It thus becomes vital to locate potential markets for the products of the arms industry – an undertaking hitherto beyond the ability of its heads. The same point was made by Egyptian general Dr Nabil Ibrahim Ahmed, who claimed that there had been occasional proposals for a joint Arab arms industry to be located in Egypt. The possibility came up mainly in the form of a revival of the Arab Organization for Industrialization. Dr Nabil held this to be pointless, for the loans and grants to the Organization would tempt it into making products that would end up in warehouses, because nothing was being done to win purchasing contracts for them. In part, the problem lay in the preference of the Arab and Islamic states – the leading potential customers of Egypt's munitions industry – for weapons from sources outside Egypt, on the assumption that they would be of higher quality, or from political considerations.[13] During the Afghan civil war, for example, it was the common view that, of the numerous types of 7.62 mm calibre weapons, the Egyptian-made Kalashnikov rifle was the least efficient.[14]

The Egyptian munitions industry's marketing difficulties were exacerbated in consequence of Iraq's invasion of Kuwait and the ensuing war. Iraq, formerly a major consumer of weaponry, was no longer a market. In addition, the other Gulf states deferred or cancelled orders, due to financial difficulties. Thus, Kuwait scrubbed an order for 150–200 Fahd armoured combat vehicles. Financial difficulties made the Gulf states more choosy in their weapons purchases. The Egyptian arms industry's sales to the Gulf states are estimated at $70–80 million annually.[15] Marketing difficulties were further compounded when Egyptian-made arms failed to perform well on the battlefield. These difficulties left some of Egypt's munitions plants operating at no more than 10 per cent of capacity.[16]

In recent years, the heads of Egypt's arms industry have tried a number of ways to grapple with these difficulties. One is to pinpoint new customers outside the traditional Arab market. In 1992, arising from these efforts, Egypt effected a first-time sale to Rwanda of D-30 122 mm cannon, mortars, ammunition and additional equipment.[17] Another way is conversion of some arms industry production lines to manufacture for the civilian market. This trend was already in train in the late eighties, when 'the National Organization for Military Production' and the 'Egyptian Industrialization Authority' began to channel 40–50 per cent of output to the civilian market. In 1990, the Authority's chiefs decided on further expansion of the production lines for the civilian sector, diversifying the range of products designated for it.[18]

One example of conversion to civilian production is the 'Helwan Co. for diesel engines' (Plant 909) which managed to export some of its output of engines to countries such as Morocco, Algeria, Zimbabwe, Kenya, Japan and Australia. Coincidentally, the Ministry of Military Production worked out further plans for the company. The projects included: adaptation to natural gas operation of bus engines for the public transport authority, which is owned by the armed forces; conversion of the American 'Cherokee' jeeps manufactured by the Egyptian Industrialization Authority, from 6-cylinder petrol engines to 4-cylinder diesels; manufacture of engines operating on natural gas, particularly engine type 116. An additional Industrialization Authority project still at the design stage calls for production of a novel 'national engine', of which Plant 909 plans to manufacture 75,000 annually for installation in cars produced or assembled in Egypt.[19] It should be noted that the 'Helwan Co. for diesel engines' has taken a hand in a number of civilian projects, some in domains with no direct link to engine manufacture. For example, it shared in supply of power units to the phosphates project at Abu Tartur, and the 'Cable and Wireless Communications Authority'. In addition, it provided irrigation units for the country's new agricultural lands. 'Helwan' also supplied special dredging units for cleaning up the canals owned by the 'Egyptian Public Authority for Sewage Works'. According to the minister of military production, the company would also take part in the Sinai development project, supplying the irrigation units required by the 'Egyptian Ministry of Works and Water Resources', and power units for the areas around Dahab, Noweiba, Ayun Musa, Ras Sadr and Raffah.[20]

Egypt does not seek to resolve the difficulties besetting its munitions industry by selling off the plants, even if recent years have found privatization applied in various sectors. The Egyptian government appears to have decided in principle against privatization of industries and assets connected to national security. This view was supported in May 1996 by the Minister for the Public Business Sector, Dr Atef 'Ubeid, who stated that the munitions industry, like the Suez Canal, the oil companies and banks, is not for sale and will not be privatized.[21]

Non-conventional weaponry

Little is known about Egypt's capability in the field of weapons of mass destruction. Egypt was the first Arab state to acquire chemical weapons, employing them in the Yemen war in the sixties. In the early seventies, Egypt supplied Syria with small amounts of self-produced chemical weapons (see at length below in the section on Syria). In the eighties, Egypt, in collaboration with Iraq, stepped up its efforts to manufacture chemical weapons. In the early nineties – though its chiefs deny the fact – Egypt's munitions industry engaged in production of chemical weapons, employing raw materials imported from various countries including India and Germany.[22]

In the early sixties, Egypt's first chemical weapons factory – Plant 801 – went into operation, with Soviet and German experts assisting with the transfer of chemical and biological weapons technology. Between the years 1963–67, the Egyptian airforce employed chemical weapons in Yemen.

After the 1967 war, strategic cooperation between Egypt and Syria extended to chemical weaponry. In 1972, Egypt supplied Syria with chemical weapons, including Sarin and mustard gas. Neither country employed these weapons in the 1973 war. In the late seventies and early eighties, Egypt and Iraq maintained strategic cooperation extending to chemical weapons technology. A few months prior to Iraq's invasion of Kuwait, Egypt justified Iraq's acquisition of chemical weapons, arguing that it reflected Iraq's right to self-defence. These claims are in line with the Egyptian view of chemical weaponry as an essential element in achieving parity with Israel's nuclear edge.[23]

Over the years, various Arab sources have published reports of the existence of surface-to-surface missiles equipped with chemical warheads. In this domain, Egypt appears to have collaborated with North Korea.

In the sphere of nuclear arms, Egypt made a number of attempts over the years, but apparently has yet to chalk up any genuine achievement. According to the Egyptian opposition newspaper al-Ahrar, Egypt's leadership during the rule of Gamal Abd al-Nasser made efforts to achieve a nuclear capability, pursuing those efforts in 1956 with the purchase of a Soviet-built 2 megawatt research reactor that went into operation five years later. Egypt sent scientists abroad to specialize in nuclear physics, a project that trained at least 380 experts in this field.[24]

In the seventies, Egypt made attempts to extract the uranium to be found within its borders. The project, directed by the 'Committee for Nuclear Resources', employed a special helicopter to pinpoint uranium deposits. The committee also intended to produce thorium, a component of nuclear reactor fuel. Egypt imported equipment for extraction of zirconium, but failed to use it.[25] On conclusion of the peace treaty with Israel in the late seventies, Egypt curtailed efforts to acquire nuclear weapons.

A report published by the Egyptian Shura council (parliament) in July 1987 claimed that the difficulties besetting Egypt's nuclear programme are not economic or technological, but rather stem from efforts of outside parties to block acquisition of the required technology. It was a direct reference to the policy of the United States, which has declined to assist Egypt's nuclear programme with technology or financing.[26] Various circles in Egypt have recently adopted an 'activist' position on the nuclear issue: refusing to rest content with the reasons for the failure of the nuclear programme, they prefer to use them as a point of departure for future application. Dr Izat Abd al-Aziz, an Egyptian expert on nuclear energy, is convinced that the Arab states, Egypt above all, should acknowledge their backwardness in the nuclear field. In his view, Egypt and Libya have accumulated some limited nuclear know-how that could serve as basis for joint efforts in that area. Along with putting that knowledge to use, the Arab states should develop their own technology in this field. Such an aim can be attained by using the nuclear expertise and technology to be found in the former Soviet republics and the countries of the one-time Eastern bloc. That know-how is now on the market. So far, nothing is known of Egyptian approaches to former Eastern bloc countries for nuclear assistance. One country from which Egypt managed to receive assistance in this area was Argentina, where Egypt commissioned a 22-megawatt research reactor due for delivery in 1997.[27]

Summary

Egypt's arms industry was created out of economic and military motives, and for reasons of prestige. In economic terms, it was designated to attract the foreign investment and advanced technology required for the development of Egyptian industry. It can be stated that Egypt's munitions industry failed to achieve those objectives; indeed, it largely attained the opposite outcome. It attracted large numbers of Egyptian employees with suitable technical skills, but did not lead to large-scale expansion of local industry, which currently contributes no more than 20 per cent of the domestic product, i.e. less than the farming sector. Furthermore, the munitions industry has failed to meet military requirements, its products not being rated high quality. This finds expression in the fact that 20 per cent of Egypt's external debt stems from military expenditure.

The predicament of Egypt's munitions industry is reflected in the solutions the Egyptian authorities have sought since the early nineties: diverting production lines to the civilian sector, and ongoing efforts to locate fresh markets. Unless Egypt is embroiled in direct military confrontation with one of the states in the region, there will probably be no substantial change in the functioning of that industry in the short term. In other words, it may be expected to continue diversion of production lines to the civilian sector. In time, this trend could have detrimental effects for Egypt's civilian market, currently accustomed to an intake of products from the military industry. Any increased need to turn out military products will be at the expense of civilian production by the munitions plants. In any case – from political considerations above all – the Egyptian government is not expected to approve the sale or closure of these plants. It should be recalled that the arms industry is headed by former senior officers with close ties to the regime; they would interpret anything that impairs the standing of the munitions industry as a direct blow to their own personal and political status.

The future of Egypt's munitions industry is the subject of internal debate in that country's military circles. Notable in this respect is an article by Dr Nabil Ibrahim Ahmed, which points to the Israeli–Arab conflict as a significant consideration. Despite the peace treaty in force, Israeli–Arab rivalry is regarded as Egypt's prime challenge, particularly as Israel enjoys a military edge arising from its nuclear capability. Accordingly, the development of Egypt's arms industry should aim to achieve the following objectives:

1. Reducing Israel's lead over Egypt in the domain of military production.
2. Manufacture of weapons systems that could have a favourable effect on other industrial sectors.[28]

Dr Ahmed is trying to say that development of Egypt's military industry will cut the existing technological disparity between Israel and the Arab states overall, Egypt in particular.[29]

IRAQ

Up to the second Gulf war, Iraq's munitions industry occupied second place – in size and diversity of products – among the arms industries of the Arab states. In the late eighties, it had some 100,000 employees, similar to the number employed by its Egyptian counterpart. However, the true dimensions of Iraq's munitions industry, its capacity and planned expansion – particularly in relation to non-conventional weapons – only began to emerge after the end of the Gulf war, when Iraq was forced to open up its manufacturing and storage installations to UN representatives.

Iraq began fostering its munitions industry in the mid-seventies; but commencing in 1984, during its war with Iran, development was markedly accelerated. One of the principal factors inducing the Iraqis to divert more numerous resources to expansion of the local munitions industry was the resolve of the world's arms manufacturers, France principally, to suspend military aid to Iraq until it paid its debts. In the course of its eight-year war with Iran, Iraq imported arms and military equipment to the tune of over $30 billion; accordingly, Iraq had to find alternate sources of arms supplies. In spite of its debts and the economic difficulties incurred during the war and subsequently, Iraq managed to find the capital required for development of its munitions industry. To this end, it drew upon oil revenues, and credit extended by various banking sources (for details, see below).[30]

Since the mid-eighties, the Iraqi munitions industry has manufactured a variety of conventional weaponry and military equipment, including ammunition, light arms, artillery systems, surface-to-air missiles and various electronic components. It also produced a broad range of non-conventional weaponry, including biological and chemical weapons. In addition, its development plans for nuclear weapons reached an advanced stage.

The Gulf war was exceedingly harmful to the Iraqi economy overall, its munitions infrastructure in particular. The blow to the arms industry stemmed from the Security Council's April 1991 resolution banning delivery of anything associated with the design, development, manufacture or use of weapons, and imposing supervision on plans for production of biological weapons, chemical materials and ballistic missiles.[31]

The following survey principally describes the achievements of Iraq's munitions industry up to the Gulf war, drawing upon information brought to light in its wake.

Conventional weapons

Iraq's arms industry is under full state control and ownership. Munitions plants are subject to the Ministry of Industry and Military Industry – a merger of two bodies formerly operating separately: 'the Military Industrial Authority', founded in the latter seventies and responsible for the munitions plants; and 'the General Organization for Technical Industries', charged with promoting technological projects under the guidance of the industry ministry. The 'Commission for Development and Science', another body involved – up to the Gulf war – in promoting the munitions industry, was charged with the task of improving the equipment in service with Iraqi army units. Also linked with the munitions industry were civilian offices and special commercial procurement agencies operating abroad.[32]

Iraq's leaders hoped that the munitions industry's relatively high standards would influence civilian industry; in particular, they hoped to expand subsidiary civilian sectors such as steel and electronics. In fact, these industries did show some development in the late eighties. Thus, a $240 million deal concluded with Egypt in March 1989 provided for construction of two iron and steel works in Iraq.[33]

In the realm of conventional weaponry, Iraq's arms industry engaged in producing ammunition, and light and medium arms of various types (including cannon, mortars, shells etc.). Much of its efforts to this end hinged upon revamping ageing models of weapons and munitions in service with the Iraqi army, mainly of Soviet manufacture. Prominent in the conventional weaponry domain was the sector manufacturing the tactical ballistic missiles that Iraq employed in its war with Iran. The Iraqi plants engaged in perfecting Soviet Scud B missiles to produce the 'al-Hussein', 'al-Hijara' and 'Abas' types. The most advanced was the 800–900 km range 'Abas', but its use during the Gulf war against Israel proved that its probable margin of error is broad. Iraq also attempted, in association with Brazil, to develop a longer range missile named 'Walid'; but its completion appears to have been cut short by the Gulf war. Iraq was also involved in the project for an exceptionally long range 'super-cannon'.

Another important field that Iraq pursued was development and manufacture of armoured combat vehicles. In this context, we should mentioned the projects for local manufacture of the Soviet T-72 tank, and developing the T-55 and the BMP-1 armoured troop carrier, likewise of Soviet manufacture. In addition, Iraq engaged in developing various aerial bombs and naval mines. In electronics, Iraq's munitions industry manufactured various components for ground-units and the airforce: these components were in service in the fighting with Iran.

One sector less developed in Iraq – despite ambitious plans for its expansion – was the aircraft industry. In this sphere, Iraq adopted an approach resembling that of Egypt, commencing with partial local manufacture under licence in preparation for acquiring full manufacturing capability. Accordingly, Iraq focused its efforts upon improving imported aircraft, manufacture of RPV and pilotless planes. In 1990, Iraq concluded an agreement with France including a licence for partial production and assembly of 50-60 Alpha-Jet planes and a similar number of Mirage 2000. Simultaneously, Iraq negotiated with Egypt for aid in manufacture and assembly of Alpha-Jets and Gazelle helicopters. Iraq also acquired from Brazil a licence to manufacture its Tucano training plane.[34]

It should be stressed that Iraq's plans for arms design and manufacture in the eighties relied upon foreign countries and companies from the West, Egypt,[35] North Korea and Yugoslavia. During the same period, Iraq also employed a variety of ruses to bypass Western governments' restrictions on sales of equipment required for its munitions industry.[36] Western contributions, from private companies, were channelled mainly to the conventional field; but as would emerge subsequently, they also went to the non-conventional domain. Thus, companies from Germany, Switzerland and Italy assisted in construction of a steel complex north of Baghdad, which produced artillery barrels among other goods. British firms sold equipment to ammunitions factories, while the US Hewlett-Packard corporation sold computers, and control and measurement equipment designated for the military research centre near Mosul. These deals were pursued in compliance with the law; the companies involved not always being aware that the equipment was designated for military use.[37] Overall, Iraq pursued its activities in a sophisticated manner, taking care to purchase its requirements from the largest possible number of unconnected sources. In addition, it laid stress on purchase of individual items rather than entire systems.

In the acquisition of know-how and technology, Iraq developed an equally sophisticated technique, buying foreign high-tech companies with which it maintained ramified commercial ties. Thus, in the late eighties, it purchased over 90 per cent ownership of the British Matrix Churchill company, which was to contribute to Baghdad's efforts to develop nuclear weapons (see below).

Along with acquisition of equipment and technology, Iraq employed a sophisticated technique to solicit credits for development of its munitions industry. The system rested upon an international network of procurement and finances, conducted from Baghdad or by means of Iraqi-owned companies abroad. They drew upon credits issued by foreign banks, the most prominent being the Atlanta, Georgia branch of the Italian-owned Banca Nazionale del Lavoro. During 1988-89, the bank granted Iraq credits totalling some $3 billion.[38] Another source of credit for Iraq's expanding munitions industry was the Bank of Credit and Commerce International. This fact came to light when the bank collapsed in 1991.[39]

Non-conventional weapons

Iraq is the only Arab state known to have engaged simultaneously in the development of chemical, biological[40] and nuclear weapons.

Chemical weapons were manufactured in Iraq as far back as the sixties, ahead of the development of conventional weapon production. Up to the Gulf war, two principal Iraqi plants produced chemical weapons – the expansive plant at Samara, 100 km north-west of Baghdad, and a smaller unit at Faluja, 65 km to the west. These plants manufactured mustard gas;[41] later, in the eighties, they began turning out more advanced nerve gases – Sarin, VX and Tabun. Information available sets Iraq's overall annual production at over 1,100 tons, of which 250 tons are VX gas. The chemical agents were introduced into artillery shells, bombs and 'al-Hussein' missiles.[42] In April 1990, a few months ahead of the invasion of Kuwait, Iraq already test-fired a missile with a chemical warhead.[43]

Iraq has never formally admitted to possessing any biological weapon capability.[44] However, the data provided by the Iraqi general Hussein Kamel Hasan, who defected to Jordan in the summer of 1995, reveals that Iraq engaged in development and production of biological weapons in not inconsiderable amounts over the years. Among other components, Iraq appears to have cultivated a virus that causes anthrax. In addition, Iraqi scientists pursued research into forms of botulism which cause paralysis, and alfatoxin that affects the kidneys and liver.[45] Another biological weapon that Iraq possessed was the lung-damaging ricin; and enterovirus, causing blindness and haemorrhaging. It should be stressed that, in testimony to the Security Council in late 1995, the UN inspector on Iraqi arms, Rolf Ekeus, claimed to have no evidence that these weapons had been destroyed.[46]

Iraq invested extended effort into the development of nuclear weapons, commencing as far back as the seventies in disregard of international restrictions. In retrospect, conflicting assessments make it impossible to determine how close Iraq came to its ambition of developing nuclear arms.[47] These assessments range from a stress on the enormous disparity between plans and actual achievement,[48] to the view that the objective was close to attainment.[49]

After the Israeli airforce bombing of the reactor at Osiraq in 1981, Iraq began examining an ambitious and innovative nuclear weapons programme. To this end, its leaders considered five different technical approaches: gas diffusion; electro-magnetic isotope separation (EMIS); uranium enrichment by chemical means; uranium enrichment by laser beam; and employment of a gas centrifuge. Experiments with gas diffusion and chemical enrichment of uranium were abandoned as early as 1987. A year later, the Iraqi leadership adopted a decision to commence serial production of nuclear missiles as soon as 1991, using enriched uranium that Iraq had received legitimately from France for operation of the reactor that Israel destroyed. With the aim of implementing these aims, Iraq decided to concentrate upon two methods: EMIS and the gas centrifuges, while at the same time continuing to upgrade the 'al-Abas' missile to render it capable of bearing a nuclear warhead.

At the time of the Kuwait invasion in the summer of 1990, a large project to house the EMIS process was in advanced stages of construction. The technique gave disappointing results, and the amounts of enriched uranium were small and inadequate.

By contrast, the technique that achieved the highest level of development in Iraq during the eighties – with the help of scientists from Germany and Austria – used gas centrifuges. Research on gas centrifuges was conducted at Rashidiya, in Baghdad's northern suburbs. The initial Iraqi plan was to exploit civilian production as a cover for large-scale purchases of machinery required for development of nuclear weapons. In practice, it became necessary to settle for a more restricted purchase of machinery which, while not fully compatible with Iraq's nuclear plans, did lay the foundations for local production in the nuclear domain.[50] Western publications name Matrix Churchill – under Iraqi control since the eighties – as one of the companies involved in supplying components required for the construction of gas centrifuges[51] in the period from November 1988 to April 1990.

After delivery of the required machinery, Iraq constructed a centrifuge factory at al-Furat, 30 km south of Baghdad. The plant was partly completed at the time of the Gulf war. After the war, Iraqi attested that the factory was capable of manufacturing 200 centrifuges annually, but UN inspectors estimated production ten times higher, possibly reaching 5,000 a year. Self-evidently, such a number would have enabled Iraq to extract enriched uranium on a significant scale, allowing for construction of several nuclear devices each year. It should be noted that a shipment of additional components was seized in Jordan during the war, under the embargo imposed on Iraq.[52]

After the Gulf war

Iraq's munitions industry and the plans for its expansion suffered a setback in the wake of the Gulf war. The sanctions imposed following the war do not allow easy access to foreign sources for equipment, know-how and technology. Supplemented to this is the US blacklist specifying companies and individuals who had aided Iraq in weapons supplies and financing. All the same, there are currently breaches of the sanctions by Western European commercial firms, seizing on loopholes in the wording of the sanctions, and the indifference of their governments.[53] It was alleged recently that Iraq has renewed the operations of its secret network for purchase of components and equipment for weapons of mass destruction. In other words, West European commercial companies defy UN resolutions to supply Iraq with equipment and raw materials.[54]

The Gulf war's devastating impact on the national infrastructure induced Iraq to recruit its munitions works to aid in reconstruction. To this end, the plants turned out, *inter alia*, industrial machinery, farming equipment and pumps.[55] In addition, engineers from the Organization for Military Industry lent a hand in reconstruction projects, particularly in transportation (rebuilding bridges). Furthermore, there is testimony of arms factories diverting production lines to various products designated for the civilian sector, such as refrigerators.[56] During 1995, the Iraqi government's industrial office approached Jordanian businessmen to purchase arms works and convert them to civilian factories. The offer referred to a number of giant workshops and an ammunitions plant. However, the offer evoked no apparent response as potential buyers would not be permitted to remit their profits out of Iraq.[57]

If and when the embargo is removed, Iraq would be able in the future to reconstruct its capacity in the realm of light industry, particularly production of ammunition and spares, which does not call for advanced technology. In addition, it should be possible to reconstruct the electronic equipment sector, which functions in proximity with the civilian market. Third World countries and former Soviet republics possessing the required experience and technology would probably be willing to assist Iraq in these capacities.[58]

A CIA report dated 1994 points out that Iraq's technological infrastructure makes it possible, when the embargo is lifted, to embark upon independent manufacture of long-range missiles. The commander of US forces in the Persian Gulf, General Binford, estimated that, on removal of the embargo, Iraq would rearm with large quantities of weapons of mass destruction, and may also seek to complete the nuclear programme curtailed by the Gulf war.[59]

Should Iraq wish to re-establish its munitions industry after the embargo is lifted, it would appear to possess the required economic potential. Firstly, it should be recalled that the Iraqi population is among the most highly educated in the Arab states. Secondly, Iraq's oil reserves, estimated at 60 billion barrels, are the world's second-largest (after Saudi Arabia). Prior to the Kuwait invasion, Iraq produced 2.8 million barrels a day. Accordingly, its oil revenues, along with development of its agricultural sector and the country's natural wealth, offer a rosy economic future. Self-evidently, part of those resources could be channelled to restoration of the munitions industry, particularly completion of the nuclear programme, so as to serve Iraq's objective of achieving regional hegemony.

SYRIA

Syria's munitions industry is limited in size and types of product. In comparison with its counterparts in Egypt and Iraq, it is not advanced, notwithstanding past Syrian ambitions of striking a strategic balance with Israel. Syria's economic difficulties, and its lack of an advanced industrial base, forced its leaders to rely upon imports of relatively cheap weapons (from the Soviet Union up to the early nineties) along with a stress on developing surface-to-surface missiles and chemical weaponry.

Syrian industry is backward, employing low-level technology, contributing about 10 per cent of the national income, and generally focusing on production of consumer goods for the local market. Accordingly, the arms industry has made advances principally in producing ammunition for light arms, machine-guns and mortars. In the past, Syria manufactured self-propelled 122 mm howitzers (the Soviet D-30 cannon fitted in the T-34 tank).[60]

Syrian leaders stress local production of conventional and non-conventional weaponry capable of reinforcing its military clout in relation to its neighbours. This refers mainly to production of chemical weapons (which in the past Syria failed to acquire from the Soviet Union) and development of long-range missiles in collaboration with China and North Korea, and to a lesser degree, Iran. Syria relies mainly on these states, but resorts to the West in developing its own chemical weapons capability; at present, the country is unable to shake off its dependence on external suppliers and foreign aid.[61]

Non-conventional weapons

Chemical weapons

Significant development of Syria's chemical weapons industry commenced in the course of the eighties. Its achievements in this domain outstrip those of Egypt;[62] according to American experts, Syria has the Arab world's most advanced chemical weapons programme.[63] Syria's capacity for production of chemical weaponry is currently estimated at several tons a year. This development is relatively swift, considering that Syria possessed no weapons of this type in the early seventies.[64] Syria has three centres of chemical weapons production – in the Damascus region, near Homs and near Aleppo.

Syria took a significant step towards production of non-conventional weapons in the early seventies with construction of the 'Scientific Studies and Research Centre' (SSRC). Launched as a civilian scientific centre, in practice the Centre invested considerable effort into development of non-conventional weaponry. Towards the late seventies, the Syrian military command decided to embark upon local production of chemical weapons, because, among other reasons, Syria's then strategic partner, the Soviet Union, declined to supply them. Development of chemical weapons commenced in the SSRC chemical and biological department. Plans worked out at the Centre set the first stage objective as manufacture of aerial bombs containing Sarin gas. Efforts to manufacture the gas were shared by East Germany. Israeli sources located the plant manufacturing the gas near the north Syrian coastal town of Latakia.

In its efforts to achieve strategic parity, Syria attached importance to surface-to-surface missiles with chemical warheads, alongside the aerial bombs. In the mid-eighties, the Syrian army began stockpiling chemical warheads. At the same time, Syria embarked on production of cyanide, which was employed in putting down the Moslem Brotherhood uprising at al-Hama in 1982.

In the latter half of the eighties, Syria kept up its chemical buildup, spurred by Iraq's offensive chemical capability as illustrated in the war with Iran.[65] The setbacks Iraq inflicted on Iran with its use of aerial bombs containing Sarin made the Syrians draw conclusions, inspiring them to adapt VX-type chemicals – a nerve gas more powerful than Sarin – for installation in aerial bombs and surface-to-surface missiles. Here too Syria received assistance from East Germany. The Western press located the VX manufacturing plant at Homs.[66] According to a Russian report, Syria also manufactures mustard gas, employing local raw materials.[67]

Reports published in Germany in June 1996 related that Syria, with the assistance of German arms traders, was constructing a new chemical weapons plant near Aleppo. Satellite photographs in the possession of the United States and Germany show the plant to be identical with the factory under construction at Tarahouna, Libya, the resemblance being attributed to the involvement of German arms dealer Joachim Roz in their construction.[68] The aspiration to develop chemical weapons is expected to persist as long as Syria senses itself strategically inferior to Israel's nuclear might.

Biological weapons

American experts are convinced that Syria is developing biological weapons of the 'botulin' or 'ricin' type, as well as an agent of anthrax, even if there is no specific proof thereof.[69] Production is carried out at two centres, one of which is situated in Syria's coastal region. Most of the research and development of biological weapons is pursued at the 'SSRC' institute.

Development of ballistic capacity integrating chemical weapons

Syria's production of chemical weapons in recent years has gone hand-in-hand with the ambition to beef up its long-range missile capacity – an ambition reinforced when Syrian decision-makers completed a close study of the reactions of the Israeli population during the Gulf war.

Up to mid-1991, Syria had received delivery of 24 North Korean long-range Scud-C missiles. Beyond acquiring missiles, the two states agreed on construction of missile manufacturing plants in Syria;[70] components vital for their construction indeed reached Syria early in 1992. The subterranean plants are situated in areas close to Aleppo and Homs; there is no information on the volume of production. It is clear however that the Syrians intend the missiles to bear both conventional and chemical warheads. Their missile development is at an advanced stage, explaining the test firing of a Scud C missile in August 1996.

SAUDI ARABIA

Conventional weapons

The Saudi munitions industry, restricted in output relative to its counterparts in Egypt and Iraq, confines itself to specific fields of production (ammunition, light arms, etc.). The Saudi government plays a limited role in fostering its arms industry, sanctioning private sector involvement in joint projects with foreign companies, the latter being responsible for providing know-how and technology.

Sharing in the attempt to establish the 'Arab Organization for Industrialization' in 1975, Saudi Arabia pulled out in 1979. In the early eighties, Saudi Arabia embarked upon promoting its own independent arms industry, with the following aims: acquisition of the advanced technology associated therewith; diversification of income sources; and a reduced dependency upon foreign arms suppliers. However, prestige was a prominent factor in the wish to discharge – to a degree – the role Egypt had formerly played as leader of the Arab world. Financially, Saudi Arabia enjoyed a pronounced edge over Egypt at that time and could consequently afford large-scale investment in an arms industry, regardless of the country's traditional lack of an adequate industrial base and suitable manpower.

Under supervision by the 'General Establishment of Military Industries' (GEMI) founded in 1982, the Saudi plants manufacture ammunition and light arms. By the mid-eighties, they already contrived to supply 60 per cent of the Saudi army's needs in ammunition and light arms.[71] Factories employing more advanced technology were not fully state owned, generally being joint projects created with the assistance of foreign companies.[72]

Saudi Arabia's arms industry is largely concentrated at al-Harj, south-east of Riyadh. As already noted, the first factory set up there was an ammunition plant, expanding in time to what is now known as 'the al-Harj arsenal'. The Saudis have yet fully to implement plans to extend it to five factories, research and development centres, administrative buildings and everything required to house employees and their families. Correct to now, al-Harj manufactures principally light arms.[73] A new factory inaugurated at the al-Harj complex in May 1993 produces uniforms and equipment for the kingdom's military units and security forces.[74] At the formal inauguration, leading Saudis declared that part of its products would be exported to neighbouring Gulf states and other Arab countries.[75]

Saudi joint projects with foreign companies, including those in the arms industry, were part of the 'economic balance' programme,[76] a strategy worked out in the first half of the eighties. The Saudis acknowledged that expansion of the kingdom's industrial base would oblige them to rely on foreign companies possessing the necessary technology. Accordingly, the plan provides for cooperation resting on the principle that the foreign companies are committed to reinvesting – in industry, commerce or services – a certain percentage of the value of the project to which they are signatories. For its part, the Saudi government is committed to granting private entrepreneurs grants and easy credits, so as to coax them into taking part in setting up the projects.

The strategy was first applied in the 'Peace Shield' programme concluded with the United States in March 1985. The plan was subdivided into four projects with an overall value of $600 million. Worthy of mention among the prominent joint projects set up under this plan is the 'Centre for Modernizing of Aircraft'. Founded in Riyadh with Boeing Corporation assistance to the tune of $100 million, the Centre was intended to provide repair and maintenance services for planes and helicopters in civilian and military service. A further joint project is the works for overhauling and maintaining aircraft and helicopter engines. The works, likewise located in Riyadh, was built with the assistance of General Electric.

One prominent joint project is the 'Advanced Electronics Company' (AEC) which manufactures various types of electronic equipment for the military and civilian sectors. Amongst other products, AEC produces components for tactical communications systems and printed circuit boards (PCBs) for US-made 'Abrahams' tanks in service with the Saudi army.[77] This is a joint Saudi–British project, one of the partners from the British side is the Racal company.[78] Founded in 1988 with capital of $168 million,[79] AEC commenced production in 1991. The company factory, situated in Riyadh, employs 330 workers, of whom 195 are Saudi.[80] In recent years, the company has concluded a number of supply contracts for the equipment it produces. Thus, early in November 1994, it signed a $7 million deal with the US Northrop Grumman company for manufacture of air-combat systems for F-15 S combat planes, the project to extend over four years.[81] That same year AEC also signed a $6.5 million contract with the Hughes Corporation for manufacture of components for the APG 70 radar system designed for the F-15 S.[82] Among its products for the civilian market, the company makes components for telephone exchanges and PCBs.[83]

Over and above the joint projects, private Saudi companies engage in manufacturing goods and products for the military sector. These companies are generally small by comparison with the joint projects. In this context, we should mention the 'National Company for Vehicle Industries', some of whose shares are owned by the Mercedes company. The company sells its trucks to the Saudi army. Another example is the 'Abdullah al-Faris Co. Ltd for Heavy Industries' which engages, *inter alia*, in manufacture of armoured combat vehicles.[84]

The notion proposed in Yezid Sayigh's book, that the Gulf war stimulated expansion of the Saudi arms industry, is among various assessments not borne out. On the contrary: following the war, Saudi Arabia laid greater stress on import of military equipment (from the US especially) to the tune of billions of dollars annually. The kingdom's military expenditure grew to an estimated $13 billion out of an overall budget of some $40 billion in 1995. But the GEMI allocation did not increase, coming to just under $90 million that year.[85]

Judging by the state of the Saudi economy, no significant expansion of the kingdom's munitions industry is to be expected. The enormous outlay caused by the Gulf war, and the decline in income due to the drop in oil prices on the world market, induced the Saudi government to adopt a policy of restraint over the past two years. This policy found expression in the years 1994–95, when government expenditure was cut by 25 per cent. The Saudi government can hardly be expected to enlarge its investment in development of the arms industry, which requires extensive resources. Furthermore, the Saudi munitions industry has yet to prove that it rates expansion as a significant source of income; in 1994, the kingdom's income from sale of the military equipment it produced came to $130 million – less than 0.001 per cent of the national income overall.

Creation of a munitions industry has not given Saudi decision-makers the hoped-for results in reduced dependency upon external arms suppliers, nor in technology transfer nor diversification of the industrial base. The Saudi industrial base is underdeveloped. The industrial sector's contribution comes to less than 10 per cent of national income, while oil contributes some 35 per cent. Despite the Saudi authorities' recent efforts invested in stepping up employment of Saudis in the governmental and private sectors, the kingdom remains dependent upon foreign workers, currently estimated to number 6 million.[86] Self-evidently, it is difficult to base defence industries on workers who are not nationals. Overcoming the problem of manpower quality in industry calls for prolonged effort. Training technicians and engineers abroad will not provide an instant response to the need for manpower with practical experience.[87] In view of all this, it seems reasonable to assume that Saudi Arabia will continue to opt for importing arms rather than developing a local munitions industry, which will continue to function in its present format.

SUMMARY

The munitions industry in the Arab states is not advanced; this stems largely from the environment wherein it functions, i.e. an unsophisticated industrial sector.

Conditions in the Arab states after achievement of independence included an absence of democracy and political stability, with the Arab–Israeli conflict and inter-Arab disputes dictating diversion of significant resources to the armed forces. These were among the factors that limited the capital available for creation of an industrial sector capable of a significant contribution to the national economy.

The rise of the oil sector, in the Gulf states particularly, along with the soaring prices of 'the oil decade' (the seventies and early eighties) transformed these countries into consumer states with the stress on welfare. The oil states' income for the years 1973–82 totalled $1,112 billion,[88] an enormous revenue that was used to expand consumption, public and private. This state of affairs did not spur the countries under study to create a firm industrial base. On the contrary: with a marked preference for imported goods in the oil states, the sharp rise in per capita income served to undermine the standing of local industry. One reason for the failure of an advanced industry to emerge in those countries was the absence of inducements for its creation. No country maintained a supervised import policy to protect local industry.[89]

After the drastic drop in oil prices in the eighties, the Arab states, including the oil states, tried to foster industrialization, but their prime success was in petro-chemicals[90] and vehicle assembly.

The drop in oil prices also hit those Arab states that are not major oil exporters, due equally to cuts in the financial aid they received from the oil states, and the decline in the stream of remittances from their nationals temporarily employed in those states. These factors induced Arab states to recognize that they must grapple with development of an industrial base. It should be recalled that those Arab states not rich in oil possess the manpower required for rapid industrial expansion, even if they lack the required capital.

All in all, the sharp drop in oil prices prompted the Arab states to stress industrialization, but achievements in that sphere vary from country to country according to circumstance. Overall, it may be stated that the process did not achieve great success in the Arab world, particularly as industrial growth failed to keep up with the growth of the work force by creating sufficient jobs. The expansion of industrial activity does not reflect upon the quality of industry in the Arab states. Their industrial sector does not focus upon heavy or advanced industries available for exploitation for military production; rather, it concentrates on production of food, textiles and other light industrial products.

At a declarative level, the Arab states aspire to develop a munitions industry, both national and pan-Arab, stressing the importance of local manufacture that precludes dependency upon external suppliers. Although the arms industries are of long standing in the Arab states, their achievements over the years have been limited. The prospects of pan-Arab cooperation likewise appear dim, in view of past experience and the less-than-cordial relations between different portions of the Arab world. It should be stressed that prestige was a prime motive of the Arab states in founding and developing an independent arms industry. In view of the economic difficulties the Arab states are experiencing nowadays, this is no longer the decisive factor in governmental considerations.

Arab governments' freedom to allot major resources to military production – which requires capital on a large scale – is hamstrung by the economic travails besetting the Arab world, and pressure for economic reform from international bodies such as the IMF and the World Bank. The reforms generally include structural changes in the economy, with the aim of limiting the public sector's functions therein. With the arms industry virtually dominated in most countries by the governmental sector, governments are accordingly unable to bear the burden of expansion. Faced with the urgent necessity of meeting its economic difficulties, even Iran has adopted an extraordinary step: opening up free trade zones with the aim of attracting foreign investments, including Western companies.

In view of the condition of the region's munitions industries, one can comprehend the emerging trend of recent years in countries like Egypt and Iraq, which are diverting some production lines in their arms factories to the civilian market. With that, not a single Arab state has included its munitions sector in its process of economic reform. Acting on national security and political considerations, the Egyptian government adopted a resolution of principle to exclude the munitions industry from the process of privatization it has pursued in recent years.

To a degree, the governments find themselves in a somewhat delicate predicament. On the one hand, development of a munitions industry did not accomplish a significant expansion of the industrial sector, or reduction in military expenditure. On the other hand, albeit that some plants operate below capacity and are unprofitable, governments prefer to avoid eroding their status lest it be construed as an affront to the military establishment and its leaders. At a declarative level, Arab policy-makers are particular to stress the importance of the munitions industry and the necessity of its expansion. In practice however, there is a great disparity between declarations and their practical implementation.

The munitions industry has also failed in one of its major objectives – introduction of advanced technology. Significant development of the arms industry thus depends upon the willingness of outside parties to convey such technology to the countries of the region. Since the early nineties, the following states can be singled out as the principal assistants in developing the region's munitions industry: Germany,[91] India, North Korea and China. Their assistance reaches the private and government sectors. The aid is variegated and includes joint projects of production and development; in this category, China and North Korea stand out for delivering the input vital for a munitions industry.

The Gulf war and the character of the fighting accompanying it also affected regional policy-makers' views on the munitions industry. Rather than invest large sums of money in expanding and diversifying their arms industry, the countries of the region understood that it makes more economic and military sense to focus on those branches and products capable of enhancing their strategic clout. This explains the great efforts invested in recent years by Syria and Egypt (formerly, by Iraq also) in developing their non-conventional weapon capability, and their stress on long-range surface-to-surface missiles, biological and chemical weapons, and nuclear weapons.

ACKNOWLEDGEMENTS

I take pleasure in thanking a number of persons who aided me in preparing this chapter. First and foremost, I wish to thank Mr Doron Peskin of Bar Ilan University, who laboured tirelessly and with great resourcefulness to help me in all stages of my work. My thanks also to Mrs Ruthy Rosenthal, and Professor Efraim Inbar, director of the Begin–Sadat Center for Strategic Studies.

NOTES

1. Alan Richards and John Waterbury, A Political Economy of the Middle East (Boulder: Westview Press, 1990), p. 73.
2. Yezid Sayigh, Arab Military Industry (London: Brassey's, 1992), p. 45.
3. Ibid., pp. 57–8; Ha'aretz (11 September, 1995).
4. Yezid Sayigh, pp. 46–53; Gil Feiler, 'Economic Relations Between Egypt and the Oil States of the Arabian Peninsula', Doctoral Dissertation (Tel Aviv, May 1989), pp. 129–35.
5. Yezid Sayigh, pp. 54–5, 58, 99
6. MENA news agency, Cairo (22 October 1995).
7. Ruz al`Yusuf (28 November 1994).
8. Cooperation between Egypt and North Korea in developing surface-to-surface missiles was no novelty; such cooperation goes back as far as the mid-seventies. The two countries engaged jointly in extending the

range of the Scud missile.
9. *Ha'aretz* (23 June 1996), pp. 1–2.
10. Yezid Sayigh, p. 57
11. *Al-Difa* (1 May 1995).
12. *Al-Itihad* [UAE] (6 April 1991).
13. Yezid Sayigh, p. 98; see also Nabil Ahmed Ibrahim, 'The Arms Industry in Egypt and the Challenges of the Nineties' (title translated from Arabic), *Al-Siyasah al-Dawliyah* 100 (April 1990), pp. 165–6.
14. David C. Isby, 'Continuity and Change in the Egyptian Defence Industry', *Jane's Intelligence Review Yearbook 1994/1995*, p. 68.
15. IPR Strategic Business Information Data Bases.
16. David Isby [14].
17. Ibid.
18. Yezid Sayigh, pp. 54, 58
19. A number of factories in Egypt currently engage in vehicle production and assembly. Their productive capacity is 100,000 vehicles annually; however, actual production in 1995 did not exceed 30,000.
20. *Al-Hayat* [London] (6 August 1995); *Ha'aretz* (11 September 1995).
21. *Al-Itihad* [UAE] (21 May 1996).
22 Yezid Sayigh, p. 120.
23. See: Dani Shoam, *Chemical and Biological Weapons in Egypt and Syria* BESA Mideast Security Studies 31 (Ramat Gan: Begin–Sadat Center for Strategic Studies, 1995).
24. *Al-Ahrar* [Egypt] (23 May 1995).
25. Hassan Tahsin, *Saudi Gazette* (30 May 1995).
26. Khalid Muhammad Ghazi, 'The Balance of Power with Israel, Why Do the Arabs not Possess Nuclear Arms?' (translation from Arabic), *al-Watan* [Qatar] (21 June 1996), p. 10.
27. Hassan Tahsin, *Saudi Gazette* (30 May 1995).
28. Dr Nabil Ibrahim, 'The Arms Industries in Egypt and the Challenges of the 1990s' (title translated from Arabic), *Al-Siyasah al-Dawliyah*, 10 (April 1990), p.160 [Arabic].
29. Ibid., pp. 162–3.
30. Yezid Sayigh, pp. 103–5.
31. Ibid., pp. 103, 130.
32. Ibid., pp. 106–8.
33. Ibid., pp. 128–9.
34. Ibid., pp. 108–19, 128.
35. During the 1980s, Iraq, Egypt and Argentina collaborated in developing the 1000 km range Condor-2 missile. Egypt ultimately dropped out in 1989 due to financial difficulties.
36. Yezid Sayigh, pp. 121–4.
37. Alan George, 'Saddam's Supply Routes', *The Middle East* (April 1991), pp. 20–22.
38. Ibid.
39. Yezid Sayigh, p. 122.
40. Reliable information on Iraq's development of biological weapons only became available after the defection of Gen. Husein Kamal Hassan to Jordan in the summer of 1995.
41. In the course of the eighties, production of mustard gas was stepped up by

means of a shipment from Germany at an estimated value of $8 million.
42. Yezid Sayigh, p. 120.
43. Reuven Pedatzur, 'Saddam "Whistles" at the World', Ha'aretz (8 April 1996).
44. Yezid Sayigh, p. 121.
45. The Independent (12 October 1995).
46. Ibid.
47. Yezid Sayigh, p. 121.
48. David Albright and Robert Kelley, 'Massive Program, Meagre Results', The Bulletin of the Atomic Scientists (November/December 1995), p. 56.
49. Reuven Pedatzur, 'Saddam's Bomb', Ha'aretz (12 May 1996).
50. David Albright and Robert Kelley, pp. 56–60.
51. Ha'aretz (14 December 1996).
52. David Albright and Robert Kelley, pp. 56–60.
53. Reuven Pedatzur, 'Saddam "Whistles" at the World', Ha'aretz (8 April 1996).
54. Ibid.
55. According to the Iraqi Military Industrial Organization, a lathe by the name of 'Jihad 1' was developed to serve in the manufacture of tractor engines. The lathes were designated for the 'General Institute for Mechanical Industries'.
56. Iraqi News Agency (26 September 1995).
57. Ha'aretz (29 June 1995).
58. Yezid Sayigh, p. 130.
59. Reuven Pedatzur [53].
60. The artillery pieces were produced at army workshops, not at arms industry factories.
61. Dani Shoam [23].
62. Ibid.
63. This was reported at a US House of Representatives hearing held in July 1996 on Syria's support of terrorism.
64. According to Shoham, Syria first received chemical weapons from Egypt prior to the 1973 war, in two phases. The first phase included small quantities for research purposes; the second – chemical weapons for operational purposes, including Sarin (nerve) gas and mustard gas.
65. Dani Shoam [23].
66. The New York Times (3 May 1992).
67 Dani Shoam [23].
68. Ha'aretz (5 June 1996).
69. Jane's report as quoted in Ha'aretz (12 August 1996).
70. International Defence News Vol. 1 (1994), p. 21.
71. Okaz [Saudi Arabia] (30 September 1986).
72. Yezid Sayigh, p. 137.
73. According to existing information, Saudi Arabia has not hitherto been involved in production of non-conventional weapons, despite one sole testimony, of uncertain credibility, as to Saudi intentions of acquiring nuclear arms. A Saudi diplomat who defected to the West reported that the kingdom had set up its first office of nuclear research in 1975, in the Suleil area near al-Harj. According to him, the Saudi authorities sent out secret feelers to Iraq on the matter in the mid-eighties, but the invasion of Kuwait

ultimately precluded any possibility of nuclear collaboration between the two countries.

74. Shares in the company were held by 'The General Establishment of Military Industries', 'The National Industrial Company', 'The Saudi Company for Advanced Industries' and the Gulf Investment Corporation.
75. Saudi News Agency (31 May 1996).
76. Yezid Sayigh, p. 138.
77. Al-Wasat [London] (24 August 1992); Al-Iqtisadiyah [Saudi Arabia–London] (31 January 1996); Defence News (19 March 1995).
78. Yezid Sayigh, p. 138.
79. Al-Hayat (10 March 1996).
80. Al-Iqtisad wal-`Aamal [Lebanon] (April 1996).
81. Al-Iqtisadiyah (2 November 1994).
82. Al-Hayat al-Iqtisadiyah [London] (11 October 1994); Al-Iqtisadiyah (31 January 1996); Aviation Week and Space Technology (31 October 1994).
83. AEC signed a $252 million contract for manufacture of printed circuits for AT&T, which is responsible for the mammoth task of expanding the Saudi Arabian telephone network.
84. Yezid Sayigh, p. 138.
85. Saudi News Agency (31 May 1996).
86. See Al-Wasat [London] (18 December 1995).
87. Yezid Sayigh, pp. 139–42.
88. Gil Feiler, 'Arab Labour Mobility in the Middle East in a Period of Economic Recession, 1982–1987', Middle East Contemporary Survey 11 (1987), p. 299.
89. Gad Gilbar, 'A Decade of Oil in the Middle East', in Yaakov Goldberg and Yoseph Kostiner (eds), A Decade of Reduction: The Middle East In the Shadow of a Receding Oil Industry [title translated from Hebrew] (Tel Aviv: Skirot, 1987), p. 6.
90. The petro-chemical industry emerged back in the seventies, but it too is export-inclined, just like oil.
91. On 23 April 1996, the German government approved a law permitting German companies to collaborate in arms production abroad even if the identity of the final user is unclear. According to the resolution, such permission does not include manufacture of arms for Middle Eastern countries.

9

The Rise and Fall of Arms Industries in Argentina and Brazil

ETEL SOLINGEN

INTRODUCTION

This chapter examines the most important sources leading to the development of a weapons industry in Argentina and Brazil. International market and political conditions, domestic economic and political determinants, and regional contextual factors explain the evolution and makeup of the military industrial complex in these countries. I examine all three sources in the following section, and provide a summary profile of the arms sector in each country. Developments in the 1980s and early 1990s along domestic, regional, and international dimensions have resulted in the near-collapse of the arms sector in Argentina and Brazil. I explore this dramatic contraction and its potential implications in the third section. The conclusions look at some of the ramifications of the rise and fall of Argentine and Brazilian arms industries for the Middle East.

THE RISE – THE SOURCES OF ARMS INDUSTRIES IN ARGENTINA AND BRAZIL

International Market and Regimes: Permissive Conditions

The initial impetus for the development of arms industries in Argentina and Brazil goes back to the 1930s and 1940s, when the armed forces took incipient steps to create an indigenous capability in weapons production. However, it was not until the 1970s and early 1980s that Brazil's aircraft and arms industries were consolidated and their export capacity became more significant. Declining global arms markets in the early 1980s strengthened this export capacity, in a technical sense. Opportunities to strengthen political and economic relations with developing countries, fierce competition among producers, and national prestige considerations fuelled an aggressive arms trade and lowered the resistance of traditional suppliers to diffusing technological and productive capabilities to such second-tier producers as Argentina and Brazil. In other words, changing patterns in arms trade helped shape a new international division of labour, expanding access to arms and technology markets for a group of such emerging third world arms producers as Argentina and Brazil.[1] These conditions increased the ability of recipients to maximize indigenization in weapons production through assertive bargaining. The effective growth of Brazil's arms exports began in 1976 and lasted until the early 1980s, while Argentina's production, hitherto negligible, despite an initial effort in the 1950s, surged slightly in the late 1970s. Middle Eastern countries' demand for weapons during that period made them a major target of Brazil and Argentina's arms industries.

International financial conditions at the time were beneficial to the development of arms industries in these countries. On the one hand, the 1973 oil shock and its aftermath increased constraints on domestic financing in oil importers such as Brazil, which now required efforts to expand exports. On the other, it also provided Middle Eastern and other oil producers with windfall petrodollars capable of funding the modernization of their armed forces, expanding the pre-1970s third world arms market. Euromarkets flooded with recycled petrodollars were now a source of loans and suppliers' credits to finance domestic arms production and purchase of technology for such countries as Argentina and Brazil.

Finally, international regimes related to arms transfers were fairly inactive during that period, imposing few constraints on arms exporters. Thus, international political, strategic, commercial, and financial conditions point to an overall permissive environment for the development of arms production among emerging suppliers during the 1970s.

Domestic Determinants: Import-Substitution Industrialization, Statism, Military Rule, and an Independent Foreign Policy

An ideology of 'national security' has prevailed in Argentina and Brazil since the 1960s, when the military ruled more often than not and military budgets and ancillary activities became privileged.[2] The historical origins of the ideology run yet deeper. Import-substitution as the overarching industrialization strategy was the name of the game. State entrepreneurship was at the heart of this strategy. Its expression in the military sector was the seeking of as much military independence from suppliers as was possible. Arms embargoes begot even stronger import-substitution efforts (in the case of Brazil, as a reaction against US President Carter's human rights prerequisites for arms sales). Domestic arms production and exports were regarded as an important means to 'great power' roles, '*grandeza*', 'equidistance' from the superpowers, and non-alignment. In the words of a former Brazilian officer (the director of Brazilian War Material Enterprise-IMBEL): 'We will sell to the left, to the right, to the centre, up above and down below.'[3] The ideology of national security permeated the foreign affairs bureaucracy as much as it did the military institution itself. Arms exports held the promise of increased international leverage *vis-à-vis* suppliers of raw materials, oil, and technology.[4]

The Regional Setting: Rhetorical Closeness, Distant Neighbours

Brazil and Argentina never went to war, but relations between the two giants in the Southern Cone have never been very close. Despite the classic rhetoric of pan-American solidarity (mostly directed against the United States), a tacit historical competition between the two countries occasionally developed into a more open exchange of expressions of mutual distrust. Military institutions helped exacerbate the relatively cold bilateral relations. No genuine cooperative economic schemes ever took hold until quite recently, as we shall see below. The relationship was best characterized as lukewarm, with neither militarized conflict nor effective cooperation. It is important to remember that the Argentine–Brazilian rivalry has largely been overplayed, and that it never reached more than a measured competition. Argentine–Chilean military rivalry was more pronounced, leading both countries to the verge of war over the Beagle Channel. However, in the grand scheme of factors affecting weapons production in the Southern Cone, regional considerations played a rather marginal role in the evolution of the arms industries.

Brazil: A Profile

Under the international, regional, and domestic conditions just described, Brazil developed an arms and aircraft industry characterized by an effective partnership between the state and private sector.[5] The industry succeeded in achieving impressive rates of indigenization, allowing Brazil to leap into being one of the world's largest exporters of conventional arms in the mid-1980s. Concrete strategies in Brazil's arms industry involved a policy of 'market reserve', state financing, and technological support to private firms through the Centro Técnico Aerospacial (Aerospace Technical Centre; CTA) and the army's Technical Centre (CTEX, created in 1979, emulating the air force's CTA). The state reduced entrepreneurial 'strategic' and market uncertainty through its procurement of guaranteed shares, often at higher prices than their market value. It financed private R&D, built part of the infrastructural requirements, trained engineers, mediated between foreign technology suppliers and national firms, and transferred new technologies to private firms.

The air force concentrated in missile development, airplanes, and guided systems, the army in armoured vehicles and artillery; and the navy in electronic systems, communications, and computers.[6] In the late 1970s the Ministry of the Navy initiated activities in shipbuilding and nuclear-related technologies, including a nuclear submarine. IMBEL was established in 1975 under army sponsorship, as a state-owned holding of seven major producers (and 55 private companies), administering army arsenals and factories. The anti-statist movement of the latter part of the 1970s, and an extant private infrastructure in automobile manufacturing, acted as an effective barrier against state expansion in this area. By the early 1980s, IMBEL had a semi-privatized cooperative structure, and was granted tax exemption for most of its imports.

The three major enterprises accounting for most Brazilian arms exports at the time were Embraer, Engesa, and Avibrás.[7] The Air Force developed the state-owned firm Embraer in 1969 as the national champion of the aircraft industry, out of the CTA, the locus of technological research in aircraft design and production. The Ministry of Aeronautics manipulated Brazil's domestic market for civilian and military aviation to Embraer's advantage, through providing it procurement power, R&D support, and protective tariffs. The Ministry not only had effective control over Embraer itself, but increasingly concentrated – throughout the 1970s – R&D, training, financial, fiscal, marketing, regulatory, and international bargaining (for technology) related to the sector. By the late 1970s, the Ministry managed to camouflage Embraer as a mixed enterprise, as a result of a tax incentive scheme – a deduction of 1 per cent in corporate income tax to purchase Embraer's shares – that provided the firm with low-cost, long-term, intervention-free capital. Embraer was thus considered a mixed enterprise; state-controlled, 90 per cent privately-owned, with 246,937 shareholders.

Embraer began producing a variety of planes (air frames, parts, and navigation equipment), and licensed aircraft technology abroad (Tucano to Egypt and the United Kingdom). By the early 1980s Embraer was the sixth largest aviation company in the world (outside the United States), producing the Xavante jet trainer and ground-attack (Italian licence); the AMX fighter-bomber (a joint venture with Aermacchi and Aeritalia, 80 per cent Italian), sold to Brazil and Italy's air forces; the trainer 'Tucano' (sold to Libya, Egypt, and Iraq, among others, and produced in Egypt by the Arab Organization for Industrialization, with Brazilian technology); the civilian

Bandeirante (Pratt & Whitney engines) (over 500 Bandeirantes sold to 34 countries); Brasilias (hundreds sold); three medium-sized general purpose aircraft (Xingu, Tapajó, Araguaia); and Ipanema (agriculture). Some models were the product of skilfully negotiated industrial cooperation agreements with a foreign supplier, designed to achieve rapid market penetration without excessive technological dependence.[8] Preferred modes of technology transfer included co-production arrangements (with the Italian Aermacchi for the Xavante jet-trainer and with Aermacchi and Aeritalia for the AMX fighter) and licensing (from Piper for different light aircraft). The Tucano trainer and the Bandeirante are of national design, but more than 50 per cent of the value of a Bandeirante was imported from the United States and Canada.[9] Efforts at nationalization of inputs resulted in the diffusion of technological capabilities to 300 suppliers.[10]

The Ministry of Aeronautics, but more so the army, nurtured the private firm Avibrás in missile technology, turning Brazil into a designer of ground-ground missiles, including guidance systems. Founded in 1961, Avibrás was a pioneer aerospace company which produced the first Brazilian composite propellants in the 1960s. It developed the Sonda I, II-B and II-C rockets, worked on the second stage of Sonda III and the first prototype of Sonda IV, and converted the Sonda series of sounding rockets into artillery rockets for exports.[11] The Astros II rocket-launching system became its most successful product by 1983. Avibrás' annual production grew from $6 million in 1978 to $391 million in 1987, and its work force expanded from 250 to more than 6,000. Orbita was created in 1987 as a joint venture among private firms (including Engesa) and Embraer, although it never materialized from the planning stages. It was designed originally to consolidate missile-development activities: to convert the Sonda IV space rocket into a missile with the help of extensive technical assistance from West German and French firms, and to develop the Leo anti-tank missile and the Piranha air-to-air missile, which never entered the production stage.[12] By the latter half of the 1980s Brazil was estimated (perhaps exaggeratedly) to have developed a potential nuclear delivery arsenal, including ground-based SS-300 missiles (which never materialized) and Barracuda sea-launched missiles for tactical warheads.[13] Brazil's Satellite Launch Vehicle (SLV), capable of launching a 440-pound payload into a 435-mile orbit, was scheduled to be ready by early 1996, but this was postponed. In 1993, some 200 Brazilian companies (including Avibrás and Embraer) joined in the Aerospace Industries Association of Brazil, in order to promote exports.

Another private firm, Engesa, became a major producer of armoured vehicles, with more than 90 per cent of its production oriented towards exports. In the early 1970s Engesa was still a small firm with little in-house research activity; by the end of the decade it had become the world's largest producer of such vehicles – including the Urutu, Cascavel, and Jararaca – exporting to more than twenty countries. Engesa relied on domestically developed technology (approximately 17 per cent of its sales were invested in R&D: $1 million in 1980), or on carefully selected and negotiated co-production agreements with several suppliers. Most engines were from Mercedes Benz do Brasil. Engesa's armoured vehicles were sold to Libya, the People's Republic of China, Iraq, Iran, Nigeria, and Sudan, among others. The planned Osorio tank never went beyond a 1985 prototype (one of which went to Saudi Arabia).

In sum, the sector reflected a cooperative structure among state (particularly military), private-sector, and research institutions. It succeeded in achieving relatively high levels of national design and indigenization of components and in using add-up engineering, integrating imported components into a new system.[14] In excess of 90 per cent of its production, including armoured vehicles, aircraft, sophisticated rocket systems, and missiles, was exported to more than 50 countries (15 per cent of it to the United States). Buyers included Australia, France, the United Kingdom, the United States, Canada, New Zealand, Australia, France, Iraq, Jordan, Kuwait, Saudi Arabia, Gabon, Cameroon, South Korea, Uruguay, Chile, Bolivia, Paraguay, Mexico, Venezuela, Peru, Nigeria, Togo, Sudan, and Mauritania. Some fifty core firms employed roughly 50,000 workers.[15] Brazil's exports in this area are said to have comprised close to 40 per cent of all third-world arms exports by the late 1980s. Between

1980 and 1983 Brazil accounted for 94.4 per cent of the combined arms exports of Brazil, Chile, Argentina, and Uruguay.[16] Between 1976 and 1982 these exports amounted to $530 million (in constant 1975 prices).[17] By 1984 Brazilian sources estimated exports to be in excess of $1 billion, although experts concur on the general overestimation of the value of military exports for political purposes.[18]

According to some sources, military exports accounted for 25 per cent of Brazil's trade surplus of $8 billion in 1983. Arms Control and Disarmament Agency (ACDA) data suggests that exports peaked in 1982 at $749 million. By 1986 military exports were estimated to account for more than half of all Brazilian manufacturing exports, although SIPRI reports on exports of major weapon systems in 1987 for only $491 million. Some assessments aver that the $10 billion military-industrial complex constituted about 5 per cent of Brazil's GNP during those years.

During its growth phase, Brazil's arms industry developed extensive connections with Middle East clients.[19] Brazil's military exports to Algeria, Libya, Egypt, Morocco, Qatar, Saudi Arabia, Tunisia, and the United Arab Emirates had turned this area into its major extra-regional market, followed by Africa (Gabon, Nigeria, Upper Volta, and Zimbabwe). Brazil's heavy oil dependency had lubricated these connections, leading to barter and counter-trade agreements exchanging oil for weapons. Engesa's international debut was in armoured vehicle shipments to Iraq in 1977. Between 1979 and 1982 Engesa delivered to Iraq almost 800 Cascavels, in addition to more than 300 Jararaca and 300 Sucuri, turning Iraq into the recipient of a third of all Brazilian arms exports.[20] A package of tanks, missiles, and aircraft equipment ($1 billion) with Saudi Arabia followed in the mid-1980s. Embraer licensed the Tucano for production in Egypt (110 units) in 1983, with resales to Iraq. Over 90 per cent of Avibrás' exports went to the Middle East, principally Iraq and Libya (also Saudi Arabia), including the rocket system Astros II (range 40–70 km)[21] Libya ordered nearly $1 billion worth of rocket system Astros II. By 1989 Brazilians were assisting Iraq in rocket aerodynamics, flight testing, the control of rocket trajectories, on-board electronics, and rocket propellants.[22] Brazil revealed in

1990 that, since 1980, it had provided Iraq with enriched uranium and with assistance in uranium enrichment, with the prospecting of uranium ore, and with a facility for converting yellowcake into uranium oxide.[23] In 1993, UNSCOM inspection teams in Iraq were studying samples of nuclear material believed to be of Brazilian origin.[24] Brazil was also suspected of providing Iraq with designs for centrifuges and even with an actual centrifuge.

Brazil's relative success in arms production and exports, even if far less impressive than estimates at the time implied, could be traced not only to an effective reading of market signals, but also to the suitability of its planes for third-world conditions (due to size, price, low operating costs in short commuting routes, and low maintenance requirements); the versatility of its armoured vehicles; simplicity in design (again, low maintenance requirements); adaptability to poor climate and terrain; and reliability. Finally, as a third-world supplier during the Cold War era, Brazil's no-strings-attached partnership was particularly appealing.

Argentina: A Profile

Argentina's arms industry was traditionally owned and controlled by the state. By 1945 the military conglomerate National Directory of Military Industries (DGFM) controlled fourteen state enterprises (including the first pig iron factory, Altos Hornos de Zapla) and 20,000 employees. Efforts to develop arms industries (including aircraft) started in earnest in the early 1950s, when Argentina ranked first among third-world producers. A de facto tripartite division of the state among the three armed forces since 1955 placed the DGFM under the control of the army.[25] Some 80 per cent of DGFM's output in the 1960s was for civilian use by major army-controlled enterprises (YPF, Gas del Estado, Ferrocarriles Argentinos) and private industry. The expansion of DGFM reflected the dominance of a statist orientation in the army, which became the dominant political force from 1963 on. Statism inhibited private entrepreneurship in the arms sector.[26]

The military de-emphasized indigenous arms production after the downfall of Peron and until 1976, when investment in state arsenals surged. The best-known export output at the time was the TAM (Medium Argentine Tank), commissioned for design by the West German firm Thyssen-Henschel in 1973. Among recipients of TAM were Iran (about 100), Peru, Panama, and Jordan. Efforts at reducing dependence on foreign technology and licensing in the military complex run by the army were negligible. This is particularly striking if one compares the relative shares of R&D funds from the central budget allocated to the three forces, with their technical achievements. The navy's export share of total R&D investments in 1978 was 0.2 per cent; the air force's export share, 1.72 per cent, and the army's, 18 per cent.[27] There was no shortage of army R&D agencies, which included twelve institutes under the supervision of the Council for the Armed Forces for R&D.[28]

The state-run aircraft industry created in 1927 became the National Mechanical and Metallurgical Industries (IAME) in 1952. In 1957 it became the National Bureau of Aeronautical Manufacturing and Research (DINFIA), and since 1968 it has been known as the Military Aircraft Industry (FMA). Formally the air force's province, it was effectively under the control of the army's DGFM. The recurrent reorganizations reflect attempts at strengthening the sector and stand in sharp contrast with the remarkable continuity of the navy's Atomic Energy Commission. FMA was far less dynamic than its Brazilian counterpart. It relied heavily on foreign licenses after a period of intense design activity by former German Luftwaffe engineers in the 1940s and early 1950s. Although considered an indigenous design, the Pucara was inspired by a US model and was highly dependent on imported parts. Limited numbers of Pucara were sold to Uruguay, Iraq, the Central African Republic, Venezuela, Morocco, and El Salvador.

The Armed Forces Technical Research Centre (CITEFA) started working on missiles in the early 1970s. With mostly German technical assistance (MBB) and Egyptian and Iraqi funding, it was engaged after 1982 in the development of a medium-range (600 miles) surface-to-surface ballistic missile

(Condor II), with a payload of 1,000 pounds.[29] Developed by the air force at Falda del Carmen, the Condor II project was estimated to have absorbed $300 million.[30] Iraq and Egypt were to acquire 200 Condor II each (labelled the Badr 2000 in Egypt and the Saad 16 in Iraq). The Argentine government admitted delivering eight Condor II prototypes to Egypt in 1991.[31] Argentina also produces an unguided multiple launch (200 km) rocket, the Alacran, capable of delivering a 100 kg payload, far below the MTCR (Missile Technology Control Regime) threshold.

The navy controlled the nuclear sector and the National Atomic Energy Commission's ambitious nuclear programme. The navy's liberal orientation followed the British and American models and was evident in its emphasis on 'state subsidiarity', to which the nuclear programme gave effective meaning by developing private firms in heavy components and other inputs for nuclear plants and fuel processing facilities. The structure, sources, and a more detailed account of the export performance of the nuclear sector in Brazil and Argentina are discussed elsewhere.[32]

As with Brazil, Argentina's arms industry also aimed at the Middle East, seeing it as a most promising market. There is the almost comic case of two Argentine provinces competing for sales, with Cordoba's independent foreign policy pushing for Pucara plane sales to Iraq, and Entre Ríos opposing the sale, to protect its rice and tea exports to Iran (worth $500 million). Among other transactions in the 1980s, when nuclear exports were part of the nationalist diplomatic kit, Argentina supplied nuclear materials and services to Middle East countries. This included assistance in completing the two Iranian reactors at Bushehr and exporting large amounts of uranium dioxide to Algeria.[33]

Argentina arms exports amounted to $217 million between 1976 and 1982. By 1985 Argentina's revenues from arms exports were as high as those from meat exports. All in all, Argentina's arms industry historically was shackled by a statist orientation, and for the most part it was unable to translate copious investments into technologically and commercially significant capabilities.

THE FALL – THE DOMESTIC, REGIONAL AND GLOBAL LOGIC OF ECONOMIC LIBERALIZATION

International Constraints: The 1980s and Beyond

The end of the Iran-Iraq war in 1988 also ended a primary market for Brazil's arms industry. By the end of the 1980s the international arms market became saturated – with declining demand – a situation made even worse by the end of the Cold War and the ability of traditional suppliers to adjust to the requirements of third world clients. In 1990 Saudi Arabia was ordering Abrams tanks, not Brazilian Osorios, despite Engesa's effort to get a $2.2 billion deal by calling the tank the al-Fahd tank. International financing for arms industries had dried up. Iraq stopped paying Engesa's bills in the late 1980s, contributing to Engesa's financial collapse in 1990. Avibrás' sales dropped from $350 million in 1987 to $10 million in 1989, leading to its bankruptcy in 1990. Even Embraer, which could still rely on civilian exports, became heavily indebted by the early 1990s, forcing it to cut its projects and labour force dramatically.

Thus, the brief success of Argentine and Brazilian arms exports ended with a 'double whammy': the sharp contraction of international demand on the one hand and the heightened levels of supply on the other.[34] In addition, the emergence of international regimes aimed at controlling international arms transfers and sales, such as the Missile Technology Control Regime (MTCR) placed additional political and technological constraints on the relative freedom of operation which Argentina and Brazil had enjoyed in the preceding decades. For example, Argentina's Condor II and Brazil's VLS programme had come under heavy MTCR pressures. The Condor II project with Egypt and Iraq was Argentina's best known military cooperation project in the Middle East. Condor II-related components were discovered by UNSCOM in 1993.[35] It is argued that Argentina helped Iraq in solid fuel technology and guidance systems, increasing the range of Iraq's Scud missiles. Guidance and control systems were, however, Argentina's own bottleneck in the development of the Condor II. The programme was deactivated under heavy US pressure, with its components shipped to Spain's National Airspace Technical Institute (INTA) in 1993. In the area of nuclear exports, Argentina was still alleged to have transferred low-enriched (20 percent) uranium fuel and nuclear-related services to Tehran by 1993. However, both Brazil and Argentina's nuclear exports came under stricter supervision in the 1990s, and Argentina even joined the Nonproliferation Treaty (NPT) and the Nuclear Suppliers' Group, with its strict guidelines.

A New Domestic Political Economy: The Rigours of Economic Liberalization

Following democratization in both countries in the mid-1980s, the armed forces aimed – ultimately unsuccessfully – at exchanging the right to rule for the right to nurture military industries.[36] The service heads of the army, navy, and air force in Brazil resisted the cancellation of their ministerial status and of the hitherto secure budgetary autonomy of their economic fiefdoms. In Argentina, President Alfonsín challenged those prerogatives with limited success, as evident in Alfonsín's inability to curtail the air force's Condor programme in 1985. By the late 1980s and early 1990s, Brazil and Argentina were posed for what, in time, amounted to genuine revolutions in the countries' political economies. This was to weaken the military as an institution and an industrial complex, together with the influence of the old strategic thinking about regional threat perceptions that had emanated from military academies and war colleges.

The political coalitions backing presidents Carlos S. Menem and Fernando Collor de Mello endorsed effective economic liberalization, privatization, military contraction, and structural adjustment, with unprecedented vigour. Following decades of import-substitution industrialization, a progressive and genuine liberalization began taking hold, most consistently in Argentina, where the neoliberal programme brought about privatization, low inflation, balanced budgets, and an average growth rate of close to 8 per cent annually in the early 1990s. Arms and ancillary industries were now prime targets for privatization and conversion into civilian-oriented production. Economic reform lagged in Brazil with the ascension of Itamar Franco, who wooed a statist-populist constituency and the military, attacking international institutions and their domestic allies. This phase was superseded by the election of Fernando H. Cardoso in 1994. His coalition set out to embrace much of the grand political-economic strategy of Argentina's Menem.

The military sector – a recipient of state subsidies, fiscal incentives and R&D support – was a primary casualty of the contraction of state expenditures and entrepreneurial activities. Fewer resources narrowed the political space for military expenditures and forced a redefinition of priorities.[37] Although Brazil had been spending less than 1 per cent of its GNP on the armed forces, among the world's lowest rates (Argentina spent 2.4 per cent), there were hidden costs (i.e., investments beyond those showing in the military budget) and opportunity costs in the expansion of the military-industrial complex, which had pushed itself ahead of other infrastructural and educational targets. Among the most important political costs was the expansion of the armed forces' influence, and its resistance to contracting the state. In Argentina, DGFM accounted for up to 5 per cent of the country's GNP,[38] swallowed over 7 per cent of the national budget,[39] and accumulated over $1.5 billion in foreign debt.[40] Already by the mid-1980s, pressures to privatize DGFM were mounting. The Condor II programme was estimated to have absorbed between $3 and 5 billion, although Iraq provided most of the funding.

Economic liberalization had a beneficial effect on the military's disentanglement from political and economic sources of power. Both in Brazil and Argentina, such institutions as the air force's CTA (Brazil) and IIAE (Instituto de Investigaciones Aeronáuticas y Espaciales, Argentina), and the navy's IPqM (Brazil's Instituto de Pesquisa da Marinha) and national nuclear energy commissions had enjoyed enormous bureaucratic autonomy.[41] Reduced significantly were the level of political insulation and budgetary rent-seeking of military-related enterprises, and even further reduction is likely with the expected 'Argentinization' of Brazil's political economy under President Cardoso. By 1994 Cardoso had cut off funding for missile development. Brazil's VLS satellite launch and nuclear submarine programmes were stalled, while Engesa itself had ceased to exist. The eventual cancellation of the Condor II project symbolized the triumph of the new liberalizing agenda under President Menem over old power competitors in the Argentine political system, such as the air force.[42] Both countries continued promoting space research – with very limited resources – having placed their respective commissions for space matters directly under the president's supervision.

Finally Menem, in contrast to Alfonsín, scrapped the Condor II project, dealing a severe blow to the last military programme with a potential for redressing decades of Argentine failure in military production. The Menem administration played a clever game of occasionally pointing to foreign pressures and tradeoffs in dismantling this programme, but in reality the external benefits of increased US support and international recognition complemented a domestic priority of killing the vestiges of a historically powerful statist rival: the military-industrial complex.

Thus, the relatively dense network of military cooperation that had developed between Argentina and Brazil on the one hand, and Iraq, Iran, Egypt, Algeria, Libya, and Syria on the other, came to a virtual end. With the contraction of state agencies and military budgets, this network faced significant threats. However, private actors, including former military officers and entrepreneurs continued to offer their services to Middle Eastern arms programmes. Former Brazilian CTA and Orbita personnel were allegedly involved in plans to build a nuclear version of the Piranha air-to-air missile for Iraq, although the Piranha itself had never even entered production.[43] Argentine scientists were reported to be assisting Iraq's rocket programme as well.

Regional Breakthroughs: Mercosur

The leap in economic liberalization was matched by a leap in bilateral cooperation. Following decades of Argentine–Brazilian estrangement and failed attempts at genuine political and

215

economic cooperation, the administrations of Carlos S. Menem in Argentina and Fernando Collor de Mello in Brazil laid out a blueprint of cooperation, beginning in 1990, involving every issue-area, most notably economic integration and regional denuclearization. This was an unprecedented definition of regional cooperation in the Southern Cone, with Mercosur as an essential component. This time, integrative schemes were not mere rhetoric, but effective policies. A genuine economic integration process was in place, after many failed attempts during these countries' import-substituting and hybrid (including weakly liberalizing) phases. A mutual commitment to renounce nuclear weapons, and the accession to the Treaty of Tlatelolco stipulations and to the NPT (in the case of Argentina), have replaced three decades of nuclear ambiguity and competition. A highly cooperative regional context weakened even further the justification for extracting societal resources to maintain military-industrial complexes. Moreover, the commercial excuse for export-oriented complexes had withered away.

All in all, the contraction of arms production in Argentina and Brazil was overdetermined by international, regional, and domestic considerations. All three are linked by the process of economic liberalization. These arms industries are definitely down, and perhaps even out.

CONCLUSIONS

The external dimension of the transformation of Brazil and Argentina's political economies included not only an unprecedented embrace of liberal trade rules but also the abandonment of historical nationalist foreign policies across the board. By the early 1990s Argentina had joined an array of international regimes (including NPT and MTCR), severed its membership in the Nonaligned Movement, and sent a naval contingent to join the multilateral force in the Gulf war.[44] The infamous Condor II project was put to rest in 1993, paving the way to increased Argentine access to investment, technology, and trade. Argentina's new credentials also became evident in its caution and deference to nuclear export guidelines and to the political sensitivities of the international community regarding what are often referred to as 'rogue' states. In 1992 President Menem barred the transfer of nuclear reactor components, including uranium conversion and purification equipment, that Argentina had agreed to supply to Iran in 1987. Argentina joined the Nuclear Suppliers' Group restricting the supply of sensitive nuclear materials in 1994.[45] By 1995, Chancellor Guido Di Tella was ready to cancel the (internationally legal) sale of an experimental nuclear reactor to Syria, with an uncharacteristic flexibility that revealed the source and nature of Argentina's new policy.[46] Whereas the Atomic Energy Commission once had a virtual monopoly over Argentine nuclear policy (including exports), a refurbished foreign ministry had become pivotal to the implementation of the external aspects of Menem's liberalizing grand strategy. The Brazilian government became similarly committed to passing a Congressional bill improving export control mechanisms for sensitive technologies. Brazil became a full MTCR member in October 1995 and has since received advanced missile technology from Russia, which cannot be re-exported.

Domestic political shifts away from the policies embraced by the Menem and Cardoso administrations are possible, but not likely in the near term. Political challengers and casualties of the new liberalizing agenda, including former President Alfonsín's Radical party in Argentina and sectors of the military-industrial complex in both countries, have criticized the demise of the military sector. However, even if challengers manage to replace current administrations, the likelihood of a comeback for the arms industry is fairly low, given the global, regional, and domestic logic that accelerated their downfall in the last lustrum.

NOTES

I would like to acknowledge the support of the John D. and Catherine T. MacArthur Foundation's Programme on Peace and International Cooperation, as well as the helpful comments on earlier versions of this work by Ken Conca, Scott Tollefson, Patrice Jones, and participants in the January 1996 Conference at Bar-Ilan University.

1. D.J. Louscher and M.D. Salomone (eds), *Marketing Security Assistance*

THE POLITICS AND ECONOMICS OF DEFENCE INDUSTRIES

(Lexington, MA: Lexington Books, 1987).
2. Alfred Stepan, *Rethinking Military Politics – Brazil and the Southern Cone* (Princeton: Princeton University Press, 1988).
3. Brazil did ban arms exports to Cuba and South Africa, however, mostly for domestic reasons.
4. On the role of arms exports in the broader context of foreign policy during those years, see Etel Solingen, 'Technology, Countertrade, and Nuclear Exports', in W.C. Potter (ed.), *International Nuclear Trade: The Challenge of the Emerging Suppliers* (Washington, DC: Heath Lexington Books, 1990) and Etel Solingen, 'Managing Energy Vulnerability: Brazil's Adjustment to Oil Dependency', *Comparative Strategy*, vol. 10, no. 2 (1991).
5. Patrice F. Jones, 'The Brazilian Defence Industry: A Case Study of Public-Private Collaboration' (PhD dissertation, Department of Economics, University of Notre Dame, 1988).
6. Clovis Brigagao, *O Mercado de Seguranca – Ensaios sobre economia politica da defesa* (Rio de Janeiro: Nova Fronteira, 1984); Kenneth L. Conca, 'Global Markets, Local Politics, and Military Industrialization in Brazil' (PhD dissertation, University of California, Berkeley, 1992).
7. Renato P. Dagnino, 'Industria de armamentos: O Estado e a tecnologia', *Revista Brasileira de Tecnologia*, 14:3 (1983), pp. 5–17, and Renato P. Dagnino, 'A Industria de Armamentos Brasileira: Condicionantes e desenvolvimento', in A. O. Herrera *et al.* (eds), *O Armamentismo e o Brasil* (Sao Paulo: Brasiliense, 1985); Conca, 'Global Markets'.
8. Carl J. Dahlman, 'Foreign Technology and Indigenous Technological Capability in Brazil', in Martin Fransman and Kenneth King (eds), *Technological Capability in the 3rd World* (London: Macmillan, 1984), pp. 3–30; Jones, 'The Brazilian Defence Industry'.
9. Jones, 'The Brazilian Defence Industry'.
10. Etel Solingen, *Industrial Policy, Technology, and International Bargaining: Designing Nuclear Industries in Argentina and Brazil* (Stanford: Stanford University Press, 1996).
11. *The Risk Report*, 1:3 (April 1995), p. 6; Conca, 'Global Markets'.
12. *Jane's Defence Weekly* (1/11/1987). The Roland and Cobra missiles were licensed by West Germany and France.
13. *The Nonproliferation Review* (Fall 1995), p. 155.
14. Michael Brzoska and Thomas Ohlson (eds), *Arms Production in the Third World* (London: Taylor and Francis, 1986).
15. Daniel Chudnovsky and M. Nagao, *Capital Goods Production in the Third World* (New York: St. Martin's Press, 1983), p. 99; Brigagao, *O Mercado*. Conca (1995) provides updated and reliable estimates of the industry's size and performance.
16. Stepan, 'Rethinking Military Politics'.
17. *SIPRI Yearbook*, 1987.
18. *O Globo* (10 December 1984).
19. A more detailed discussion of Brazil's relations with Middle East countries can be found in Solingen, 'Managing Energy Vulnerability'.
20. Jones, 'The Brazilian Defence Industry', p. 176; Scott D. Tollefson, 'Brazilian Arms Transfers, Ballistic Missiles, and Foreign Policy: The Search for Autonomy' (PhD dissertation, Johns Hopkins University, 1990).
21. *Aviation Week and Space Technology* (17 August 1987).

22. Gary Milhollin and David Dantzic, 'Must the US Give Brazil and Iraq the Bomb?', *New York Times* (29 July 1990), p. 19.
23. *Eye on Supply* (Spring 1991), p. 13.
24. *The Nonproliferation Review* (Fall 1994), p. 121; (Winter 1994), p. 101.
25. Alain Rouquié, *Poder militar y sociedad política en la Argentina: 1943–1973*, vol. II (Buenos Aires: Emece, 1982); Victor Millán, 'Argentina: Schemes for Glory', in Brzoska and Ohlson, *Arms Production*. The army also controlled the state steel firm SOMISA as well as DINIE (a group of 38 formerly German firms, primarily in pharmaceutical and chemicals, that were taken over as enemy property at the end of World War II), and also firms in the iron ore, timber, and construction sectors (through majority shares). The army also supervised the aircraft industry and the navy's AFNE yards; see Laura Randall, *An Economic History of Argentina in the 20th Century* (New York: Columbia University Press, 1978).
26. On the statist tradition of the army, its aversion to privatization, and its consistent preference for foreign equipment and technology, see R. D. Mallon and J. V. Sorrouille, *Economic Policymaking in a Conflict Society: The Argentine Case* (Cambridge, MA: Harvard University Press, 1975).
27. Victor Millán, 'Argentina'.
28. A group of researchers at the army's R&D centre (Citesa) was never able to influence the army and the DGFM in the direction of industrial promotion and technological investments.
29. London *Sunday Times* (22 May 1988). More than 20 European companies from West Germany, Italy, France, Spain, Switzerland, and Austria were supplying the Condor II programme with technology; see Scott D. Tollefson, 'Argentina and the Missile Technology Control Regime: A Reassessment' (paper presented at the 34th Annual Convention of the International Studies Association, Acapulco, Mexico, 24–26 March 1993).
30. FBIS Latin America (24 August 1993), p. 31.
31. Tollefson, 'Argentina', p. 17.
32. Solingen, 'Technology', 'Managing Energy Vulnerability', and 'Industrial Policy'.
33. *Eye on Supply* (Spring 1992), p. 5; (Fall 1992), p. 3.
34. *SIPRI Yearbook*, 1994.
35. *The Nonproliferation Review* (Fall 1993), p. 95; (Winter 1994), p. 144; (Spring-Summer 1994), p. 155; Tollefson, 'Argentina'.
36. Stepan, *Rethinking Military Politics*.
37. For a detailed examination of the impact of economic liberalization on the military-industrial complex worldwide, see Etel Solingen, 'Democracy, Economic Reform, and Regional Cooperation', *Journal of Theoretical Politics*, 8:1 (January 1996).
38. Daniel Poneman, *Argentina: Democracy on Trial* (New York: Paragon House Publishers, 1987), p. 101.
39. Paul H. Lewis, *The Crisis of Argentine Capitalism* (Chapel Hill: University of North Carolina Press, 1990), p. 451.
40. Augusto Varas, *Democracy Under Siege* (New York: Greenwood Press, 1989), p. 53. More than $7 billion had been invested in military industries, *El Desarrollo* (1985), p. 166. By one estimate, 25 companies run by the armed forces producing weapons and planes received $300 million annually from the national budget (13 per cent of the total for state firms).

41. Erber attributes the self-reliant characteristics of the computer and aircraft programmes in Brazil to the relative autonomy of institutions within the state, especially those pertaining to the military establishment; see Fabio Erber, 'Technological Development and State Intervention: A Study of the Brazilian Capital Goods Industry' (PhD dissertation, University of Sussex, 1977), p. 349.
42. Menem went as far as placing retired Brigadier General Ernesto Crespo under house arrest for his public statements criticizing the cancellation of the Condor II programme, Tollefson, 'Argentina', p. 38.
43. Eye on Supply (Winter 1990–91), p. 6; (Spring 1991), p. 14; Los Angeles Times (9 December 1989).
44. Roberto Russell (ed.), La política exterior Argentina en el nuevo orden mundial (Buenos Aires: Facultad Latinoamericana de Ciencias Sociales, 1992).
45. Argentina was still scheduled to export 20 per cent-enriched U235 to Algeria and Egypt. Argentina's INVAP SE also services a turnkey reseach and radioisotope production reactor it supplied to Egypt in 1993; see Nonproliferation Review (Fall 1994), p. 119.
46. The Argentine reversal on the Syrian reactor is particularly significant in light of President Menem's own family background (Syrio-Lebanese). President Menem is the first Argentine president to visit Israel and has arguably maintained unprecedentedly close relations with Israel.

A version of this chapter first appeared in International Politics 35 (March): 31–47. I acknowledge Kluwer Publishers for their permission to reprint the original with some revisions.

Index

For Product Safety Concerns and Information please contact our EU
representative GPSR@taylorandfrancis.com
Taylor & Francis Verlag GmbH, Kaufingerstraße 24, 80331 München, Germany

www.ingramcontent.com/pod-product-compliance
Ingram Content Group UK Ltd.
Pitfield, Milton Keynes, MK11 3LW, UK
UKHW020935180425
457613UK00019B/403